THE COACH'S
GUIDE TO TEACHING

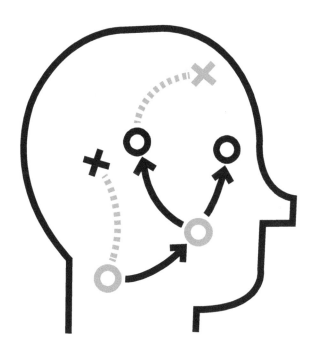

DOUG LEMOV

Illustrated by Oliver Caviglioli

JOHN
CATT

First Published 2020

by John Catt Educational Ltd,
15 Riduna Park, Station Road,
Melton, Woodbridge IP12 1QT
UK

Tel: +44 (0) 1394 389850

4600 140th Avenue North,
Suite 180,
Clearwater, FL 33762
United States

Email: enquiries@johncatt.com
Website: www.johncatt.com

ISBN: 978 1 913622 30 5

Set and designed by John Catt Educational Limited

 # CONTENTS

FOREWORD

What is great coaching made of? What separates the planet's best coaches from the rest?

For the past century or so, the traditional answer went like this: *Great coaching is a mysterious gift possessed by rare individuals.* We believed that great coaches—John Wooden, Vince Lombardi, Johan Cruyff, Pat Summitt—were different from regular coaches in exactly the same way that Babe Ruth was different from regular ballplayers, or that The Beatles were different from regular rock bands. Great coaches possessed an inborn X-factor, a golden twist of DNA and destiny, that propelled their success, and that could not be copied or stolen. Wanting to be a great coach was like wanting to win the lottery: everyone was welcome to try, but only a lucky handful could be chosen.

In the past few decades, thanks to the work of countless scientists and researchers, we've learned that this traditional model is absolutely, positively, 100% wrong. We've looked inside the brain as it learns, we've assessed and tracked effective interactions, and we've learned that great coaching only *appears* magical. In truth, it's a complex combination of skills—a kind of sociobehavioral sport, whose fundamentals are knowledge, communication, and leadership. We've learned that these skills aren't magical, but can be built with the right tools.

In all, we've learned that great coaching isn't about the *who*; it's secretly about the *how*.

That's where Doug Lemov comes in.

I met Doug after reading his first book, *Teach Like a Champion*. Its premise was irresistible: he systematically observed highly successful teachers, then distilled those observations into a toolkit of 62 techniques that drove student achievement. The simple, powerful moves Doug described—"Check for Understanding," "Plan for Error," "Right is Right"—have been absorbed, employed, and shared by hundreds of thousands of grateful educators around the world. More than that, the book functioned as a mystique-busting X-ray, peering beneath the surface of teaching to reveal its essential machinery. And it led straight to a question: if these tools worked in the classroom, where else might they be applied?

Not long after his book came out, I contacted Doug and asked if he would speak with the coaches of the Cleveland Indians, a team I consult for. Unlike richer major-league teams, Cleveland doesn't have the budget to buy great players—instead, they build them, and thus depend utterly on developing players through coaching. The timing of my call was poetic, because, as I shortly learned, Doug was already heading up an effort to strengthen the U.S. Soccer

Federation's licensing and training program for coaches. In other words, he was deep into exploring the transfer of his teaching concepts to the sports world—a world that is famously skeptical, risk-averse, and resistant to new ideas and outsiders. The question was, would it work?

The answer was a massive and unmistakable yes. It took about two minutes, and it happened when one of the coaches brought up the old saying *The game teaches the game*. It's the kind of mantra coaches love to say and repeat, because it sounds irreproachably true, and it also gives them an out, because if the game teaches, you don't have to. Doug listened, then he spoke.

"Everyone says that—*The game teaches the game*—but is it really true?" Doug paused—what I would come to see as a Lemovian pause—warm, expectant, giving everybody a chance to reflect. Then he continued.

"I was just at a [soccer] workshop and we were talking about making runs off the ball—basically getting yourself open to receive a pass. At the workshop, I learned about the different types of run that you could make, and why. [Lemovian pause.] I've been playing and coaching soccer for decades and no one ever *named the different types of runs*—or that one of key types of runs is when you split the two central defenders. *No one told me that*—or told me from a defensive point of view that it was critical not to get split."

The group started nodding—they got it. Then Doug asked if there were similar frameworks in baseball and the group started speaking up. Turns out there were lots of frameworks, hidden just beneath the surface: there are six ways for a catcher to block a ball, five ways for a baserunner to round first base. The room started to buzz. You could feel the ideas start exploding to the surface, coaches seeing their role in a new way.

"So maybe the game isn't the best teacher," Doug summed up. "It's an unequal teacher. If you let players just play, some may get it and some may not. But if you give players frameworks to understand, they can adapt and apply them, and become better problem-solvers." Shortly afterward, a major-league hitting coach and the head of player development signed up to attend a *Teach Like a Champion* workshop that winter, marking what might be a historical first: professional baseball personnel sitting attentively in a fluorescent-lit classroom, shoulder to shoulder with public school English and math and social studies teachers, learning together.

That's Doug's power: he gives you fresh ways to see the interactions between teacher and student and the game, and provides the tools to make an impact in the learning process. With each insight, he is teaching us an overarching lesson: great teaching is great teaching, whether it's in an algebra classroom or on a soccer field.

Doug's other power is that he's always learning. That is, he has a rare ability to relentlessly explore new science, new contexts, and new ideas, and to draw useful connections. We see this power in ways that are obvious—for example, in the way Doug rethought and rewrote his original book to produce *Teach Like a Champion 2.0*. We also see it in ways that are harder to measure—for example, how he and his team adapted to the pandemic by developing remote-coaching models that helped teachers and learners work closely together despite the distance. Doug's work serves as a reminder that coaching isn't about being the all-knowing guru on the mountaintop, but rather about being the curious seeker.

So let's return to our original question: what's great coaching really made of?

(Lemovian pause)

I think one answer might be: *Great coaches are learners who are obsessed with giving you the tools and support to make yourself a little bit better every day.* And that's precisely why we are incredibly fortunate to have a coach like Doug Lemov, and a toolkit like the one you now hold in your hands.

* * *

DANIEL
COYLE

INTRODUCTION

A few years ago, I was in a conference room with a group of educators, getting ready to show a video of a high school math teacher when I was suddenly overcome with panic, which might seem like a strange reaction.

For the previous ten years, I had been studying teachers, and in particular teachers who were "positive outliers." These were teachers who worked with students from impoverished neighborhoods where only a fraction of students graduated high school, never mind went on to college, and where typically only 10% or 20% of students might pass a given state test (an incomplete but still important measure of progress) in math or reading in a typical year. And yet working in that same landscape, the teachers I was studying helped their students achieve at a dramatically higher rate than anyone would have predicted: they might have double the number of students passing...or four times the number of students passing. Sometimes every single kid passed. Sometimes they had more kids score "advanced" than teachers in surrounding schools had kids score "proficient." Their results often closed the gap between kids born to poverty and kids born to privilege, their scores equaling or exceeding those in districts where educations were supplemented by trips abroad and private tutors, and where the walk to school was made along tree-lined streets that were rarely dirty and never dangerous.

I wanted to understand how those teachers could take a group of students who some skeptics said couldn't perform at the highest levels, "didn't care" and "didn't have the skills," and achieve transformative results. There were predictions of what was "possible," in other words, and then there were people like Denarius Frazier, the teacher in the video I was about to show, who broke all the models. In Denarius's classroom, it seemed like anything was possible. I had spent hours watching and re-watching videos of his lessons, noting how he managed time, gave feedback, built relationships, assessed

1. This ultimately became a book, *Teach Like a Champion* (now *Teach Like a Champion 2.0*...and soon to be *Teach Like a Champion 3.0*. There's a lot to learn from studying teachers so the book requires constant updating.)

how much everyone was learning. I did that with dozens of exceptional teachers like him, then took the videos and chopped them up into short clips of two or three minutes—"game films."[1]

So what was the headline? What was the secret to great teaching? There wasn't one. What characterized those classrooms wasn't one big thing but a lot of little things. "There is no 100% solution, only one hundred 1% solutions," is how a colleague of mine, Brett Peiser, put it. The power was in the aggregation of small improvements—what some people call marginal gains. That's both good news and bad news.

Good news because, as James Clear discusses in his book *Atomic Habits*, marginal gains compound over time in a curve a bit like this:

It's surprising. "If you can get 1% better each day for one year, you'll end up thirty-seven times better by the time you're done," writes Clear. That was the secret to transformative classrooms.

Now the bad news. Mastering little things requires diligence and focus. The fact that there was no magic bullet meant that some people wouldn't do it. They wouldn't be willing to sustain their focus on small, usually not very sexy ideas when there were people telling you that there were easy, simple feel-good solutions: *Don't be the sage on the stage; be the guide on the side!*

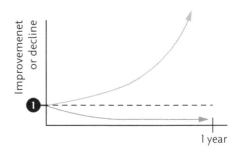

THE POWER OF TINY GAINS

1% better every day 1.01^{365} = 31.18 ↑
1% worse every day 0.99^{365} = 0.03 ↓

I'd seen a lot of guiding on the side where the lesson quality was almost criminal. I'd seen a lot of lessons where the teacher was sage-on-the-stage that were things of profound and useful beauty. "The answer is, it depends," my colleague Christian Lavers, who runs the highly regarded Elite Clubs National League, likes to say. The right strategy depends on what you are teaching to whom and when. But in the end, no matter which direction you go, the results come down to careful execution.

Here's how I summed it up in my presentation that day:

- People can outperform what is 'expected'—individually and in groups—via better teaching.
- But teaching better is technical; it requires sustained focus on things that are often mundane.
- Because of that, most people won't do it.
- And because of *that*, it is an immense competitive advantage for those who will.

I have neglected to mention that the workshop I'm referring to was not for classroom teachers but rather for coaches—after all, classrooms aren't the only place where teaching takes place or where more effective learning is valuable. And soon after my first book about teachers came out, the US Soccer Federation reached out to ask if I'd be interested in presenting some ideas to coaches. I had been a fan of the game all my life. I had played in college (where I was marginal at best and where my game featured desperate panicked clearances and lots of missed tackles). I thought: "What if coaches could make athletes 1% better after every session by being more attentive to the things teachers like Denarius worried about: how you managed time, gave feedback, built relationships, and assessed how much everyone was learning? Was it possible?" I flew to Colorado and did a workshop which, I can safely say, was terrible.

I could tell coaches how to get distracted players to pay attention, but what about teaching them to make better decisions? Students in a math class have to master skills as individuals. Athletes on the soccer field have to make decisions as a group. They have to make them very quickly. Coaching is a form of teaching, but it also has different issues and challenges that required further study. There was a lot of potential in the idea but also a lot of work to be done.

So I set out to do that work: to study coaching and adapt what I knew about teaching to understand how to create positive outliers on the court and field. At the same time, I also set out to better understand the science behind learning. As I began to do more and more work with coaches, I found that some of the challenges I was familiar with from schools applied to their work as well. Sometimes the level of research and study done by coaches (and the organizations that led them) was incredible. But sometimes organizations built their teaching on myths and platitudes more than science. At one point, visiting a national coaching federation I sometimes worked with, I asked what research was behind the guidelines in their training courses. There wasn't any.

Scientists and researchers had discovered more about the brain and how it learned in the last 20 years than they had in the previous 300, and I was pretty sure the questions coaches were asking me—how you taught people to solve problems quickly in groups, for example—could be answered by research. But the research wasn't consistently making its way into the conversation. So I began reading articles and books on cognitive science. And I kept reading. The answer to so many questions in teaching is still "it depends," but that doesn't mean all answers are equal. There's still science and it will guide you towards better answers and away from lesser, sometimes more familiar ones, and even after that there is still plenty of room for "it depends." Both things are true. All of which is a way of saying that you will find discussions in this book of memory, perception, and attention, even multilevel natural selection—the idea that, in human evolutionary terms, natural selection chose based on our ability to form groups as much as our individual strengths. I apologize if it feels like too much at times, but I found it fascinating—and most importantly, highly relevant.

And so several years later I found myself standing in a conference room in Chicago, getting ready to present to a group that included some of MLS's most highly regarded coaches—guys I had watched on TV, not just coaching but many times playing; there were several veterans of World Cup rosters in the room. It was the highest-level group I had worked with, and suddenly I was very nervous.

My plan was to lead with a video from Denarius's classroom and ask them to connect what they saw there to their own manner of coaching at their clubs, but walking to the front of the room, I was now struck with suddenly clarity about the ridiculousness of that plan. I was going to ask coaches who trained world-class athletes every day (managing their egos; channeling their hunger) using the latest technology (real-time video; VR; GPS tracking)—not to mention translation services for the multiple languages spoken—to weigh in on classrooms of middle and high school students sitting in tidy rows of desks in Newark and Brooklyn.

So, coach, what can you learn from the way Denarius talks to his 9th graders to help you explain to your team—with players from eight different national teams—that you want them to press differently, or to challenge a veteran in the last phase of his career to push himself harder?

How could I have been so stupid?

By that point, though, it was too late. The coaches were looking up at me and there was nothing to do but begin. I cued up the video of Denarius and pressed play. (You can watch that video here or wait for chapter 4 when I will analyze it more fully.)

Watch "Denarius Frazier teaching math" at www.coachguidetoteaching.com

I showed about a minute and paused.

"What did you observe?" I asked. "And how does it relate to your coaching?"

It's possible that my voice was shaking at this point and I was braced for crickets—which is teacher talk for a long awkward silence—but one of the most established coaches in the league spoke up immediately.

"He's teaching everybody," he said. "Everybody."

I nodded, but in retrospect I realize that I still didn't really get where he was going. To be honest, I thought he was just trying to be gracious and say something obvious to help me through an awkward silence. But something in his voice suggested something more than a mere act of decency, and I asked him to say more.

"He talks to every single student," he said. "He's showing that he's invested in their progress, that he sees their work. He's teaching them all. We don't do that. Some guys, they barely hear from us. Sometimes for days at a time. And I'm just sitting here thinking: *Man, how does that look from their point of view?*"

Before I could respond, another coach chimed in. "You can't build relationships at this level just by being friendly and backslapping guys. They want to succeed. They want to play. You build relationships by showing you want to make them better. No, that you *can* make them better. He's doing the same thing—connecting with students by teaching them. If you can't make them better, you can give them all the high fives you want; it's not going to matter."

We were rolling.

In fact, my head was all but exploding. I had always felt a bit self-conscious about my work in the sports sector. Public education was in a national crisis and here I was indulging myself, studying what I loved but which did not help alleviate this crisis. When I came back to my office, I would often not tell people where I'd been. At least at first. But it quickly became apparent that the learning ran both ways. What great teachers did was relevant to coaches in the most profound way. And there was almost nothing out there that helped coaches think about the things that made their teaching hum—the management of seconds, the giving of feedback, the building of relationships, the assessing of how much everyone was learning. But what coaches did and knew was also highly relevant to teachers. There were a hundred teachers who were struggling that very morning because they did not understand the power of what those coaches had just said. They thought the relationship had to come first, that you could not teach until you had constructed it. They did a lot of high fiving to try to get there. But, as the coach observed, to build a long-term and substantive relationship as a teacher, you had to help people get better. You had to start teaching first. You had to teach well and use that as a tool to connect.

One other thought came to me in that moment: how humble, self-reflective and hungry to learn the coaches were. They were at the top of their profession and here I was asking them to engage in discussions they could easily have written off as irrelevant or inconsequential. They could have been excused for checking out and getting some emails done before the tactical sessions in the afternoon, but they jumped in with both feet (a description which also describes most of my attempted tackles at the collegiate level, I note).

I came to understand, starting that day, that the marker of a great coach was a constant desire to learn and grow. The people who rose in intensely competitive environments were serious about the craft and knew what was at stake. They were not smug but restless. Confident, often, but also humble. In New Zealand, for example, where the pride of a nation of five million people hinged on its ability to remain on the top of the world rugby pyramid, I showed an example of how a coach could give guidance but also preserve leeway for individual style and decision-making. It was an odd choice, potentially, because the coach and student were ballet dancers: the mentor giving feedback on arm movements to her protégé. It could have felt odd but it didn't. The rugby coaches, many of whom had played themselves for the "All Blacks," New Zealand's vaunted national team, analyzed the clip with insight and humility.

This is a topic I will take up further in chapter 6, but it was and has remained both humbling and inspiring that the coaches I am lucky enough to work with take the study of teaching so seriously. Each group of coaches I've spent time with has given at least as much as they got from the sessions, and a big part of my motivation in writing this book is to pass along the wisdom they shared.

✻ ✻ ✻

So this is a book for that class of teachers called coaches, even though some of them have never used the word "teacher" to describe themselves. It's a class of teachers that includes everyone from parent volunteers to professional coaches and private trainers—6.5 million of them in the US, according to the Aspen Institute's Project Play. It's a big tent, a messy tent—a hard one to write a book for. I'm aware that my effort to write to readers of such wide-ranging backgrounds means some examples may at first seem most relevant to some other coach: I'm talking about basics and you're a professional; I'm talking about what seems like arcane jargon when you just want to know how to get players to do what you asked. All I can do is promise that I've tried to include diverse enough examples that if what I'm talking about at the moment isn't right for you, something soon after will be.

At least I hope so. Because it was important to write a book for such a wide-ranging group.

Sports play an outsized role in our collective imagination. Increasingly, it is the way our tribes compete—as nations, cities, regions and, in a category all their own, Boston Red Sox fans. What number of children (and just possibly adults) stand in their driveway right now imagining they are LeBron James, slashing his way to the hoop as the crowd explodes? How many are wearing Messi jerseys to touch a tiny piece of his brilliance?

The economics of professional sports also show its immense influence: Lebron James signed for LA for $154 million for four years; Neymar's transfer to Paris Saint-Germain was €222 million. Like it or not, an economist would say, that's the price at which our culture values athletic performance.

However, there's more to it than that. Coaches teach our young people what it means to pursue excellence, to chase improvement, to work together to achieve common goals, to build character. The sociobiologist Edward Wilson has pointed out that the key to the human triumph among the species was not our individual evolutionary adaptations so much as our group adaptations. The genetic fitness of humans is as much a consequence of group selection as individual selection, he writes. We survived and thrived because we work together for common goals and because individuals will sacrifice themselves for those goals. We are one of very few mammals that do this. Team sports are one of the most common ways that we learn what the path of that evolution required: to seek to triumph and yet be ready to sacrifice; to want to succeed for ourselves but also remain within the group and seek its success. Sports make us more human because they echo the process of our evolution.

But the work of teaching sports is hard and complex. Coaching well involves a complex array of challenges common to all teachers. These include questions such as:

- How do I give feedback to help athletes learn better and faster?
- How do I know whether athletes have learned what I have taught them?
- What do I do when I am pretty sure they are not 'getting it'?
- How do I design and sequence activities so players will remember to execute in the game what they learned in practice?
- How do I teach decision-making?
- How can I help players become self-driven learners? How can I instill a growth mindset?
- How can I do that while fostering a love for the game and building strong character?
- How do I convince athletes to be willing to struggle and fail in the short run so they can learn in the long run?

These questions—and a hundred more like them—are daunting. A teacher's handling of them, compounded over a hundred or a thousand practices, can make or break an individual's or a team's success. And while there are thousands of excellent books and websites a coach can consult to better understand technical and tactical aspects of the game, there is almost nothing for a coach to consult that explicitly examines the teaching problems of the field, the court, the rink and the diamond.

WHAT'S INSIDE?

1. THE ABILITY TO DECIDE
2. PLANNING & DESIGN
3. GIVING FEEDBACK
4. CHECKING FOR UNDERSTANDING
5. BUILDING CULTURE
6. ISSUES IN GROWTH & DEVELOPMENT

WHAT'S INSIDE

This book consists of six chapters. The first of these, "The Ability to Decide," is about decision-making, which I call the most important proficiency of all. My discussion of it focuses heavily on the underacknowledged role of perception. Essentially, you cannot make the right decisions unless your eyes are in the right place and know what to look for. Expertise is in the eyes. How then do we develop athletes' eyes and the more advanced cognitive processes they support?

Chapter 2 is about planning and session design, both within a session and within a unit. Planning units of learning (of four or six weeks' duration, say) is far less common than planning single sessions, but at least as important because long-term memory can only be built over time. As I hope to show, the role of long-term memory is vastly underappreciated by most educators—coaches included. Consider this: you have forgotten almost everything you've learned in your life. Athletes are no different. How do you know they will remember what you've taught them when they need it?

Chapter 3 is about giving feedback, which is perhaps the single coaching action we do most. That it is so familiar to us makes it easy for us to rely on old and untested habits. We give feedback the way we do because...well, who knows. Perhaps because Coach Carlton gave us feedback that way 25 years ago. And why did he do it that way? Well, Chapter 3 is your chance to think about some of the decisions you make about feedback. The science of working memory and attention will play a key role.

Chapter 4 is about John Wooden's adage that teaching is knowing the difference between "I taught it" and "They learned it." It's among the hardest things to do in teaching and the science of perception will come back to play a key role.

Chapter 5 is about building culture. Culture is often the thing we remember best from our own sporting days, and its messages are what we carry with us longest, perhaps because our individual behaviors have evolved to be extremely responsive to group culture. In the end, you can get a lot wrong if you get culture right.

The first five chapters are about the day-to-day decisions that can bring about the marginal gains James Clear and others write about. The sixth chapter is about long-term growth and development—your players' and your own. I'll discuss, among other things, how to balance long-term learning goals with the short-term task of winning, how game-day coaching is different from coaching in practice, how to make good decisions when selecting talent, and how to make sure that you grow and develop as much as you can in your own coaching journey.

IS IT A GENERAL COACHING BOOK OR A SOCCER COACHING BOOK?

The book is intended to offer lessons and guidance that are applicable to coaches of any sporting endeavor. But because I take the domain knowledge of each sport seriously and have immense respect for how much coaches know about their chosen sport, I've chosen to write through the lens of the sport I know best: soccer. My hope is that coaches of other sports will be able adapt and apply the lessons to their own contexts without my giving direct examples from them. I do this because I "speak soccer," and am reluctant to try to provide examples from games I do not sufficiently understand. That said, while my examples are drawn heavily from soccer, you'll notice throughout the book that I've asked top-tier coaches from other sports or with different perspectives to provide reflections and context in sidebars. I asked them to reflect on how they do or might adapt and apply the ideas in this book to their own sports. I hope this will provide support and insight for coaches who seek to take some of the concepts in the book and apply them to other sports or other settings.

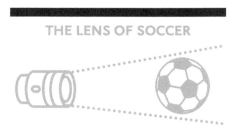

THE LENS OF SOCCER

Some caveats as you do so:

- I've always believed that teachers are like artisans, applying a wide range of tools to solve a wide range of challenges under constantly changing circumstances. The right decision depends on who the artisan is, their own style, what they seek to build, and in what setting. There is no formula and few things that are always right—either in every setting or for every person. But as I mentioned previously, just because there isn't always a single right answer doesn't mean that all answers are equal. Some things are more effective than others—it's a question of how and when you use them. Some things are ineffective. And most of all, there is still science and research that are critical to inform our decisions even if they're not all the same.

- I've tried here to walk the line between the things we know and the things we don't and to describe not a system to follow but a toolbox informed by the science of learning. I share it with you with the understanding that of all the things that cannot always be right, I am foremost on that list. It would be impossible to write a book of this length and not have gotten some things wrong. My suggestion if you think you've found one such thing (or several) is to try the idea out first and then decide. Human behavior is complex and surprising. If you try something and it does not work, you have gained knowledge. If it does work, you have gained knowledge again. Do first, then evaluate. We often rush to make up our minds when really there's no reason to hurry.

THE NEW MONEYBALL

It is the legacy of Michael Lewis's book that, at the professional level at least, every team now plays Moneyball—or versions of Moneyball. That is to say, they seek to find and exploit small competitive advantages—information about what causes or predicts success. Teaching, I think, offers its own version of Moneyball. If you could shift the way you gave feedback and make every player 1% better after every session, you would, over time, have a marginal gains curve like the one James Clear describes—rising upwards steeply. This would change your results as an organization: make a small team competitive; make a competitive team world class. That's the game now at the elite level: who can be the first to unlock the hidden advantages of some critical but overlooked aspect of building performance? Ironically it is the same game we have (or should have) been playing all along at the youth and lower levels: making athletes better faster over the long run.

Here's a Moneyball moment from one of my favorite videos about coaching, in which Super Bowl-winning Seattle Seahawks coach Pete Carroll says of himself and his coaching staff: "We're really disciplined as coaches to always talk about what we want to see, the desired outcome, not about what went wrong or what the mistake was. We have to be disciplined and always use our language to talk about the next thing you can do right. It's always about what we want to happen, not about the other stuff." Part of the path to the Super Bowl for Carroll is in optimizing and systematizing across his staff a simple, mundane thing—focusing feedback on what to do, not what not to do. It's a distinction many coaches might overlook. Or one that might not feel worthy of an NFL head coach's attention. But in fact it is a game changer.

There are a hundred such aspects of teaching to optimize and systematize, each with the potential to yield remarkable returns. It's not just that teaching is a form of competitive advantage but that it is full of a hundred opportunities for a 1%-better-per-day gain that is suddenly a game changer. It is Moneyball in a hall of mirrors—suddenly, everywhere you look, another opportunity emerges. That's its true competitive advantage. And while that is as relevant to elite franchises and teams as any advanced metric, it is also accessible to the must humble local club. Refining your teaching with intentionality and craft is Moneyball for everyone. It's the effort to unlock the secrets of developing people. Some coaches do that extremely well. Some do it less well. Both could benefit from improvement because there is no limit on how much better we dream of being.

Watch "Pete Carroll Moneyball moment" at www.coachguidetoteaching.com

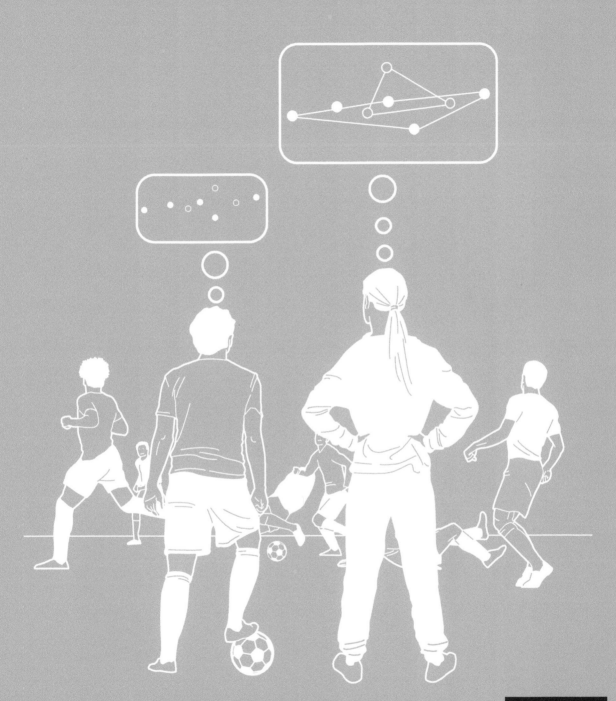

CHAPTER 1

THE ABILITY TO DECIDE

PART 1: YOUR BRAIN, INVADING

Soccer—like basketball, rugby, hockey and similar sports—is a "group invasion game." The goal is to possess and advance a ball (or similar object) through an opponent's territory. Doing so requires coordination and precision, executed under pressure, in changing contexts and often at speeds faster than conscious thought. In such games, skill alone is insufficient. Players may have speed, power, technique and even guile, but in the end the ability to decide—as an individual and among a group—is the most important proficiency of all.

"At the highest level," a former Premier League player told me, "players don't run faster; they think faster." Probably they both think faster *and* run faster, but even this distinction is not simple. The legendary Dutch soccer player Johan Cruyff once said, "When I start running earlier than the others, I appear faster." Part of being "fast" is making better decisions (like where to position oneself and at what angle to run) and making them a little quicker than the player standing a few feet away.[1]

Decision-making, though, is the hardest thing to teach, and this difficulty is compounded by the fact that its importance increases steadily over the course of a player's life. Young players can dominate based on exceptional skill or athleticism in most sports, but soon enough the opposition will learn to contain a stellar individual. There is always just one of her and 5 or 11 or 15 of them. Over time, a budding star will only shine if her decisions—and those of her teammates—get her to the right spot at the right time.

But decision-making is not like a faucet you can simply tell a player to turn on one day.

This is because it is not enough to merely want to make the right decision. Players have to perceive the signals that an opportunity is there, recognize how it must be adapted, and act on this information more quickly than the opposition can see and react. This means athletes must be looking for the right cues that inform decisions before those cues have occurred, and often while executing some other complex task. If the goal is coordination among teammates, then multiple people must be looking for similar cues and reliably reading cues in one another's actions.

1. Speed is also confidence in and clarity about decisions. Who closes a space at full speed while wondering *should I be closing now?*

PLAYER A LEARNS MORE

To state the obvious, you must first *see* quickly and effectively in order to *decide* quickly and effectively. You must recognize a signal—maybe a center-back dropping too deep—in a hundred noisy details and act on it before a window of opportunity lasting a fraction of a second closes. Much of how we see is in fact learned behavior—often learned without our awareness of the process.

This raises some questions: *Can certain people see better than others—"faster," even? Can people be taught to see better?*

The answer appears to be yes, and one key factor appears to be experience.

Any parent who has taught their child to drive knows this. A car inches out from a side road. Sitting in the passenger seat, your foot moves instinctively to the brake (even though there's no pedal on your side), but your aspiring driver's foot does not. He doesn't yet know where to look and what to focus on. He is sorting through a hundred extraneous details while you are locked in on the few that matter most. You see signal; he sees noise; and your anxiety in those slivers of a second before he reacts reminds you that tiny differences in perceptive efficiency are highly significant under performance conditions.

It takes time to wire a brain for perceptive efficiency, especially when it seeks to read what Mark Seidenberg, a leading researcher on the "other" reading (the one that involves books), calls a "quasiregular system"—one that has "statistical tendencies but not inviolable rules."[2] Written English, for example. Or open play in the sport of your choice. Tendencies but not inviolable rules means *The through ball is on.* Or *If I can get her to lean left, the backdoor pass will be on.* It's Tony Romo glancing at the formation the Patriots are in during the AFC championship game broadcast and commenting "This usually means motion and a run out wide to the right" and all of us watching, a fraction of a second later, as the motion and run to the right unfold. Learning to read (text) or "read" (movement and spacing) is learning to perceive and process visual information as fast as you can see it. This requires, first and foremost, "vast experience"—immense quantities of small trial-and-error experiments from which the brain infers statistical trends. Ten thousand interactions decoding combinations of letters teaches us to glance at text and read it at the speed of sight. Ten thousand interactions with the body shape and relative position of players teaches us to glance at a field, court or rink and read it fluently and at the speed of sight also. Perceptive capacity is context specific and built over time. By the time you realize that your athletes need to start learning to read complex patterns quickly, the hour has already gotten very late.

Coaches, therefore, run the risk of underemphasizing decision-making during the most critical developmental years because it does not yet appear necessary to success. Worse, when players demonstrate poor decision-making later on, they are unlikely to trace the issues back to teaching decisions years earlier. They can neglect the most important factor in their athletes' long-term success and *never know it.*

Part of the problem is that players constantly make decisions whether we guide them or not. This might seem like a good thing, but haphazard, ill-informed decisions accrue into habit just as readily as good ones, and unlearning poor habits is a far more difficult task than learning better ones in the first place. This explains why some of the players we teach the worst are those who dominate at an early age. They win games by doing what no

2. *Language at the Speed of Sight* (23)

Watch "Tony Romo predicting the play" at www.coachguidetoteaching.com

one else is physically able to do, not necessarily what will succeed in five years or in an environment where everyone has athleticism, so coaches often allow or encourage them to make a habit of decisions that are unsustainable or counterproductive in the long run. We all know some of these players. Remember how they used to dribble past *everybody.* What happened to them? Did they lose interest? Did they lack the heart and motivation? Or does the answer, just possibly, start with our coaching?

XAVIER

In possession, he looks to play the ball into a space where no teammate ever seems to be.

Imagine a young player. Let's call him Xavier. He is out there in the ranks of players in your area. He is small and slightly slow of foot, not without skill but seemingly always caught from behind and pushed off the ball by bigger, faster players. In possession, he looks to play the ball into a space where no teammate ever seems to be. Often, he turns and plays the ball backwards, to the annoyance of the spectating parents (and possibly his coaches). *For crying out loud, Xavier, don't play it backwards!*

Would his club invest time and effort in Xavier as much as it would his speedy teammate, flashing forward to catch up to his own heavy touch and blasting home the winning goal?[3]

Imagine: if Xavier were to play with teammates who understood how and why to be in the space where he had been looking at all those times, he might not always play backwards. But he has long since been farmed out to the periphery of the club's attention, waiting in vain for passes from the other players who are not individually dominant and whom no one takes very seriously.

Perhaps Xavier is out there today, hoping to receive, turn, and strike a pass that cuts out two lines of defense. But the "best" player on the team is on his 12th consecutive touch. He has beaten his defender, but by the time he looks up, the defense is set. Xavier's clever run has long since become irrelevant. *Why*, our star thinks, *is Xavier standing **there**?*

Soon enough, even Xavier may come to ask this question too—and perhaps stop making his runs. Why would he continue? Skill at a tactical game is hard to spot and rarely rewarded unless others are playing the same game.[4] Is it worth asking how many players' ability to play in combination goes unseen because those around them do not play in combination? How many fail to develop their early instincts because they play on a team where an insightful run rarely earns the ball?

3. (Aside: Would the club teach its super-athlete the knowledge of how to find space between lines, say, when it would be much easier to allow him to feast for a few more years on a seemingly never-ending supply of balls over the top?)

4. Johann Cruyff described a version of this. "Someone who has juggled the ball in the air during a game, after which four defenders ... get the time to run back, that's the player people think is great." Instead, he noted, "Technique is passing the ball with one touch, with the right speed, at the right foot of your teammate."

5. Xavi, aka Xavier Hernandez, is today considered to be one of the best central midfielders of all time, known for his ability to read the game, orchestrate attacks, and dictate the speed of play. He epitomized the "tiki-taka" style of soccer that won Barcelona six league titles and three Champions League trophies in eight years and won Spain one World Cup and two European Championships in the same period—all with Xavi in the driver's seat.

6. One Premier League manager even lost the locker room when he refused his players access to ketchup (too sugary).

But let's imagine that with water and sunlight—that is to say attention, teaching, opportunity, faith, high expectations—Xavier might emerge a few years later, speed and size having evened out a bit, as Xavi,[5] clever on the ball but rarely touching it more than two or three times at a stretch and instead slicing opponents apart with perfectly angled passes.

At how many clubs would he get that water and sunlight?

Don't answer out loud. We both already know the truth.

Don't get me wrong, athleticism still matters. If it didn't, professional clubs would not manage the diets of their players.[6] Yet despite the tiny margin between each player and his potential replacement, the game's most dominant players always include a variety of those who are wiry despite the benefits of muscle, small despite the benefits of size, and comparatively slow in a game where speed is king. The likes of Xavi, Andrea Pirlo and N'Golo Kante tell us that the brain is the game's ultimate source of competitive advantage.

The ability to decide is, in short, both the most important attribute of a great player and the surest test of his or her coach, not only because it requires the discipline of future-focus but also because decision-making skills are difficult to teach even for those who believe in them.

What kind of "thinking players"?

One reason it is difficult to teach thinking is that it is difficult to recognize when thinking happens. This might seem like an absurd statement, but as David Eagleman points out in *Incognito: the Secret Lives of the Brain*, the thinking we are consciously aware of accounts for only a tiny proportion of our cognition. The great majority of it goes chugging along without our even knowing it. One of my goals in this chapter will be to describe the cognitive processes that happen during training and competition, both those we are generally aware of and those we are not. I hope to provide some thoughts on what you as a coach might do to better develop the various sorts of thinking athletes do. My focus will be on cognitive function during group invasion games like soccer as opposed to the cognition that happens during different sorts of sporting endeavor which might involve more extensive motor learning (such as baseball or golf) or more of what you might call endurance psychology (running or biking). There will of course be areas of overlap and I hope aspects of this chapter are useful to a broad range of coaches. I note that I am not a scientist by training. Instead I have tried to take applicable research and think about it through a lens of teaching and learning.

I'll start by making a distinction between two cognitive processes that are often referred to interchangeably: **decision-making** and **problem-solving**. One (problem-solving) is generally slow and the other (decision-making) is often fast. Decision-making is the cognitive process players use more frequently during a match, but problem-solving is important in developing associations that ultimately support faster thinking during the game. Speed might seem like a relatively trivial point on which to focus, but of course it isn't trivial to an athlete. When we talk about "instincts" and "game sense" in an athlete, we are usually talking about decisions that are made faster than we can consciously think, a skill that requires its own processes.

I'll also examine the mechanics of perception. As I've mentioned, it is more complex and subjective than most people realize. "Half our brain is dedicated almost exclusively to vision," observes Irving Biederman. We can be "misled into thinking it is a very easy, simple process because it occurs so quickly and automatically." But expertise, in many ways, is knowing what to look for and where to find it.

 A study of professional pianist Daniel Beliavsky and his student Charlotte Bennett shows this connection. Sight reading a piece of new music—processing cues, deciding how to act on them, coordinating his decisions with physical motions—Beliavsky's eyes consistently move precisely to the phrase just ahead of the one he is playing, going first to the treble clef and then the base clef—something we know because in the video, he is wearing a pair of vision-tracking glasses as he plays. The range of vision—where he looks—is narrow, steady and consistent. Much steadier than Bennett's. She scans a wider range of the visual field and is not as consistent in where she directs her eyes. This is unexpected. Beliavsky, the expert, is taking in less visual information to guide his decisions than his student. But this is because he knows exactly where to look to find the right cues, and he locks in on them earlier. His perception captures more signal and less noise. What's more, he does this unconsciously. "I wasn't even aware that I did that," he notes, watching his eye movements on the screen.

Watch "Pianist vision-tracking" at
www.coachguidetoteaching.com

DANIEL BELIAVSKY

There are at least two things that differentiate an expert from a very good but still developing apprentice. First, his expertise comes from subconscious knowledge about where to look. Second, he can process what he sees efficiently because what his hands do is automatic and fluid and so his working memory is free to focus almost exclusively on what he perceives.

Studies have found similar trends among teachers. Compared to novices, *veteran teachers looked at less but saw more*. Their eye movements, like Beliavsky's, were steadier and narrower. With experience they had come to know where to look to reliably see the important variables.

For athletes, the mark of expertise is often the habit of consistently and unconsciously looking in the right place: find the signal; ignore the noise. A recent vision-tracking study of Cristiano Ronaldo (widely regarded as among the game's top two or three players, for those who aren't soccer fans) shows him doing essentially this in keeping a ball from a defender—focusing on cues from the hips and knees of the defender, locking in on the key data in a methodical way and reacting with a deeply encoded skill. ▶ Critically, he is unaware that he does this. Experts see differently from novices. They are quite literally seeing different things and watching a different game.

Watch "Cristiano Ronaldo vision-tracking" at www.coachguidetoteaching.com

7. A colleague who coaches basketball at the collegiate level recently sent me an interview with one of the Navy SEALs responsible for the raid that killed Osama bin Laden. In describing how the team successfully reacted to the disastrous crash of one of its two helicopters as they landed at Bin Laden's compound in Pakistan, he noted: "I think what SEALs are good at is what I consider pickup basketball. You know … We all know how to move efficiently and tactically. And we can communicate clearly. So when something goes sideways, we're able to play the pickup basketball and just kind of read off each other."

8. Willingham, D. (2010) *Why don't students like school?* San Francisco, CA: Jossey-Bass.

Another form of decision-making involves the coordination of individual decisions within a group. This relies on a mildly strange idea: while individual players engage in problem-solving only infrequently during live play (it happens too slowly), teams constantly solve problems during games. By understanding and anticipating the decisions of those around them more efficiently than the opposition, good teams predict and react to one another optimally[7] and achieve something that is similar to problem-solving or perhaps artificial intelligence.

Finally we'll examine one of the key factors that can cause a group's problem-solving behavior to happen. Knowledge forms the foundation of all higher order cognitive functions including critical thinking, problem-solving and decision-making. "Data from the last thirty years lead to a conclusion that is not scientifically challengeable," writes University of Virginia psychologist Daniel Willingham.[8] "Thinking well requires knowing facts, and that's true not simply because you need something to think about. *The very processes that teachers care about most—critical thinking processes such as reasoning and problem-solving—are intimately intertwined with factual knowledge that is in long-term memory (not just found in the environment)."*[9] (My emphasis)

It's important to note that factual knowledge's role as the basis of understanding, critical thinking and even creativity is all but consensus among cognitive scientists, but popular opinion—and often the opinion of educators—leans the opposite way. Learning facts to them is a "lower order" activity, a waste of time in a world where you can google anything. The assumption is that problem-solving and critical thinking are abstract skills that can be applied across different domains once learned. They are, in the words of a cognitive scientist, "transferable."

I understand why this idea is so compelling. The notion that, once learned, critical thinking could be applied flexibly from one setting to another is a beautiful idea. Unfortunately it is also at odds with the realities of brain function. Critical thinking and problem-solving are heavily context specific. You can think critically only about those areas where you have knowledge. To think critically about Napoleon's decisions at Waterloo, you need to know about Napoleon's personality and motivations, his relationships with his generals, the nature of the British and Prussian commanders, and their position on the field on June 18, 1815. Without this knowledge, you could try to think critically about why he attacked and whether it was reckless, but in the end you would be guessing, and *guessing is not critical thinking.*

For it to be useful in thinking, knowledge must be encoded in *long-term memory*. Working memory—things you are consciously thinking about—is preciously small,[10] and trying to think about or remember one thing reduces our capacity to think about any other thing. In other words, if you have to think consciously about something, it keeps you from thinking about other things—and from perceiving the world around you accurately, as we will discover.[11] The more we want our players to think well, then, the more knowledge they must carry in their long-term memory and the more we have to help them keep their working memory free for efficient perception.

Actually, factual knowledge does more than free up working memory for more accurate perception. Perception, too, is knowledge-based. In a study of how physicists studied complex problems, Chi, Glaser and Feltovich found that experts see deep principles when observing and deciding which approaches to use to solve complex problems, whereas novices notice superficial features that do not help them reliably solve the problems.

Decision-making vs problem-solving

Daniel Kahneman's Nobel Prize-winning research began as an effort to understand why people make predictable thinking errors. In *Thinking Fast and Slow*, he attempts to clarify the roles in the brain of two different thinking "systems," which he calls simply "system 1" and "system 2." They are connected, of course, but they function with a surprising degree of independence.

System 1 thinks fast. It has evolved in part to keep us alive in crisis situations—to see something flying at us and react faster than we can have a conscious thought. There is no time to consider, "What is that flying at me?" or even to verbalize "Watch out!" Our brains require a *duck-first-ask-questions-later* system.

9. If you don't believe Willingham, here's the National Research Council on the topic: "Over a century of research on transfer has yielded little evidence that teaching can develop general cognitive competencies that are transferable to any new discipline, problem or context, in or out of school." Cognition is not a transferable skill and is always context specific. www.bit.ly/3jw9LTR

10. Long-term memory, by contrast, is essentially unlimited.

11. Even creativity appears to be much more closely linked to knowledge than most people understand. In fact, many cognitive scientists think that creativity is a sudden association between something you perceive and an unexpected connection in long-term memory: it starts with the strange connection of two disparate ideas, one of which is in your memory. *Look at them playing 4-3-3 at Old Trafford. It's like Napoleon at Waterloo!*

"System 1 is more influential than your experience tells you," writes Kahneman, "and it is the secret author of many of the choices and judgments you make." This is not limited to decisions where speed is of the essence. It is constantly assessing and processing our surroundings in ways we are not aware of, and many of the things we do out of instinct are governed by this portion of the brain. In *Incognito*, David Eagleman describes an example: a study where men were shown pictures of a group of women and asked to score their attractiveness. Half of the pictures featured women with dilated pupils—an indication of arousal—and the men reliably picked these women more often, but without recognizing their dilated pupils. They were conscious only of picking who seemed attractive. Net: perceptions we are not conscious of having exert a constant and far-reaching influence on our decisions.

One of system 1's other important characteristics is that it is always on. We cannot suppress it, for the most part, even if we want to. If presented with a line of text written in your native language, for example, you cannot look at it without reading it.

No Parking

Only in unusual circumstances would you be able to glance at that sentence and not read it. This tells us that our perception automatically initiates other higher forms of thinking. It takes years to learn to read, but once you learn to create meaning out of what you perceive, you cannot turn the connection off. Because it often functions faster than conscious thought and therefore without conscious oversight, system 1 is prone to mistakes. You duck, but it's just a tree limb swaying in the wind. You slam on the brakes, but it's just a shadow.

We compensate for this via what Kahneman calls "system 2." This system thinks more carefully. It can deliberate and weigh options, test a hypothesis, change its mind. It thinks: *That could be a bird but it also could be a shadow.* It's where "critical thinking" and problem-solving happen.

But system 2 isn't perfect either. One problem is that it's tiring to use, so we are "lazy" about using system 2. We only do it when we must. Getting a group of students or athletes to turn system 2 on—and keep it on—during training takes work. Coaches and teachers have to build a culture that makes being locked-in and mentally on a habit if they want to problem-solve. (I discuss this in chapter 3.)

Another thing about system 2: it's slow—with "slow" being a relative term. It takes the brain about six-tenths of a second to have a conscious thought. By most measures, that's pretty quick. But being an athlete often requires something faster. In baseball, for example, a pitched ball arrives at home plate in about four-tenths of a second—faster than a batter can have a conscious thought in response.

For years, people presumed that reaction time was the key to hitting; faster reactions for faster pitches. But as David Epstein describes in *The Sports Gene*, the great slugger Albert Pujols was found, at the height of his prowess, to have a reaction time that was below average for the adult male population.[12] Something else must have allowed him to hit a ball moving that quickly. That something turns out to be perception: a batter like Pujols perceives visual cues from the pitcher's motion as and before he releases the ball—angle of shoulder, position of wrist, rate of hip rotation. The batter's brain processes these visual

12. The general college age population—not baseball players.

cues and predicts the pitch without his ever intentionally looking for them or *even his consciously being aware of them*. Many batters, even successful ones, still think it's about reaction time, and this is profound. The typical batter never knows what the true drivers of his success are and is not even aware that they happen. He has learned the tools of his greatness accidentally and without knowing it.

ALBERT PUJOLS

Were there experiences or even coaches that caused them to look for cues differently or better than others? Were coaches even aware of this critical function?

These questions are important because most group invasion games also feature moments when deciding faster than conscious thought is required. A space is about to open behind an opposition midfielder, and before you realize it, you have flicked the ball into the opening with the outside of your foot. You didn't think about the pass and you didn't think about the surface. You may have only vaguely realized your teammate was moving into the space. You acted before you knew you'd perceived the cue. This is system 1 at work. The moment of recognition—"I can't believe I just made that pass"—is in fact system 2 observing system 1's activity.

"The best decisions aren't made with your mind but with your instinct," is how perhaps the game's greatest player, Lionel Messi puts it. "The more familiar with a situation you become, the quicker, the better your decisions will be." The one thing I would add is that they are not *instincts* in the technical sense—i.e. innate fixed responses—but rather habits encoded in long-term memory which we associate faster than we can decide to act with a given perception. Part of a coach's task, then, is to teach players to make effective decisions when conscious thought is impractical or even counter-productive. This is often referred to as the perception-action linkage.

LIONEL MESSI

The best decisions aren't made with your mind but with your instinct.

However, just because some decisions must be made faster than conscious thought does not mean all of them must be. A striker presses the opposition's outside back. She's closing at a run. But while she must decide quickly, she is still able to think consciously about her angle of approach and adapt it to the game model. Most thinking probably involves some overlap of the two systems—it relies on a foundation of unconscious or preconscious perceptions managed by system 1, but it is further shaped by the conscious thoughts of system 2 when the action slows down slightly and so requires coordination of both systems.

This is important to recognize because the coordination of the two systems can reveal another flaw in our cognition. When working hard, system 2 can degrade the functions of system 1, especially its perceptions. Try to do something that requires conscious thought while making a left turn across traffic—adjust the climate control system in your car or talk on the phone—and suddenly you are several times more likely to have an accident. System 1, which perceives and recognizes patterns in time and space, can get worse at these tasks when system 2 is churning away.

So it's not entirely clear how much we want our striker, closing on the outside back, to actively think about her angle of approach. Perhaps we want it to be automatic. Or perhaps we want her decisions to be automatic *until something she perceives tells her the situation is atypical in some way and requires a more active decision*. Perhaps she is waiting for a cue the coach has pointed out—a bad first touch, a soft pass, a ball in the air—to tell her to strike. She sees it and suddenly locks in. This is what Berliner describes expert teachers as doing when they watch a classroom. They watch calmly, almost passively—more so than a novice—until something cues them that a situation recalls or does not match the model of what is supposed to happen. Then they attend to it consciously and carefully.

"Consciousness developed because it was advantageous," Eagleman observes in *Incognito*, "but *advantageous only in limited amounts*." (My emphasis) He is speaking in evolutionary terms, but he might just as well be speaking about athletic endeavor.

So the two systems in a player's brain work in both coordination and tension. One thinks fast and can operate subconsciously but is prone to errors; the other thinks deeply, is capable of keen insight, but moves slowly and can disrupt more pressing cognitive functions.

Ironies of a 'problem-solving game'

In problem-solving, the brain seeks new solutions to complex challenges. It often involves trial and error or deliberate step-by-step analysis. It's a system 2 task, which is to say it has a speed problem. There are flashes of insight during problem-solving, of course, but generally problem-solving is slow. By necessity, then, most thinking during a match is *not problem-solving*. And this at first seems ironic given that soccer is a "problem-solving game," but problem-solving remains critical in several ways.

First, problem-solving is one of the primary tools coaches use to support decision-making and build long-term memory. The thinking players do in a game may not always use the full capacities of system 2 but players often rely on slower critical system 2 thinking to encode and build understanding of the decisions they will adapt in the game. Memory, Willingham explains, is the residue of cognitive effort, and effortless execution is often the residue of effortful—mentally and physically—training. Cognitive scientists call this "desirable difficulty." Perversely, one of the best ways to help players think quickly in the game is probably to use more deliberate thinking—at the right times and in the right ways—during training.

Second, the aggregation of individual decisions can ultimately produce something that looks a lot like problem-solving at the team level. If the players on a team can "read" one another's decisions—if they know why teammates are making certain decisions and can anticipate what they will try next, then they can engage in a sort of group problem-solving, especially when coupled with more deliberate thinking during natural breaks in the game. What we seek, then, is not just strong decision-making from players but decision-making that is "legible" to teammates so players can read and understand one another's actions.

I'll return to problem-solving soon, but first, given that decision-making accounts for so much of the thinking players do during performance, let's examine it more closely.

Decisions and how they happen

In the words of Todd Beane of Barcelona's TOVO Academy, "It all starts with perception." The "it" here is decision-making. We are deciding even as we are perceiving a situation because we shape and select what we see right from the start.

To perceive is to prioritize. We think we simply objectively see a visual field in front of us but in fact this is an illusion—the "user illusion."[13] "You think being conscious means perceiving everything around you but in fact it means perceiving small slices of reality and … being able to switch back and forth," is how the cognitive scientist Steven Johnson describes it. When you look, your brain fills in a wide array of blanks to cause what you see to make sense. This involves its making assumptions about what's probably there. Our peripheral vision is so blurry as to be useless, for example, and there's a spot 15 degrees to the outside of the center of your field of vision where the visual nerve attaches. There are no sensory cells there. It's your blind spot. A sleight-of-hand artist can put an object right before our eyes and contrive for us not to see it at all,[14] but we never notice that because our brain fills in the blanks when it can't see. It also makes decisions about what it should pay attention to in the visual field, again often without our conscious control.

In one experiment, for example, the psychologist Alfred Yarbus asked subjects to look at a painting while he tracked their eye movements. Yarbus began asking subjects different questions about the painting, and this changed where their eyes focused. Asked to give the ages of the people in the painting, subjects unconsciously scrutinized their faces. Asked to estimate their wealth, they focused on clothing. Subjects' eyes moved in different patterns depending on what they needed to know, but crucially (and by now hopefully predictably) they were not aware they had done so. "As your eyes interrogate the world, they are like agents on a mission," Eagleman notes. "Even though they are 'your' eyes, you have little idea what duty they're on." But if subjects' brains unconsciously routed their eyes to the places in the painting that were most important, how did their brains know how to do that? The answer is experience. The tacit knowledge implicit in looking in the right place comes from ten thousand iterations of discerning people's ages from their faces or wealth from their clothes.

Your knowledge and experience tell you where to look on the playing field as well. For example, where should your eyes go to predict the pass you seek to defend? At the eyes of the player with the ball? The feet? The hips? How often do you scan among these places?

13. The term was coined by the Danish writer Tor Nørretranders.

14. Having you look at a spot on the table, she'd move the scissors into your blind spot, which you would find was huge and shockingly central to your field of vision. You don't notice it because your brain compensates for it cognitively all the time.

15. Sam Vine, University of Exeter, quoted in The Atlantic monthly: www.bit.ly/32NLm5x

How often do you scan to other spaces around you to observe other players, for example? Which spaces? You very likely don't think about where to look. In fact, you probably don't even know where you look, even if you are an outstanding defender. As one cognitive scientist put it, "People often think they're looking somewhere and they're wrong."[15] You look without knowing why you focus on what you do. What experience has not taught you to look for, you may never see.

Joan Vickers, a cognitive scientist at the University of Calgary, argues, like Berliner, that the gaze of an expert is very different from that of a novice. Her term for it is "the quiet eye" because experts' eyes lock in on the salient details within their gaze earlier in an interaction and tend to stay there more steadily and longer than novices. This is critical: sometimes players make poor decisions with full information. They choose wrong. But just as likely, they never knew what options existed. They never saw the pass they should have made because they had not learned where to look for what was important. They had not learned to see. So if we want better decisions, the place to start is with the eyes, to guide them to see—and make a habit of looking at—the most salient details of a situation.

Learning to see

If much of perceiving is an unconscious product of knowledge and experience, it means several things.

First, athletes must have extensive exposure to the geometry of the game, the benefits of which can be accelerated by instruction on how to look; that is, knowing what details—what cues—are most relevant. Second, our teaching should often focus on guiding players' eyes to find the signal amidst the noise. As I will discuss in chapter 3, asking *What do you see?* might just yield a better decision than asking *What decision should you make here?* Third, it's likely that the mechanics of looking can be improved. This is the principle behind South African researcher Sherylle Calder's work. She trains professional athletes to see better. During her work with England's national rugby team, for example, she noticed a player who was poor at catching the high balls. "If you can't catch high balls, there's a tendency to think that's just the way it is," Calder told CNN,[16] but she was able to train the player to improve his vertical peripheral vision through daily exercises. And while training peripheral vision may be more technical that most youth clubs can manage, Calder does offer some universal advice. Smartphones, she argues, narrow our peripheral vision and degrade our visual systems. The long-term effect is significant, but so is the short-term one. She suggests telling athletes to stay off their phones on days they compete.

16. www.cnn.it/34WnGOU

Finally, the crucial role of knowledge and experience in seeing explains why *you cannot turn on decision-making quickly*. It takes years of experience looking at the right things to be able to "see" or "read" the game. To return to the reading analogy, if you want to be fluent, you have to start young. In soccer, you cannot hope at age 12 or 14 to throw a switch and have players look up and start seeing the field correctly when for six or seven years they have been standing in lines or staring down at the ball they are dribbling or even playing with teammates whose movements are random and not predictive of what they will see in future games. By then it is too late. They will look but they will not see.

Geons and chunks

One fascinating attribute of the brain's visual cortex is that it can predict what things will look like even when we have never seen them before. Take a certain chair, for example, maybe one sitting across the room from you now. Once you've looked at it for as little as a tenth of a second, you can see an image of the chair from a totally different angle and, even if you've never looked at it from that angle, recognize it as *that* chair. You can extrapolate: *Oh, that's **my** chair, but viewed from below and farther away*. This is what Biederman calls "the miracle of pattern recognition," and pattern recognition is gold to athletes.

The brain can perform this miracle, Biederman says, because it can decompose complex shapes into simpler ones, which he calls "geons." "It turns out that you can model most objects in terms of a very small vocabulary of these simple shapes, numbering about 30 or 40," Biederman says. "If we represent an object we're looking at in terms of geons, then we're able to recognize what the object is from almost any viewpoint." Once your brain knows its core geometry, it can take what it knows about that geometry and apply it very quickly to new and even hypothetical situations.

Another important finding about perception involves an idea called "chunking," which is the ability of experts to process more information than novices because they process it chunks. Remembering the letters in this sequence—T ob EOR n oTOB E— is a lot easier when you see it not as 12 single points of data but as 6 words—"To be or not to be"—or even one familiar phrase. Similarly ,show an image of a chessboard to a group of expert players and they will be able to remember far more of the board than novices. This was revealed in a famous study by Herbert Simon. When he showed experts arrangements of pieces on a chess board that were typical of the middle or the end of a game for just five seconds, experts could remember where about two-thirds of the pieces had been. Novice players "could remember ... only about four" pieces, Anders Ericsson relates in *Peak*. This appeared at first to show that expert players had prodigious memories, perhaps caused by their chess playing but also perhaps a natural gift—the very thing that caused them to be so good. Interestingly, though, Simon proved that the ability to chunk was domain specific by next assessing players' ability to remember pieces on the board *when they were arranged randomly* and thus in a shape that would *not* have occurred during an actual game. In that case, Ericsson relates, expert players suddenly did no better than novices. Devoid of context of the game as it was supposed to be played, the perceptive advantage of expertise disappeared. Players had to understand what they were looking at, not just be familiar with it, or the perceptive advantage disappeared. It is not enough to stand in the middle of a swirling phase of midfield play to develop your ability to perceive. You must understand what you are looking at: the midfielder is trying to draw her opponent out of her proper shape so her teammate can sneak in behind. This is one reason why the idea that the game is the best teacher is not supported by science. The game teaches those who have first been caused to understand.

Simon argues that experts processed the positions of the chess pieces in "chunks." They saw packets of information: a rook threatening a bishop defended by two pawns was one single "thing" to them—a chunk of information. Put in soccer terms, an expert doesn't see a right back pressed ten yards above the midfield line and near the touchline and then a right center back just behind the midfield line and 25 yards in from the touchline, etc., as a novice would. The expert sees a back four shaped properly, perhaps compressed to absorb pressure. Or they see a back four compressed to absorb pressure but with the center backs too far apart. How far apart? Well, a little more than they should be. Experts used "mental representation"—conceptions based on knowledge and experience—to make sense of large amounts of information very quickly. Ericsson argues that these "mental representations" are a key to accelerating perceptive ability.

These representations also draw an expert's heightened attention when something is out of place. I experienced this myself watching a game with former Scottish international defender Iain Munro. He described the shape he expected to see in the back four as being "like a saucer." To him, looking at the back four was seeing a single image, the curving arc of a line traced across the field—a mental representation—and so he saw everything at a glance. "The left back is exposed," he said at one point as we watched a match. "He's too wide and has turned inside to correct his position. He cannot see his man." As he spoke, a long diagonal ball was driven to the opponent that the defender had ever so briefly lost sight of. Moments later, it was 1-0 to the opposition. Munro was eating a sandwich and chatting with me as he made this observation, looking out of the corner of his eye, and he had instantly seen that something was "wrong"—one of the players was not where he was supposed to be. That caused him to look closer.

Chunking, in other words, helps players see and predict more accurately, as Ericsson found when he showed soccer players videos of matches. He stopped the video when a player had just received the ball. Better players could better recall where players were, what direction they were moving and where the ball was. And they were better at predicting what would happen next.

"The better players," Ericsson related, "had a more highly developed ability to interpret the pattern of action on the field. This ability allowed them to perceive which players' movements and interactions mattered most, which allowed them to make better decisions about where to go on the field, when to pass and to whom and so on."

But there's more. As Ericsson explains, the advantage of seeing better gets bigger over time because the brain is plastic and is constantly repurposing neural circuitry to help it respond to the demands it is faced with. Brain scans of London cabbies, for example, show expanded circuitry in the portion of the brain associated with route mapping.[17] In the end, the brain perceives more of what it perceives often, and an early advantage in perception—a better mental representation—compounds over time. For this reason, it is critical to pay attention to young players' visual environment. They must gain enough exposure to the core geometries of soccer—or whatever sport they play—to be able to see at a glance and understand.[18] Once the brain knows its core shapes and can form useful mental representations, it can begin to predict how events will play out and adapt quickly.

Recent research by Geir Jordet at the Norwegian School of Sport Sciences has shown how often elite players "scan"—that is, look away from the ball to gauge the position of players and space around them—more often than less proficient players. "Those who [scan] most frequently are those with the clearest picture of their surroundings ... when they receive the ball," Sam Dean recently wrote in The *Telegraph*. "The best midfielders, Jordet has found, will scan five or six times in those ten seconds." When I shared this with coaches at several professional academies, they wrote back immediately. They were aware of the

17. Well, they did before mapping software replaced Well, they did before mapping software replaced the skill. Now their brains are expanded in the part that uses Snapchat and Twitter, just like everybody else's. The example is Ericsson's in Peak, though. the skill. Now their brains are expanded in the part that uses Snapchat and Twitter, just like everybody else's. The example is Ericsson's in *Peak*, though.

18. Several top NBA players (Kobe Bryant; Steve Nash) credit their special awareness on the basketball court to playing small-sided soccer, notes John O'Sullivan, founder of Changing the Game Project.

research and had been incorporating the requirement or encouragement to scan into exercises. It was encouraging to see coaches embracing the power of perception so proactively. It's also worth noting that while scanning seems deeply important, it's probably necessary but not sufficient. You can look but not see much, of course, because your ability to see as quickly as you can look determines the effectiveness of each scan. This may also imply that simply scanning more often may not help some players until they can perceive better.

SAM
DEAN

> Those who [scan] most frequently are those with the clearest picture of their surroundings ...when they receive the ball.

A menu of responses

Imagine that we find Xavier having finally made the first team. He's in the middle of a match, in fact, and is positioned just inside his opponents' half, facing his own goal and preparing to receive a ball played in to him by a deep lying central midfielder. Over his shoulder, he notices an opponent closing hard and two other defenders have turned slightly toward him, preparing to close if needed but obscuring their vision of the space behind them slightly. One of them moves a step or two closer. Very quickly, Xavier's brain must cue a series of reactions: a "shield the ball" response in his body shape, perhaps; a decision about where to direct his first touch. Xavier's success is predicated partly on the quality of his perception and partly on the automaticity of the required receiving and shielding skills. If he can execute them with a minimum of working memory, he will see more.

But there are a series of shared tactical perceptions happening too. Three players closing on Xavier will mean opportunity created somewhere else. If Xavier and his teammates can get the ball there quickly, they will have a numerical advantage. The pressure he feels should cause him and his teammates to perceive the cue for a sequence of tactical decisions that they will have rehearsed as often as he has rehearsed his shielding of the ball. Xavier takes a touch to lure his opponents in and then plays backwards to a nearby teammate, Beto. It's a slowish pass and in seeing it, Beto knows he must scan the field to find the place where the numerical advantage lies. The pace of Xavier's pass is telling him this. It says: *You saw the three men closing, right? I'm buying you a fraction of a second.* Beto knows he must scan before he gets the ball because his coach will have stressed that only a pass on the first touch can fully seize the advantage. Out on the wing, another teammate, Claudio, is also reading the signal. He knows Beto's pass will be coming if he can get into a position of opportunity. He suddenly cuts diagonally into a space between the lines. His defender is a step slow to react because he does not read Xavier's backpass as a signal nor understand the sequence of actions it implies. Xavier and company are now several moves ahead.

Coordinating decisions

Xavier's interaction with his teammate at midfield suggests a critical factor that enables coordinated decision-making (what you might call group problem-solving). A team with shared understanding of how they want to play and what options are preferred in specific situations will be able to "read" one another's actions faster and better than the defense can. If they have a clear shared understanding of their goals and priorities in specific situations, they will read one another's signals and communicate through their actions.

19. I'm indebted to Christian Lavers for this term.

They will read the game in a similar way, using a similar visual vocabulary. They will appear to have second sight. This is the killer app in elite soccer.

A "game model"[19] is the name for this shared understanding of *how we want to play*, spelled out in specific settings. It is as close as there is to a Rosetta Stone for group problem-solving. Such a model is a series of interlinked mental representations in Ericsson's terminology—a vision of what it looks like described in generally applicable principles. It is a more refined version of the term "principles of play" but goes beyond what coaches typically refer to as principles. As Christian Lavers, president of the Elite Clubs National League, explained it to me, principles of play are the same regardless of your style of play, but a game model is specific to a team and sometimes a setting (that is, a team could have different game models for when they are pressing and when they are lying deep). It is, in a sense, a set of team agreements. *When pressing, we will seek to prevent the ball from crossing the field left to right or right to left across the midline. When attacking through the midfield, we will seek to attract pressure and play back and out quickly.*

It is the coach's job, then, to build "knowledge": an understanding of the situations the game creates and the available solutions. This knowledge is useful to the degree that it:

- is encoded in long-term memory.
- has clear and precise names attached to it so coaches and players can recall and refer to it precisely and quickly.
- is connected to specific goals so players can coordinate their response to given situations. We can only make coordinated decisions if we understand our purpose.

Some people might see this as too controlling in a fluid game, but perhaps the opposite is true. Building knowledge and vocabulary during training allows for coordinated decision-making among players without the coach's intervention. We cannot teach critical thinking, problem-solving or decision-making in the abstract, cognitive science tells us. We can only do those things in the context of specific situations and relevant knowledge.

TOVO Academy's Todd Beane shared a favorite phrase of his father-in-law, Johan Cruyff: "Doing simple things at speed makes them seem complex." Complexity is sometimes an illusion, in other words—often to the other team (certainly to Xavier, Beto and Claudio's opponents) but even to ourselves, maybe. Perhaps Xavier's coach will have had players do so many versions of the pattern—in to pressure, back and then through—that Claudio won't even know where the idea for his run came from. Often what looks like the generation of new and unexpected ideas is in fact the use of known ideas in slightly distinctive adaptations with a high degree of coordination. This definition of creativity involves piecemeal contributions by a number of players who are reading one another's actions quickly on a sophisticated level. That may sound like a limiting definition of creativity, but consider our own genetic makeup. It is determined to a large degree by variations in the sequence of four basic chemicals in our DNA: adenine, guanine, cytosine and thymine. Vary the order and sequence of just four variables and you have sufficient creativity to create billions of unique individuals.

A last thought on creativity as it applies to sports. The creativity we seek on the field or courts is often quite different from the creativity we might seek in other settings. What we usually mean by creativity in sports is not an entirely new discovery but an unexpected application or adaptation of a common idea. These are different things. Rugby was invented when a player picked up the ball mid soccer game. Creative in the general sense of the word, but not so much if your goal is to play better soccer. The creativity we are looking for often isn't something "outside the box." It is rather an unexpected or inventive inside-the-box solution—individually or coordinated by multiple people. "A lot of people say how creative the All Blacks are or how much flair there is," famed New Zealand rugby coach Wayne Smith recently an interviewer, "but creativity is just practice that's camouflaged. It comes from hard work."[20]

WAYNE SMITH

A lot of people say how creative the All Blacks are or how much flair there is but creativity is just practice that's camouflaged.

20. www.bit.ly/2EZkB5J

Department of skepticism: all difficulty is not desirable

"Desirable difficulty" is the term cognitive psychologists use to describe cognitive challenges that result in greater learning. Learning requires effort, but this does mean that the converse is true. All mental effort does not cause learning. Learning occurs when problems are challenging but not unsolvable, and when the difficulty is focused on the task learners are trying to remember. This was borne out recently in a study of a new font called "Sans Forgetica," which looks like this:

Sans Forgetica

The idea was that if you learned more when you worked harder cognitively, why not make people work harder to read text. Sans Forgetica's designers hoped that because it was more difficult to read, people would better remember what they read. Alas, they were only half right.[21] As researchers at the University of Warwick found, Sans Forgetica *is* hard to read, "but does not boost memory." The designers had made readers work harder at a task extraneous to the content they were trying to learn.

21. www.bit.ly/2GhP0Nd

This is relevant to coaches because coaches sometimes design exercises that increase difficulty in order to speed learning, and these ideas often focus on perception, but this does not mean players will learn the intended topic better.

Bunnies and Guns is a somewhat exaggerated example. It's billed as "cognitive skills training for athletes" and promises to develop athletes' thinking skills by requiring them to complete complex multi-tasking activities—executing step patterns on an agility ladder, say, while at the same time making a pattern of signals with their hands, alternating between a bunny (two fingers up) and a gun (one finger out), say. It's full of multi-tasking and mental challenges. It seems very compelling when a "technical skills coach" weighs in about "synergies" between "our brain's left and right hemispheres." But Bunnies and Guns isn't making athletes think about the task they are trying to learn. It is adding what cognitive scientists would call extraneous cognitive load (unrelated to what you want to master) rather than intrinsic cognitive load (work focused on what you want to master). It's using up working memory perceiving and executing tasks that are largely irrelevant. Thinking better on the soccer field consists of 1) perceiving better, 2) associating a pattern in those perceptions with a rehearsed series of actions and 3) adapting and applying those actions to the specific case. Athletes who do Bunnies and Guns will get better at Bunnies and Guns and they will free themselves to think more deeply as they shuttle through their agility ladders. But that's about it.

As absurd as Bunnies and Guns sounds, it's easy to unintentionally add extrinsic cognitive load through the best of intentions, especially when we are trying to build perceptive cues into training. For example, I've observed a lot of training sessions where an athlete will be asked to react to a color or a number while executing a skill or making a decision. They receive a ball while the coach calls out "Blue!" or "Red!" or "One!" or "Two!" and then have to attack a blue or red goal or play backwards (one) or turn and play forwards (two). One downside of such examples of extraneous cognitive load is that they cause athletes to use their working memory reacting to things athletes will never see on the field. Straining to connect the word "blue" to an action and then a direction may keep athletes from using working memory to encode the skill or make observations that might be useful perceptively. It might be better to try to simulate a game cue (a defender on your back) or simply to allow players to choose a goal to attack.

Similarly many approaches to training try to build perception skills and presume

JENNY FINCH

that they are transferable. In one popular video, players wear colored vests in four different colors with the coach shouting commands during the session instructing the players to form new teams based on new color combinations during live play. First green and blue are teammates. Then, upon the coach's command, green and yellow become teammates. The same for blue and red. Players have to receive and react.

Perception, however, is also probably not a transferable skill. Learning to perceive stimuli that are unrelated to match conditions will not likely assist you in perceiving better during competition. Evidence of this can be seen in the second half of the story of major league batters told in Epstein's *The Sports Gene*. Major league hitters excel at hitting, Epstein argues, because they read the visual cues presented in the delivery motion of pitchers rather than because of fast reaction time. In other words, it is a context-specific skill (using unconscious background knowledge about pitchers' deliveries), not a transferable skill (reaction time). As evidence, Epstein describes how women's softball ace Jennie Finch barnstormed around major league baseball spring training camps one year to challenge the game's best hitters to stand up to her fastball. She had lots of takers—including Barry Bonds, then the game's elite slugger. It's not surprising they took her challenge—and did so with a bit of bravado. Even ignoring any potential gender bias, when you send 90+ mph fastballs to the cheap seats all day, you can be forgiven for not putting much credit in the idea of someone getting a softball past you at 60mph. What Bonds did not account for was that his lifetime of knowledge about shoulder position and arm speed would be useless against a completely unfamiliar delivery from a master. Finch struck him out on three pitches. Perception, too, is context specific.

PART 2: WHAT TO DO ABOUT IT

So what should coaches do to translate this information into better training?

The rest of this chapter consists of suggestions and tools to be applied differently to fit each coach and club as well as their players' age, skill and understanding. The recommendations are not a formula because there is no formula. At minimum, these ideas require application and adaptation. Doubly so because I am keenly aware that many of my readers know more about their own sport than I do.

If some of what you read sounds like familiar ideas perhaps refined and adapted, that's a good thing. There's no revolution here. Evolution is more powerful in the long run. My goal is to describe how small changes and a bit more intentionality in an environment similar to what many coaches already use can be a game-changer.

Balanced approaches

Let's start with the million-dollar question: "What's the best teaching method?"

The answer is: there isn't one—or at least there isn't *just* one. The things coaches must teach include a diverse array of knowledge and skills—from how to strike a ball to drive it over the opposition to how to play against a high press—and they teach them to professionals and ten-year-olds. Under such conditions, the methods won't be the same for everything we seek to teach and in every context. The ideal training environment should not be a monoculture in terms of methods, *no matter how effective a given method is for some purposes*. The hammer is an excellent tool. It's your go-to for attaching a baseboard. But to cut the baseboard you'll need a saw. To ask which tool is better is to miss the point of the toolbox. It's also worth noting that coaches operate in what the economist Robin Hogarth describes as a "wicked learning environment"—one in which there are often mismatches between decisions and the feedback that comes to us after we make them. In such environments, you can do the right thing and be unsuccessful (and thus have it appear that you were wrong); you can do the wrong thing and have it appear to have been right. Clarity emerges in the aggregate. Over time, you start to discern the trends. Maria Konnikova describes something similar in *The Biggest Bluff*, a chronicle of her efforts to master professional poker which, like coaching, is a long game where the apparent result of each decision is an unreliable indicator of whether it was a smart strategy over the long run, and where you win by constantly attuning to the changing signals that a hundred data points are broadcasting. She enlists Erik Seidel, one of the all-time masters of the game, as her coach, but when she asks for hard and fast rules—What is the best way to play this hand?—he advises: "Less certainty, more inquiry." One has to learn without becoming reflexive to succeed in such complex environments.

Making decisions about methods starts with defining goals, so it may be useful to categorize training activities according to their purpose. I find it helpful to think about three types: *skill-acquisition activities, game-based activities and tactical activities*. These categories are imperfect, but still useful. One of the world's top training courses for coaches, that of the French Football Federation, starts by asking coaches to make a similar distinction for activities. This causes coaches to think not about whether a training activity is "good" but about whether it helps achieve a *specific* outcome. In fact, many of the coaches I've met who've taken the French course value it specifically because it emphasizes *methods*. As Matt Lawrey of Atlanta United's academy put it, the idea is that "instead of coaching the way that you want to coach, you have to coach in the way the kids learn." Different methods—even what seem like contrasting methods—often work in synergy. Whether a method is good depends on what you're trying to get done. The answer to most questions about teaching methodology, says Christian Lavers, is "It depends."

Skill acquisition activities

Skill-acquisition activities are designed to improve players' mastery of functional tasks—a specific action or sequence of actions—and enable players to execute them at a high level. We want players to be able to strike a ball, say, or bring one down, reliably and automatically, with the thigh or chest or instep. Some people call such tasks "motor learning," a term that's useful because the purpose is to coordinate physical skills with fluidity and speed; but I think of the skill-acquisition category more broadly to include not just individual *motor learning* activities but also coordinated group actions learned to automaticity. *Passing patterns* (sequences of common ball movements coordinated among multiple players, sometimes called patterns of play) may be the best example. These types of group actions are similar to motor learning because they require fast, often reflexive reactions among a group of players who must execute like a single being.[22] A passing pattern exercise might try to encode a sequence like the one Xavier and his teammate used in the previous section: a pass in to a target man who is checking back from the ball, a simple back pass to play out, a through ball to an open teammate, a play back to the target man who has broken into space. Typically such an exercise would probably include multiple variations of this.

22. Put elsewhere: in some (certainly not all) cases, this is what Wayne Smith means when he talks about creativity being practice in disguise or what Cruyff means when he talks about simple things being executed at speed and with precision appearing to be complex. Teams play like one organism because they (sometimes) train their movements like one.

PASSING

It all depends...

Skill-acquisition activities often do not fully address decisions in a game context—when to execute a skill, why, and how in the flow of play or in a given situation. You might think this makes such exercises irrelevant in a chapter on that topic, but that's not the case. Skill mastery is still critical to decision-making because it reduces the load on working memory and allows for increased perception. When actions can be carried out with automaticity, decisions improve. If players are struggling with decisions at a specific moment in games, one response might be to further automate skills commonly required in that moment, thus freeing more capacity within working memory for perception or analysis.

Automaticity or at least fluidity of a skill is a requirement of decision-making— insufficient, of course, but still necessary. Being able to execute while thinking about something else is the hallmark of champions. A recent study of the cognition of hitters in baseball revealed something similar: "Expert hitters also tend to use their frontal cortex—a part of the brain that is generally in charge of deliberate decision-making—less than nonexperts."[23] The mark of expertise is less use of working memory.

We can often improve outcomes by placing skill-acquisition activities in environments that aid in developing perception. It may be useful in the very early stages of player development to have players in a simpler environment practice passing. This might make it easier to see the correctness and quality of execution, but once players are able to pass a ball correctly, moving them out of artificial formations into more game-like settings is critical—passing on a field in positions akin to where they'd be as a back four or some other positional group, say, or passing and moving in a 30 by 30 square with multiple other pairs also passing at the same time, or passing within rondos. These help players to look up, see space, determine the proper weight of a pass. "A pass, in and of itself, is very difficult to assess if out of context," Todd Beane told me. "Within my workshops, I have player A pass to B and ask coaches if it was a good pass. Ultimately the coaches all say, 'It depends,' at which point I know I've got them. A successful pass can only be determined by its efficacy relative to intent."

And while I would consider rondos[24] to be game-based activities and therefore most applicable in the next section, they are also an outstanding skill-development activity. In fact, they're ideal as they combine passing skills with other related game skills (receiving, body shape, angles, timing, etc.) that are just as important but perhaps slightly less visible.

23. www.bit.ly/3jKfRA4

24. Rondos are among the most common training exercises in soccer and involve a group of players (often four or five but sometimes more) playing keep-away from two in the middle. I asked coaches of other sports for examples of similar movement-based small-sided adaptable activities that were commonly used across a wide swath of the coaching sector. Some of their comparisons were "box drills" in lacrosse; "four square" in tennis; perhaps "3 on 2" or "Carolina" in basketball.

Skill-acquisition exercises should be progressive and adaptive if we expect skills to show up in performance. As I will discuss more in Chapter 2, on planning and design, performance in practice is not a reliable indicator of performance in games. To ensure that one translates to the other, training should follow a progression from blocked to serial to random practice but progressions should progress in other ways too, adding complexity and decision-making where players have to perceive the context and adapt the skill. If skill acquisition doesn't involve those things, it's unlikely to transfer to a game setting.

A final point. Many people believe that rehearsing sequences and automating actions destroys creativity and that the only way to encourage creativity is free play. This is probably a misconception. Here is the manual of the Croatian Football Federation on the topic:

> Automatism ... does not limit creativity. On the contrary, automatism is what enables and enhances a greater expression of creativity. ... The number and quality of possible solutions in the game are limited if there are [insufficient] technical skills that enable swift and proper execution. This limits players and their ability to choose. ... An example of this is a left-footed player who, when opponents or situations force the ball onto their right foot, has an extremely difficult time finding a solution because their technique with that foot is inadequate. As a result, the player does not have the confidence to consider a range of solutions, which affects their options in the game.

Another common critique of skill-automation activities is specific to passing patterns: commonly criticized for being unrealistic because they are unopposed. However, the likes of Pep Guardiola and Diego Simeone—two of the most respected coaches in world soccer—don't appear to share those concerns. They use passing patterns frequently. They don't use them exclusively and they almost assuredly don't see them as sufficient, but they use them to instill into habit patterns of action they want their players to do frequently in the game. I suspect they recognize several benefits: passing patterns build familiarity and fluidity in common sequences, thus enhancing speed of play. They allow for pattern recognition. Players are likely to recognize the basic shapes of the patterns more quickly when they appear in matches, and therefore execute them more frequently and successfully. Players are also likely to perceive more subtle cues within movements they have keen familiarity with. Subtle signals—*This back pass is for you to play out!*—are easier to read when you are more familiar with the larger action. In fact the sequence I described earlier where Xavier, Beto and Claudio read each other's intentions would probably have been facilitated by a fair amount of passing pattern work. It's one of the ways coaches ingrain the preferred actions in a game model.

Game-based activities

The second major type of training activities are *game-based activities*. These are small-scale strategic distortions of the larger game of soccer that develop players' fluency in reading and reacting to commonly occurring interactions and situations. Game-based activities provide a balance of predictability and randomness. The distortions cause certain high-value events to occur more frequently, but the occurrences vary in setting and require the interpretation of perception cues: the ball must be played wide before you can score; defenders must remain within certain parts of the grid, but attackers can move freely, etc. Game-based activities are critical because they multiply two types of events. First, they tend to be small-sided games, so they multiply the number of "mental touches" players get: the number of times they read and adapt to movements and actions of players around them with and without the ball. They are often possession based, requiring all players to be reading the game all the time. Everyone is constantly reading the foundational interactions of the game—space, movement, body position—over and over. Second, because they use constraints, they cause specific situations to occur more frequently: numerical advantages in a certain part of the field, for example. Technically, I suppose, game-based activities could reinforce almost anything, but they are most powerful at building deep and sustained intuition for foundational concepts, what you might call the 20% in the Pareto principle (the idea that 80% of outcomes are caused by 20% of causes). If your team can receive or play first time with their head up and master angles, distance, timing in interactions for 4 to 6 players, how much of everything else would fall into place?

I hope that by now it's clear how important a perceptively rich environment is, and game-based activities are excellent in this regard. This also explains why standing (or standing in line) during drills is so counterproductive. Not only are players not getting touches, but they are not reading and seeing the game. They are static and passive in all their interactions, and this means they are missing critical opportunities to learn how the game works.

So game-based activities should:

- break into smaller groups
- distort the game to make certain events occur
- be structured so that everyone is actively perceiving and reacting the whole time
- emphasize the most important foundational concepts

The distortions—often called constraints—are important too. They maximize the rate at which desired events occur, making them not random but semi-random, unpredictable but still frequent. The most basic distortion is size. Playing 6 v 6 means more time with and around the ball for players. Playing 6 v 6 in a constrained space makes for more time around the ball with decisions happening at an accelerated pace.

Other common distortions include limitations on the number of touches on the ball, the types of touches, the shape of the field or the order in which things must happen (you must play into zone A before you score). If you are scrimmaging, for what it's worth, you are not using a game-based activity—there's no strategic distortion. And while a game-based activity could be 11 v 11, they tend to be smaller.

A more scientific way of putting it is that game-based activities are especially effective at building familiarity with the core geometries of the game: space and time; how to get open and shape your first touch. Adaptable *geons*, that is, as opposed to specific tactical situations. These are among the most basic tools in reading the game. If there is such a thing as transferrable sense or awareness, it is probably developed most in these activities.

There's disagreement in the soccer world about some of the most common distortions—the presence of goals and the presence of directional play. To me, this is one of the differences between game-based activities and tactical activities. Game-based activities distort the setting to cause certain situations to occur with greater frequency. Going to

25. As evidenced by the love of and commitment to it among the greatest coaches and clubs. Its devotees include Pep Guardiola during his immense success at Barcelona, Manchester City and Bayern Munich.

26. www.bit.ly/32w9yu7

goal can be great, but going to goal can also be a distraction. Eliminating goals can allow players to focus more intently on other aspects of the game, and in so doing they can still build their decision-making fundamentals. I don't really see a scientific justification to insist that game-based activities always involve goals and/or directional play. The rondo is perhaps the perfect example. It's surely one of the best training activities.[25] Tactical play requires directional play. As far as I can tell from the science and the example of top coaches, perception and decision-making do not.

Here's how Marc Carmona, Barcelona's head of coach education put it in a recent interview:[26] "It is about games in a small space, a lot of rondos, a lot of games with possession, a lot of games 4 v 4, 5 v 5, so you can see that the ball is very important. To pass the ball, control the ball, to move with the ball ... this is the DNA in football. [Our] coaches are trying to transmit the understanding at all ages."

MARC CARMONA

It is about games in a small space, a lot of rondos, a lot of games with possession, a lot of games 4v4, 5v5, so you can see that the ball is very important. To pass the ball, control the ball, to move with the ball ... this is the DNA in football. [Our] the coaches are trying to transmit the understanding at all ages.

Is the game the best teacher?

Game-based activities often form the majority of training for many coaches. But as outstanding as game-based activities are, they are not immune from what cognitive science tells us are misapplications. For one thing, they are often conflated with a philosophy that "the game is the best teacher." This is a problematic phrase both because what people mean by it varies dramatically and because some interpretations of this phrase contradict what we know about brain architecture and cognition. If by "the game is the best teacher" you mean that games are an excellent setting—often the best setting—for both teaching and the accruing by players of experience in a perception-rich environment, then I agree. If you think it is critical to have players play in a constantly varying context—"no two touches are ever exactly the same" is how one coach put it to me—then I am with you. If you note that games are engaging and competitive for players and therefore build engagement focus and competitive spirit, I agree. And if you say that constraints can "do much of the talking"—that is, they can be used to teach players very efficiently while letting them play without breakages for explanation—then again, I agree. And if you think game-based activities are outstanding because they cause groups of players to make and coordinate decisions, independent of the coach, over and over, then I agree.

But if by the phrase you mean coaches should not guide, instruct or explain as part of games; or if you think that players should "discover" everything and that coaches talking is bad; or if you mean that games are the *only* way; or that games should not be supported by an intentional curriculum, taught in a systematic way; or that games should not have specific learning goals—if you mean any of these things, then I disagree. Games, especially carefully designed ones, are very good teaching tools. Constraints can make them even better. But they are not infallible. No teaching tool is a silver bullet and the best way to destroy the immense value of a method is to make it dogma.

Tactical activities

The final group of training activities are *tactical activities*. These recreate specific match conditions and situations in order to prepare for situations anticipated in a specific match:

Here is how we will press.

or

Here is how we will press in Saturday's game against Tigres.

Tactical activities might include reviewing specific tactical challenges and the desired response: *When they press us here, this is how we will react.* Or they might review a specific aspect of the game: how to cover on set pieces; what to do when their center backs defend narrowly. They usually use functional groupings that will occur on the field and often specify an area of the field. The topics of a tactical session might change dramatically from week to week in response to upcoming challenges.

So tactical activities are different from game-based activities in that they attempt to recreate (not distort) the game, focusing on specific and situational understanding rather than generalized decision-making. Still, it's worth noting that one of the tenets of game-based activities is constraints, and constraints-based teaching can apply to tactical exercises too. In fact, most of the subsequent concepts in this chapter can apply as well to tactical activities as to game-based activities; but before we discuss them, we must first explore the critical role of knowledge.

The game of soccer, as most coaches will know, has four phases of the game, and tactical exercises take place in one of those four phases, focusing on desired actions during the phase.

In light of that, here's a final thought on tactical activities, one that **I will take up again in chapter 2**. It comes from an insight I heard ECNL's Christian Lavers share at a workshop for coaches at North Carolina FC. Christian described a typical tactical activity a coach might do in training: an 8v6 game, in this case, where the offense attacks the goal and seeks to change the point of attack quickly to achieve and exploit numerical superiority. The most important question about the design, Christian observed, was, "How does the game start?" At first this seemed like a banal question, but in fact it turned out to be profound.

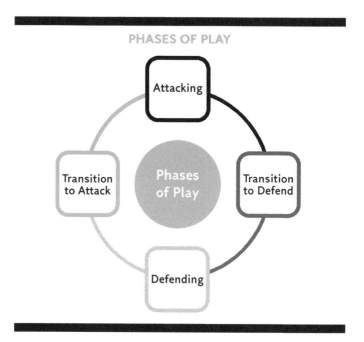

The core challenge of a group invasion game is "establishing order" (over chaos and the opposition.) In competition, you win the ball and are disorganized. You are not in your attacking shape because you have been defending. A player wins the ball but his teammates are facing the wrong direction, with some players having been pulled out of position and some not looking at the player who has won it. Perhaps they're not even aware he's won it yet. You must first keep the ball and then get yourself into a shape from which you can attack if you want your players to switch the point of attack effectively.

However, most tactical attacking activities start with the correct player having the ball and the team already nicely spread out in proper attacking shape, Lavers observed. The most common answer to his question is: the game starts with the coach (or a perhaps a player) feeding the ball into the desired player from the middle third because the exercise skips the most challenging part of execution—getting to that point—and therefore does not fully prepare players for the complexity they'll face in competition.

Here then is a good rule of thumb for tactical activities: *For an exercise to prepare players to execute in a complex environment—if you want it to "transfer" to the game—it must ultimately progress to a version that starts in a previous phase of play.* The opposition would start with the ball. The "offense" would have to win it and immediately earn the right to execute the drill by getting into the proper shape. Getting there will be hard. They'll have to do it quickly and under duress, and with defenders in unexpected places and trying to win the ball back, but establishing order is half the battle in a complex game. As I will discuss in chapter 2, most good exercises progress from simple to challenging so you probably would not want to start there, but you would want to end there before you concluded that your team was ready to execute under game conditions.

Having distinguished three types of activities, I'm now going to discuss some principles to use and adapt to the three settings. The recipe in this chapter, if there is one, is the following. To build athletes' capacity to make decisions well and quickly:

- Develop automaticity with core skills via skill-acquisition training—especially those that occur at the point of deciding (e.g. first touch).

- Develop strong foundational understanding of core building-blocks of the game—basic interactions like movement, spacing and body shape, primarily through small-sided game-based activities.

- Invest in strong background knowledge so players understand the principles of the game and can understand and learn more while observing.

- Describe shared knowledge (principles of play, game model) in clear vocabulary to allow teammates to coordinate and predict one another's actions. Automating and adapting common movements so they become natural via group skill acquisition work may also be helpful.

- Constantly stress perception. Situate athletes in settings that develop their ability to see what they will see at the point they must decide while competing as much as possible.

SEFU
BERNARD

"Before you get into the chess match, you have to have some general principles."

Sefu Bernard is the Director of Player Development for the WNBA's Washington Mystics, a job which he describes as "thinking about what and how well players are learning." Here he describes the connection between global principles, which are often developed through game-based activities, and players' ability to make tactical adjustments, usually taught through tactical activities.

As coaches, we often don't spend enough time thinking about how to design the training environment over an extended period of time (e.g. over a two-, four- or six-week period)—especially in youth sport. We tend to be day-to-day. We finish a practice, or a game, and ask, "What are we going to do tomorrow?" If we struggled with our defense we say, "We've got to work on our player-to-player defense." Then we practice it once and check the box. This is teaching to the test. It's reactive. And it lacks a long-term view that builds the competencies we want most in our athletes.

At the professional level, the game becomes so tactical. You're dealing with the highest level of athlete and the highest level of coaching acumen—both have the capacity to make in-game and game-to-game adjustments. That's a lot to prepare for. At the same time, I think it's important to differentiate between global principles, applied and applicable throughout every game in the season, and tactics, which are game-to-game adjustments.

Ball screens are the bone marrow of modern-day basketball. They're one of the most frequent interactions in today's game. The game is all about finding, using, creating and sharing advantages. Ball screens are an easy way to create an advantage. There are numerous types of ball screens and even more ways teams can get into them to trigger an advantage.

For us, we know that every team is going to run some kind of ball screen action—either to provoke poor decision-making and a breakdown in the defense or to exploit a matchup. We need to be able to defend this action; yet, even with our best scouting efforts, we can't account for every possibility.

Before you get lost in the chess match, your players have to understand some global principles for preventing and neutralizing an opponent's use of this scheme. We need to learn deeply the fundamentals of defending and reacting to a ball screen.

For instance, being able to guard the ball at an arm's length away or closer, being able to influence the direction of the ball handler, being hard to screen (i.e. avoidance), communicating and reacting to verbal cues from a teammate (e.g. direction of screen, going over or under, possibly switching, etc.). These are foundational skills and decisions that must be developed regardless of the type of ball screen and tactics an opponent employs to get into it. If you can develop a player who's a great on-ball defender and unscreenable, you don't need as many tactical adjustments.

So, for us, I'm continually asking and observing. How much time are we spending on things like on-ball defense? When and how often do we come back and revisit? Are we planning for this in advance or reacting to a feeling and the emotions of the moment?

Things get sloppy over a season. Forgetting happens. How do we plan for it such that the busyness of the season doesn't make us ignore what's most important?

One season, I started jotting down what I called "problem statements"—soundbites that we as a staff were saying: "We're not good at this"; "She's not doing that"; "We need to improve our IQ with X." I took all those phrases and presented them to the coaching staff in our off-season.

I shared with them that I'd written down the things we say that hurt us most regardless of opponent. We then had the hard conversation of unpacking those comments and revealing the overarching gaps and themes.

We were then better positioned to anchor what we did going forward around these issues. We could better prioritize and plan ahead to spend time on the things that mattered most, and also assess how we were doing toward moving the needle and improving.

Being sound on a small subset of universal principles—and the perception, communication and decision-making that fuels it—will reduce the amount of tactical in-game and game-to-game adjustments that a team needs to make.

Build knowledge

"What students know dictates what they can learn," writes teacher educator Harry Fletcher-Wood. A knowledgeable scientist looking at a diagram of ion transport understands at a glance the principles it represents and the argument it makes. She quickly and effortlessly adds details from the image to her existing understanding. A novice student of science is not so lucky. Without the same knowledge, she may stare and stare but not really understand what she's seeing and the principles it demonstrates. Experts look and see underlying principles at work; novices see superficial details. The more you know coming in, the more you learn from looking.

This profound and simple statement is one of the most easily overlooked. Knowledge, cognitive psychologists know, is necessary for problem-solving, critical thinking and even perception, and it has to be encoded in long-term memory in most cases if we want it to help. For coaches, the role of knowledge is even more important because the decision-making they seek is *shared and coordinated among a group of learners*. Only knowledge that everyone on the team has and can rely on everyone else knowing allows players to coordinate decisions optimally.[27]

For knowledge to support learning under those conditions, it must be universally understood and captured in consistent precise words that everyone can use. A player can only press effectively if she knows what actions to take and when and why to take them, as well as how to adjust her actions based on what the opposition does in response, but a *team* can only press effectively if everyone knows their specific roles and the cues that tell them when to press and how to adjust—coordination is life and death. Not just the coach but players themselves must be able to tell each other to *overload* or to *deny passing lanes* or *deny the middle*, to *press up* or to *push higher*. It is very difficult unless everybody understands the concepts the same way and has the same name for them.

It's critical then to think about what everyone should know by when and to manage that process carefully. Knowledge builds off knowledge, and gaps in what players have learned are a serious problem for individuals and the players around them. This applies between teams within a club too. If one U10 coach teaches "high pressing" and another U10 coach teaches "up-back-through," my U11 coach inherits a teaching problem, even if both of them are very good coaches and the concepts were taught well. Half of the U11 players don't know what high pressing is and half don't know up-back-through. As a team we can execute neither. Half the players will be missing signals and doing the wrong thing. And a coach can't build off of either one reliably. To teach more advanced aspects of the high press, he must go back and reteach what half the team doesn't know. If this persists, the club will always be at a basic conceptual understanding of the game. And of course the U11 coach won't even know who knows—and doesn't know—what.

There are three tools a club can use to build knowledge: a curriculum, a set of principles of play (including a game model at higher levels) and a list of shared terminology.

Curriculum (and how to use it)

A curriculum is a comprehensive document written with an eye to the long term. It describes the things players will understand and be able to do at each stage of their development. This ensures that they have both the technical skills to execute and the

27. This is a big difference between teaching athletes and teaching in the classroom. It's not just that each student needs to know how to solve for X; it's that a group of students must solve for X together and at speed.

knowledge of the game necessary to inform decisions. And it ensures that coaches know that all their players know these things by a certain point. This is important. You can't use, refer to, or expand upon a concept as a coach unless you know confidently that all players understand it already. Few coaches have this luxury. They refer to an idea and hope that most of their players know what they're talking about with no way to know for sure. This is ironic because most clubs have curiculums. They just aren't very good and rarely get used.

An ideal curriculum is specific as to what level of mastery of what content by when. Players will probably spend years understanding pressing. But to develop advanced understanding among 17-year-olds, a club must establish clear mastery points. What about pressing they will know and be able to do by U14, and by U16? This is the greatest challenge with any complex skill: to break it out into yearly *mastery points*, allocating skills to specific times in players' development so they are mastered at the right time but also so that there is clear focus on a manageable number of skills at each age level—in other words, you want to make sure you do few enough things to get deep mastery of everything you cover.

Spiraling is a common term in the world of schools to describe certain curricular programs. A program that "spirals" causes topics to appear and then reappear over the course of a year or even multiple years. If you are working on a topic now, you will leave it and then work on it again in a few months. Or perhaps another coach will work on it next year. It's a productive idea because mastery is rarely achieved in one interaction, and even if it was, the forgetting would begin as soon as you stopped practicing. You'd need to teach it again to get mastery that lasted. So the principle is good, but the risk with spiraling is that it's too easy to say, "Oh, we'll come back to it later," or "That's good enough for now. They'll master it the next time around." The result can be that skills never get mastered. So the challenge is to make it really clear to the U13 coach exactly what she has to master in that year and to the U14 coach what exactly she will add to that base knowledge.

A second challenge of curriculum—which is partially in conflict with the above—is to balance breadth with depth. We need to clarify the things we want players to master in any given year, but we also want to focus on true mastery of the most important things. Of the 100 things you might teach players, there are probably 20 that are important enough to obsess on. Another hour focused on that 20% of most important things probably yields more benefit than introducing something from the remaining 80%.

The final risk of curriculum is specific to soccer and probably other sports. It's easy to focus too much on what players can do with the ball when they get it and not what they do away from the ball. Most of the decisions that matter—the ones that break open the game—are initiated by a player without the ball. She sees the space and moves into it to create the opportunity for a pass. Or she pulls a defender away. Or she distracts the defender by making her unsure of where to be. She denies an opportunity by covering perfectly as a second defender. Great players are great—and make their teams greater—based on what they do when the spotlight is not on them, but you'd never know it from looking at most curriculums.

But the news isn't all grim. Curriculum is one place where technology holds particular promise in changing how we work. Video is an outstanding way to ensure knowledge and understanding outside of and in synergy with what happens in practice. Jesse Marsch recently discussed this in an interview with Gary Curneen. "Video is the only way for players to fully understand how we want to do things." A club could take advantage of this idea by pairing each competency in its curriculum with exemplar videos. The key of course would be in getting the videos into circulation among players, perhaps via phones. *We're working on recovery runs in training today. Here are examples of what elite players look like when they recover. Watch them and send me two observations before training.* Now players (and coaches) have a consistent image in their minds of the things they are trying to learn. They have shared knowledge. A group of coaches I admire are working on this idea at scale: a video-based curriculum that matches high-level examples to each concept so players can see what they look like at the highest level. And so training, rather than simply seeking to develop conceptual understanding of (say) breaking lines, starts with conceptual understanding and quickly moves on to application. From a learning perspective, that's an idea that's worth its weight in gold.

Principles of play/game model

Unlike a curriculum, which guides decisions about what to teach from the background, the purpose of principles of play is to make goals shared and public. Coaches interact with a curriculum; players interact with principles of play, or in more advanced cases a "game model." Principles of play distill the overarching tactics, strategy and style of play a team pursues into a small number of concrete actions that players should remember. They frame priorities simply and memorably so coaches and players can refer to them during training. A game model is more specific. It describes how this team seeks to play. It breaks down principles into more specific details that have to do with style and philosophy—we'd expect clubs to have different game models—and often with descriptions of changes made in specific tactical situations. The way we play is different if we are pressing high or defending deep. A game model says, *When we are pressing, here is what we seek to do...*

Here's a small section of a document FC Wisconsin used to define its game model:

GAME MODEL

		U8 (4v4)	U9 (7v7)	U10 (7v7)	U11 (9v9)	MAXIM
QUICKLY CIRCULATE TO UNBALANCE	MOVE BALL ACROSS CHANNELS	1: CREATE SPACE AWAY FROM THE BALL	+2: BODY POSITION OPEN TO FIELD	+3: RECOGNIZE DEFENSIVE OVERLOAD	+5: FIND A PLAYER WHO CAN PLAY FORWARD	"SEE THE TRAP"
	CREATE COMBINATION PLAY	1: TRIANGULAR SUPPORT FOR THE BALL 2: SHIELD TO BUY TIME	+3: CREATE WALL-PASSES +4: CREATE OVERLAPS	+5: DRIBBLE TO ENGAGE DEFENDER	+6: BE OR FIND THE THIRD MAN	"MAKE THEM CHASE"
	GET UNMARKED	1: GET AWAY FROM THE DEFENDER	+2: DECIEVE THE DEFENDER	+3: PULL THE DEFENDER TO CREATE SPACE	+4: COMPLIMENTARY MOVEMENT	"BE SLIPPERY"

You could describe "circulate to unbalance" as a principle of play. But the club has taken that and divided it into three sub-principles. It's then mapped these sub-principles to years when concepts will be taught. You could argue it's principles of play, game model and curriculum in a single document. This is a club that is serious about how it plays and how it teaches to play.

THE ABILITY TO DECIDE

When a team defines its principles of play (or a game model), it must write them down—there's a document somewhere—but mostly the principles should live in the interactions and conversations of the team (or club). The goal is for coaches to constantly reference them, to have players know them without having to read them.

There might be different versions of a principles of play document within a given club. For young players, there should be fewer simpler priorities in easy to comprehend language—perhaps two or three principles each for offense and defense.

Perhaps something like this:

On defense we:

- Get narrow and compact;
- Block the direct path to the goal;
- Always mark goal side.

For older and more advanced players, principles would naturally be more complex and sophisticated, likely divided into the four main phases of the game—attacking; defending; transition to attacking from defending (winning the ball); transition to defending from attacking (losing the ball)—with four or five principles for each phase. There might be other specific settings that warrant principles: pressing, say, or counter attacking. But more is not necessarily better. It's critical that the principles must contain a manageable amount of information in simple direct language because they will form the basis of much of a coach's questioning. Players will be asked not only to recall them but also to use them. This means players will have to memorize them so they know them cold and can always access them.

Once players know their principles—and helping them to know them through a bit of retrieval practice (e.g. light quizzing) from time to time is probably a useful idea—they can be used to make questioning more efficient and more focused on solving specific problems. For example, let's say a U16 team has divided its principles of play into four parts. They have three principles for transition to offense (having just won the ball):[28]

28. These are deliberately simplistic principles for the purpose of illustration.

- Play immediately away from pressure
- Spread the field—fast (to stretch the defense)
- Find numerical advantage in as few passes as possible

A coach could then use these principles to help players make and understand effective decisions during training with short sequences of questioning like this:

Pause. Blue team. We have just won the ball. What's our first principle?

Play away from pressure.

And if I don't have the ball?

Stretch the defense.

OK, so Carlos won the ball. Where is the pressure?

Here, where Kelvin and Paul are.

Yes. So a better first ball would be?

To Matty.

Because?

It's away from pressure.

And Matty, when you get it, where are you looking to play?

Where we've got numbers.

OK. Let's see if we can do that. Play again from Carlos. Go!

Or:

What phase are we in?

We just won the ball.

OK, so assess our decision as a team there.

We played back into pressure.

OK, what's the best way to fix that?

Or:

Our first principle is to play away from pressure. Look at how we were positioned. Why were we unable to accomplish that goal?

The key here is that principles of play make questioning productive and efficient because they reduce guessing. If I did not have principles of play and I said, "We just won the ball, what do we want to do here?", players would likely guess wrong, which wastes time and dilutes focus from the real problem-solving of figuring out execution.

Another way of thinking about principles is that they shift the emphasis of player thinking from *what to do* to *how to do it*. Some coaches may not like this. The idea of allowing players to discover principles has many advocates. And I think there is legitimacy to allowing players to occasionally derive principles for themselves. But generally speaking, the intellectual challenges of the game have more to do with implementing an idea once you know it than deriving the idea itself. We know we want to press. The whole team is pressing. I don't want my players to derive a new defending strategy or to define a different role for themselves within the press. The problem-solving I want is "How do I react when the opposing goalkeeper is excellent with the ball at his feet or when my own teammate reacts slowly?" It may be useful to spend 30 minutes having players "discover" that they should play away from pressure but really learning *how* to play away from pressure under a variety of circumstances is a more productive focus for problem-solving. Figuring out how to adapt to the setting is the difficult part.

St. Louis Cardinals' hitting coach Jeff Albert described how he combined principles with problem-solving. The key for him is not to try to explain everything right away: "I try to get the mental representation first. Have them understand the concept and what it looks like. Name it, give them a few suggestions, and then instead of overexplaining it, get out of their way for a little bit. Let them try it and capture them while they're doing it, live or ideally

"What I've learned the most about in teaching the technical side of football is vocabulary," FC Red Bull Salzburg head coach Jesse Marsch told me. "Vocabulary streamlines communication and expresses the technical aspects of who we are as a team. The first thing in coaching is you have to have a plan. The details of how you play and what you are about. The second thing is you have to have the words."

on video, and show it back to them. Let them see what they look like when they are connecting the pieces." The goal was to start with a clear vision and discover over time how to bring it into fruition. But if you start with a clear vision—a very good mental representation—the problem-solving is much more effective because everyone knows what they're trying to accomplish.

Having simple memorable names for ideas is deeply important. If I explain what should happen when we win the ball or even if I let my players derive this idea, they will have a hard time replicating and applying their learning in future situations unless they have a clear phrase to describe what they seek to do. Having a name for an idea increases the likelihood that players will remember it. And using the same phrase for all such situations allows them to connect the greatest number of examples and build a broader understanding of the game: *This "play away from pressure" situation is different from the others I have encountered in training this week but I group and compare them mentally because they are all in the same category.* Players make connections better and learn faster when they have words to define the concepts they are applying.

If players know their principles cold, coaches can consistently reference them during practice, and they can question more efficiently and therefore more frequently if they so desire. They can build understanding and thus foster more autonomy, not less.

Shared vocabulary

"What I've learned the most about in teaching the technical side of football is vocabulary," FC Red Bull Salzburg head coach Jesse Marsch told me. "Vocabulary streamlines communication and expresses the technical aspects of who we are as a team. The first thing in coaching is you have to have a plan. The details of how you play and what you are about. The second thing is you have to have the words. They carry the specific instructions of how to do what you do when and how. Being concrete and clear through vocabulary. That lets you build understanding." (In chapter 5, you can read more about how Marsch uses this concept.) His approach is built around the idea of developing a unique phrase to describe each aspect of his team's tactical approach. *Ball-oriented* means staying compact when pressing and controlling space in front of the ball, for example. He coins his own terms so he can control the definitions and thus the details of concepts.

Teaching technical vocabulary intentionally and standardizing its usage across a team or club is one of the fastest ways to accelerate learning. When players can name something—touch-tight defending; playing between lines, receiving side-on—they become more explicitly aware of it as a concept and suddenly they can see it more readily when it happens.They notice players defending touch tight or receiving side-on more often because the phrase makes the idea concrete for them. If coaches and players are consistent in using the same phrase for a concept every time, players will remember the idea better and associate a greater number of relevant experiences with the concept. Steve Freeman, director at Black Watch Premier, is very consistent about using the phrases "above the ball" and "below the ball" to refer to players' positions when not in possession. This gives him—and the rest of the club—a simple tool to talk about how players position themselves differently depending on where they are. This is most relevant during questioning. The first question to a player is often, "Where are you relative to the ball?" This is usually enough to allow them to answer the next question—"Where should you go? or "What are your choices?"—as well. Since Steve and his coaches use the phrase consistently, players are able to associate a greater number of experiences with the idea. If they didn't, players might learn something but not connect it to being "above the ball." That small piece of knowledge would remain disconnected from other knowledge and thus be less useful. Players learn faster when language helps them connect what they are learning.

Similarly, I recently watched US Military Academy head men's soccer coach Russell Payne run training. One of his focuses was the angle a back pass should be played at to allow its recipient to choose among options upon receiving it. He called a ball played diagonally back rather than straight back a "short switch," and having defined it he was able to ask for it or praise it or explain how it applied time and time again. He took a subtle and abstract aspect of passing angles and named it into being for his players. And this was only one example of his healthy obsession with vocabulary. The result was a team with uniquely efficient ability to discuss their own actions and decisions.

In fact, shared vocabulary is so important that a team will likely need more terms than the principles—which must be kept short—can encode. So they would do well to basically build a vocabulary list. This ensures that we all understand what it means to *press on*. Or *receive side on*. Or *open up*. Or *close the space*. Or *keep your depth*. Or use your *back foot*. Because of course every player likely does not understand some proportion—large or small—of the terminology used around him or her in training. They likely don't understand the way their conceptions of those terms are wrong, and if they're confused, they're not likely to mention it. So no one knows which terms which players don't know in most cases. As a result, every conversation is eroded for some group of players—a different group for every word.

At almost every club I have observed, coaches insist that their players "communicate." They recognize that this is critical to the game. But if they truly value this idea, they should first make sure their players can all speak the same language by managing terms—the phrases set out for everyone to understand and the ones implemented along the way (e.g. *touch tight*). Consistent vocabulary is necessary to consistent execution.

Another case where vocabulary is critical is in cueing. One of the most common things coaches do to undercut performance is to try to explain to players what they want them to do during live play. This is often counterproductive. A player who is trying to listen to his coach is either degrading his on-field performance—system 2 in operation degrades the perceptions of system 1—or is learning to ignore his coach. I think it is possible to remind a player—during short breaks—of ideas encoded during training. But I am confident that a coach cannot teach players new things during games. If you find yourself shouting directions that do not reference ideas that you have explicitly trained on, it's probably better to write it down so you can add it to next week's training. But if you have taught it, you want to use consistent and efficient terminology to recall it for players. One top coach I know described how he and his colleagues spent "hours talking about the words we use for concepts."

The following image is a few lines from a document that coaches at an MLS academy developed as they sought to standardize vocabulary to facilitate communication. If you try to build one for your club, you'll facilitate conversations and accelerate learning, but keep this one piece of advice in mind. The easiest way for it to go wrong is to get too long to be useful. Better to have 12 technical terms that every single person has memorized than 45 words that only some people really get. Obviously, every club would want to have a different vocabulary list, but it is vital for coaches and players to use the same words for the same concepts.. This is, to me, one of the most important concepts you could take from this chapter.

STANDARDIZING VOCABULARY

ATTACKING	DEFINITION
HALF-TURN – BODY SHAPE/SCAN	WHEN POSSIBLE, OPEN YOUR BODY UP, CHECK TO SWITCH OR PLAY FORWARD
TURN THEM	PLAY BEHIND THE OPPOSITION
STRETCH THE GAME	LONG TO PLAY LONG AND FORWARD
BREAK THE LINE	RECEIVE OR PASS/DRIBBLE IN BETWEEN DEFENSIVE LINES AND FORWARD
BREAK/COUNTER	FIRST THOUGHT, TO PLAY/RUN FORWARD QUICKLY
LOOK FORWARD	FIRST THOUGHT CAN I PLAY FORWARD
MANAGE THE GAME	WHEN WINNING – LATER IN THE GAME – KEEP POSITION – NO RISK MENTALITY
CHECK SHOULDERS	TAKE A LOOK AND KNOW WHAT'S AROUND YOU BEFORE YOU MOVE OR RECEIVE

Now let's push forward with tools you can use as you run a typical session.

Build perception

One of the most important times to build perception is during "stoppages": breaks in play where you give athletes feedback or ask them questions. As I will discuss much more extensively in chapter 3, this is an ideal time to guide athletes' eyes. A question like "What do you see?" or "Where should you look?" may be more valuable in the long run than "What could (or should) you do?", but such a question only works if players are actually looking at what they might see during the game. That is, if your stoppage doesn't recreate the visual field for the discussion, you're probably not getting much out of it from a decision-making point of view. Or rather than asking what players see, you might simply stop and guide them to notice a common cue. This could be the sole purpose of a stoppage. "Pause. Eduardo has the ball on the far side. If you are on the near side your eyes should watch his hips. He can only strike a long ball into the space behind you if he pulls back his hips. That's your cue." Or to use an example from rugby, a top coach recently explained to me what to look for when closing to tackle: a runner with two hands on the ball is preserving his optionality—that means drop back and delay committing; a runner with one hand on the ball has now committed himself—close aggressively. As a rugby novice, I found that profoundly useful. It would be one of the first things I'd want to know in learning the game.[29]

29. The third part of chapter 3 discusses much more extensively how to use stoppages to build perception and decision-making abilities.

Another way to build perception is to put players in situations that replicate what they will perceive during the game as often as possible. Reading the game is the result of millions of interactions where athletes unconsciously infer the statistical tendencies of complex, "quasi-regular" systems. If you want to be a great reader, one of the biggest drivers will be how much time you spend reading. The idea of situating activities in a context that looks like that game is sometimes called "ecological dynamics." A common misconception about it is that the exercise must look exactly like the whole game. Perception happens within a variety of spheres of focus, however. Sometimes an athlete is looking at a visual field involving 14 or 15 players, but sometimes she is looking at a visual field involving a smaller functional group, or a few players clustered around the ball. Sometimes she is reading tactical space—where are the gaps she can exploit?—and sometimes she is reading body language cues like where someone intends to play their next touch. All of these are important and immersing exercises and ecological dynamics can help with all of them. But while a rondo cannot accomplish the former, it accomplishes the latter as well as any drill I know. There are no lines, there are no goals, there are not 11 players, but it is foolish to presume it is not ecological and perception-building. In fact it is especially effective at building perception of the "geons" of the game: its fundamental replicable shapes.

The net on this is that a good coach should recognize the need for a variety of exercises to build perception, and perhaps *how* it will build perception is a question that should be asked of any training exercise. To me, perception is the (or at least a) primary purpose of game-based activities, and they in turn are the primary tool through which perception is built. That said, because they tend to be small sided, they tend to teach perception within a fairly small range of distance from the ball, and players must also learn to look far away. So tactical activities—and game-based activities of varying sizes—will also be needed to stress perception in larger settings. Essentially there are a series of concentric circles of perception. Those close up are used most frequently, but good players are often undone by asymmetrical perception skills; they can perceive cues well within a narrow circle (and succeed based on them) but often miss cues—and therefore opportunities that are especially critical at the elite level—that occur farther away. This is a really useful thing to think about in stoppages. Instead of asking "What should you do?", you might try (as I describe in chapter 3) "What do you see?"; and depending on what your athlete answers, you might then respond with "And what do you see if you look farther away?"

In the previous section, I made the case for the critical role of background knowledge in decision-making—doubly so in shared decision-making. I'd also like to point out the critical role of knowledge in perception. Consider this video that I've excerpted from a longer one made by Cedarville University women's basketball assistant coach John Leonzo. The video shows two of the team's core principles of play: "Pass where the help came from" and "Penetrate, pass, pass." These simple and engaging videos make those principles visible to players and cause them to be more likely to notice them—and notice details about them—when players around them use them. What you understand is what you see, and the more you know, the more you make sense of what you are looking at. This concept is sometimes called the Tetris effect, based on the observation that obsessive players of the video game Tetris start to see its shapes everywhere in their everyday lives. "Playing hour after hour of 'Tetris' actually changes the brain," as cognitive psychologist Shawn Achor describes in his book *The Happiness Advantage*.

Watch "John Leonzo
principles of play" at
www.coachguidetoteaching.com

"It rewires to perceive what it knows." And so by giving athletes clear and repeated images of the building blocks of the game, Leonzo is causing them to perceive those actions and their variations as they happen. He's making them more perceptive by informing their eyes.

A final way to build perception is to think intentionally about what players are doing when they are not actively playing. Athletes spend a lot of time *not* training in training sessions and *not* playing in games. They are on the bench. There are three teams of 8 rotating through and theirs is out for five minutes. What are they doing then? Watching, perhaps, but probably not as carefully and intentionally as they might. Physical downtime or rest time can still be productive cognitively. What if you gave "observation tasks" to the players in the team that was off? Perhaps there are general tasks—"Let's all watch for and grade the first touches." Then when you stop for coaching points, you could call on girls who were out: "OK, who was watching for first touches? How did Ava do there?" Not only would this engage them in watching more intentionally, but it would teach them to watch the game technically.

Or you could individualize the tasks. Maybe everyone gets a card with an observation task.[30] Give girls a player at their position to watch. Or give them a skill they are struggling with to watch for. Margaret, whose first touch is often static, gets the "watch the first touch" card or even the "watch to see whether and how players change direction with their first touch—be ready to share excellent examples" card. You could even be transparent about it: "I'm giving you this card, Margaret, because it's the next step for you to take your game up a level. Watch carefully and learn!"

30. I got this idea from observing the very excellent coaching of Mike Ellicott at Empire United's girls academy in Rochester, NY.

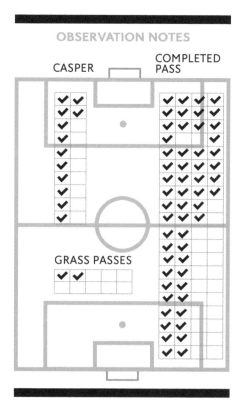

OBSERVATION NOTES

Or you could make it a group task. Consider this picture:

It's the observation notes Ruth Brennan Morrey's U12 girls took during a match in Rochester, MN. "I had the resting players huddle around the clipboard together and watch for completed passes," Ruth told me. "I also had them watch for 'Casper passes'—passes that go directly to a defender in the passing lane (as in: the only way it would get through was if the defender was a ghost).

"On the opposing team's bench, the girls were saying 'Oh, I'm glad we don't have practice tomorrow' or 'Are you going to the carnival next Friday?' or simply 'Good job, Sarah!' But on our bench, suddenly girls were actively watching the game when they were out." There were discussions about whether a pass should be counted as complete. It was social and it was focused.

Ruth shared a few other observations about the effects. "Once we labeled the Casper ball, there were fewer Casper errors, almost immediately, on the field; and the more the game progressed, the more successful they became at completing passes. The girls improved their play, not just their understanding, and their critical eye became their own teacher."

It's worth noting that there are potential technological developments that could assist with the degree and accuracy with which we can show a problem. A colleague recently visited a club in the Bundesliga and noted a giant screen next to the training ground where practices were shown live. The coach, pausing, could walk to the screen, roll it back 15 seconds and say: *See? Danilo, where is the space?* Not only does this help more with teaching but it gets Danilo and company back to playing more quickly. You might not have the jumbo screen, but you could capture a lot of the power of it with an iPad at a fraction of the cost. I watched Kelvin Jones do this with a group of boys in Virginia. "What do you notice?" he asked, holding up the iPad to the gathered players. They could suddenly see and analyze much more precisely.

A caveat. The bet here is that we can improve athletes' unconscious processes of looking by making them more conscious. That's a decent bet but not a sure one. "Good players look at the nose of the ball when they kick," a rugby coach told me. There's a reasonable chance that telling young players to look at the nose of the ball will improve their kicking, but it could also, in making an unconscious process conscious, disrupt them. Or it could be that where good players' eyes go is more correlation than cause. Simply changing that effect wouldn't change the key action. All of which is to say that I think it's a bet worth taking—but it's still a bet. In light of that, here's a cautionary tale told to me by a performance analyst at Scotland Rugby. A world class skier—sorry, I don't remember which—tried to use GoPro footage shot from a camera on another skier's helmet to prepare for an important and challenging race. She wanted to know the course like the back of her hand, to see it in her sleep. The experiment, however, was not a success. What she found on race day was that the subtle difference in visual angle between her GoPro on the top of the helmet and where her eyes actually were threw her off. It was more harm than good. She'd learned the wrong course, in a sense.

We're going to have to go through some trial and error ourselves before we've got perception figured out. VR technology is probably one of the avenues to explore. Is there potential for it to help develop players' eyes? Yes. Are we likely to get a lot wrong too? Yes,

I'd argue. I'm guessing the first three things on the market will be well intentioned but flawed. I might not be the first adopter.

Use platforms and progress

Geons, research tells us, are critical to perception. The game is made up of a series of smaller games—small groups of players, often just two or three—covering, balancing and preventing penetrating passes on defense; working in combinations on offense, observing and reacting to space behind and beside defenders; creating space and timing runs. If players can come to develop a strong familiarity with these common and foundation interactions—the "shapes" of the game—they will be well equipped to understand the interactions within a more complex visual environment. Mastering geons sets you up for (but of course is not the same as) mastering more complex tactical ideas. They will be able to predict and anticipate movements and interactions in a more predictable way. They will be armed to leverage the "the miracle of pattern recognition." It's the equivalent of teaching reading comprehension—when you can do that at a sophisticated level, all advanced concepts are at your fingertips.

So as much training time as possible should be invested in activities like rondos that recreate the basic interactions of players and space in their foundational forms over and over. They are geon-building exercises. And rondos have added benefits. As Matt Lawrey, U15 head coach at Atlanta United's academy, put it, one benefit is that "a rondo is a microcosm of the game. It has attacking, defending, and transition. How you manipulate these moments of the game can tactically focus the rondo on a different principle or focus." Rondos not only allow you to recreate the core interactions of all four phases of the game; they are also endlessly adaptable—you can adapt them to have a particular technical or tactical focus while you build perception.

Matt's comments point out that one of the benefits of game-based activities—rondos, small-sided games, etc.—is that they are what I call a "platform." They are a basic format of activity that you can install and teach players to execute at a high level with almost no downtime. Once you've done that, you can engage players by repeating the most productive activities with minor strategic variations instead of constantly introducing new ones. This makes you more productive and your players more focused.

Let's say you often divide your players into three groups who play possession rondos: 6 in one box, 6 in an adjacent and a third team defending. You call these "possession rondos". By the third or fourth time you run this drill, you should be able to say, "Set up in groups of three. Possession rondos. Be ready to play in 15 seconds. Go!" Not only will your players be ready quickly but they will know the drill. There won't be downtime while they figure out how basic logistics work.[31] But now that you have a platform, you have an opportunity to layer on details and complexity. To reuse the platform does not mean you are repeating the drill. In fact you can not only make small changes each time you use a platform, you can also make progressive changes during a session. And this brings us to one of the key attributes of a good decision-based session. Some coaches think that once they are doing game-based work, they are reinforcing decision-making. I suppose they are. But by changing the focus during the drill, you can get even more out of it.

31. I You can see Steve Covino doing this in the video of him called "SteveCovino.StartStop" in chapter 5. At 1:50 in the video he says simply: "When I blow the whistle i want you to get into your "Barcelona" set up." At the sound of his whistle they dash happily and quickly off. The platform is second nature to them by this point.

A recent session of Matt's at Atlanta United's academy was a great example of this. He started with a 5 v 2 rondo. Almost every session of his starts with a rondo, so from the moment he said go, players knew exactly what to do and were productively engaged. He let them play for a bit with standard rondo rules—defenders who won the ball switched with the player who lost it. Then he shifted the rondo so that if the defenders won the ball they both got "out" and the player losing the ball and the teammate to his right went in. This subtly shifted the dynamic to emphasize teamwork: since both players benefitted from winning the ball, the incentive was to coordinate rather than gamble. Next, Matt worked on teamwork even more. If the attacking team could hit a ball that split the two defenders, defenders had to stay in a second round. After they won the ball, they had to give it back, and then defend again. This taught them to think about coordinating cover and balance. If they both attacked, they would surely pay the price. Next Matt placed a cone outside the rondo square. The two new defenders had to sprint around the cone and enter the square. This created a dynamic that was more like pressing. They had to close space quickly together. Next there was a challenge. If a defender won the ball, he could earn his partner's way out if he completed a pass to him, but if he failed, they both remained in. On the other hand, he could simply win the ball and earn his own way out and leave his partner. This round socialized the boys to attempt to win the ball and play a pass quickly. It also socialized loyalty and other team values. Boys who had the opportunity to play their teammate out and elected not to were often goaded by the group for putting self above team. Matt had also planned a round when the defenders had to be silent and concentrate on reading each other's movements to coordinate their positions. In this way, Matt constantly changed the focus and emphasis but continued to build perception of the game's core interactions.

This of course is by no means the only or even the most common set of rondo variations—more typically, variations involve space parameters: connect a certain number of passes successfully and then try to connect a longer pass into a different area where other players continue the game, for example. But part of what's so interesting about Matt's variations was how he focused on defensive aspects of play.

And if you take a few minutes to think about it, you could probably come up with 20 other variations to subtly shape the dynamics of the session. The platform doesn't change but the focus does.

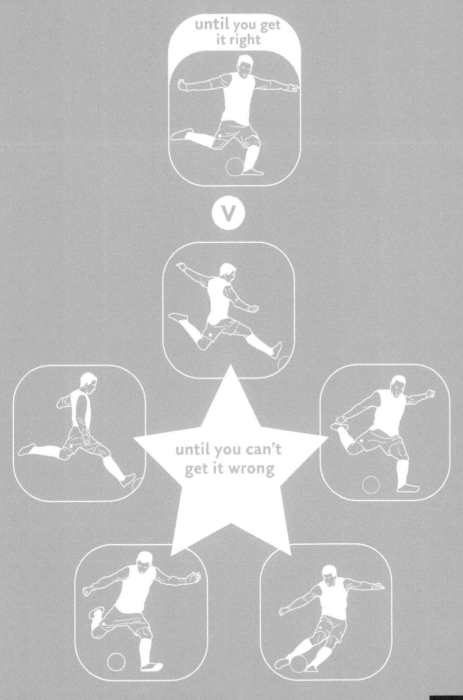

until you get
it right

until you can't
get it wrong

CHAPTER 2

PLANNING AND DESIGN

THE BATTLE AGAINST FORGETTING

"The major function of instruction is to allow learners to accumulate critical information in long-term memory."

Sweller, J., van Merrienboer, J. J. G. and Paas, F. (2019) "Cognitive architecture and instructional design: 20 years later," *Educational Psychology Review* 31 (2) pp. 261–292.

You have almost assuredly forgotten most of what you've learned in your life. For example, you remember only a fraction of what you learned in school. If you don't believe me, have children, wait 15 years and try to help them with their math or history homework. Learning is a constant battle against forgetting—and so, therefore, is teaching. In this chapter, I will discuss key factors in learning design: how to structure training activities and training sessions to ensure that the process ends with understanding. But the first topic in that discussion—memory and its antithesis, forgetting—requires a bit of a deeper dive.

Here's an example of one way forgetting happens. Imagine you are standing at a party talking to a group of people and are introduced to someone new: Alex. "Nice to meet you," you say. You chat briefly and enjoyably. As you talk, you are relying on working memory, the part of the brain that you use to think consciously about the world around you, to carry out complex reasoning and subtle acts of perception. In a split second, you discern that Alex's remark about how easy it was to park was ironic; you smile and laugh. At the same time, you have inferred from pronunciation that Alex grew up somewhere in the Midwest.

Working memory is a marvel of higher order thinking and perception. It enables the kind of problem-solving that allowed humankind to conceive of string theory and discover penicillin—not to mention conceptualize the overlapping center back. But working memory has one huge limitation. It can only hold a tiny amount of information at a given time. Try to think about too much at once and you begin to think poorly or forget. So, for example, all it takes is turning and chatting briefly with another friend who's just arrived, and you realize you have forgotten Alex's name.

The limits on working memory are no secret. Phone numbers are seven digits because that's as much as the typical working memory can hold. For ideas more substantive than digits in a sequence, the limitations are much more draconian. We can probably only think about one or two ideas of any substance at a time; after that, making a shopping list for the lasagna you're going to bake will cause you to be unable to think about that email to your boss—it's one or the other. And even that reflects our capacity under *ideal* conditions, with even very common situations counting as "less than ideal." The slightest shift in our attention—loud music or a glance at the TV—and what you were thinking about can slip away. Unless we get knowledge encoded in a different and separate part of our brain called long-term memory, we are likely to lose it.

The failure to transfer knowledge into long-term memory[1] is only one form of forgetting, however. Imagine that you are driving home from the party and hear a song a decade or two old on the radio. *It's Kool & The Gang!* You have not heard the song in years but suddenly the words come flooding back.

1. It's worth taking a second to explain what I mean by "knowledge" here. First, it refers to factual knowledge and also physical knowledge—skills like receiving a ball. Second, "factual" includes both abstract and concrete things. "It would include," writes Daniel Willingham, "the idea that triangles are closed figures with three sides and your knowledge of what a dog generally looks like." In an athletic setting, there's a lot of abstract knowledge—knowing how to recognize space in which to pass the ball, for example. Is it possible that because we are less likely to recognize this as a form of knowledge, we are less likely to treat learning as a knowledge-driven endeavor?

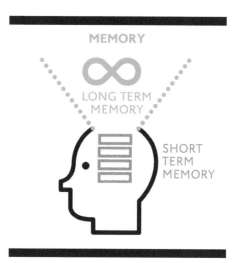

You find you know every verse and voice inflection. And strangely there are additional memories that come back to you with the song—where you were when you heard it last and the people you were with, perhaps.

Your knowledge of the song was there all along, sitting in your long-term memory without your knowing it. Then suddenly you were able to access something you had forgotten you knew, a memory you did not know you had. This process of recalling things into working memory is called retrieval and it is complex, fallible and immensely important to athletes. For now, let's recap the key points: You "forget" some knowledge because you never encode it in long-term memory, but other knowledge you "forget" *despite its being encoded in your memory* because you are not able to access it when you need it. You occasionally realize this when the right set of reminders grant you access to a lost memory. For much of the knowledge you've stored, however, the right reminders never come along and you may never manage to retrieve it.

Here's something else the memory of that old song can teach us: the capacity of long-term memory is almost unlimited. There are hundreds of old songs stored in your memory, not to mention details of the nights you heard them. You are almost entirely unaware of them now, but a brush with the right cue would connect you once again to this knowledge. How many old songs are there in your head? It's impossible to say; most of them will remain hidden forever, a vast jukebox awaiting retrieval.

The fact that long-term memory is all but unlimited has both drawbacks and advantages. On the upside, learning more about X or Y rarely keeps you from learning about Z. In fact, knowing more about a topic generally makes it *easier* to learn and recall other knowledge on the same topic. Ideas make sense quickly when connected to other things you know; they become connected through their recall and application, so as you remember one you remember others. The more knowledge you have on a subject, the more ways back to any single piece of information.

The limiting factor, writes cognitive psychologist Michelle Miller, "is not storage capacity but rather the ability to find what you need when you need it,"[2] and the challenge of finding knowledge stored in memory is multiplied for an athlete who generally needs it

2. Quoted in James M Lang's Small Teaching, p. 28.

instantaneously. Under performance conditions, the speed with which you can find it is the critical factor in your ability to use it. And for the most part, you can only find quickly what you have practiced finding many times before.

Memory and the athlete

Athletes must be able to recall both knowledge and skills automatically, reliably and in a flash while they are busy doing and perceiving other things. If they "know" something but they cannot recall it seamlessly, it's not much use to them. *They must know it and be adept at retrieving it*, and this fact has huge implications for how we design learning environments. If coaches don't pay attention to the process by which athletes learn to recall back into working memory what they know—a process known as retrieval practice—they risk developing athletes who fail to remember what their coaches are sure they know. It is easy for this to happen because we tend to assume that recall is relatively automatic. Having seen athletes do something, possibly multiple times, we tend to think the work is done. *If I've seen you do it, you must know it. Therefore you will remember to do it. If you do not, it must be because you lack in concentration or motivation.*

In fact *athletes themselves* often think this. They know they are capable of doing something; they understand a concept and they intend to use that knowledge during performance. But they will just as likely fail to and not know why.

One of the most important distinctions in education is the difference between performance and learning. Performance is what you know or can do while being taught; learning is what you know or can do later on. As Harry Fletcher-Wood puts it, "Student performance while being taught is a poor indicator of lasting learning." If we were making a movie of your life as a coach, thunder would clap as you read that line. Since we're not,

As Harry Fletcher-Wood puts it, "Student performance while being taught is a poor indicator of lasting learning."

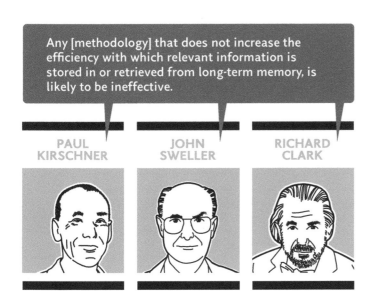

Any [methodology] that does not increase the efficiency with which relevant information is stored in or retrieved from long-term memory, is likely to be ineffective.

PAUL KIRSCHNER   JOHN SWELLER   RICHARD CLARK

3. There are of course other reasons beyond forgetting why something athletes trained on might not transfer to the game. Fatigue, nerves, and the failure to practice it at a challenging enough level come to mind.

4. www.bit.ly/3IGB7YZ

5. I'll discuss these challenges more in chapter 4, "Checking for Understanding."

I'll just repeat it, slightly translated: *Performance in training is a false signal. What an athlete demonstrates she can do during a training session does not indicate what she will be able to do in a match.* As coaches, we observe training and conclude that the level of proficiency we see then is what we are likely to see in the game. However, during training, athletes have not yet begun to forget; as soon as the session ends, that process begins, and forgetting is a ruthless and tireless enemy.[3]

The educational psychologists Kirschner, Sweller and Clark summarize it this way:[4] "Any [methodology] that does not increase the efficiency with which relevant information is stored in or retrieved from long-term memory is likely to be ineffective."

Understanding what you can do about that will be a major focus of this chapter; but before we dig deeper, I want to point out that there is a recipe for recrimination and blame hidden in the misunderstanding of how memory works. If we assume that athletes "know" something because we have seen them do it in training, then we are at risk of believing that their failure to use it during competition must reflect some intrinsic flaw: lack of concentration or desire, a poor attitude. There are, in other words, relationship risks when coaches do not fully understand the role of forgetting.[5] To be clear, I am not saying that a failure to execute is not sometimes the result of poor concentration, attitude or lack of desire on the part of an athlete. It may well be. But coaches should remember that it's easier and quicker to blame the learner than it is to ask a hundred questions about teaching, memory and the learning environment. Coaches who diligently hold themselves to task and assess whether they've gotten not only the *teaching* but the *learning design* right before presuming there is some attitudinal failure on the part of athletes will build better relationships in the long run.

Before we go on , here is a summary of what I hope to have established so far:

- Retrieving what you have learned back into working memory is a separate but related function from learning it in the first place.
- Ease of retrieval determines whether athletes can use what they know quickly when they need it.
- It's easy to overlook the uncertainty of retrieval because performance—temporary learning during training—fools us.
- Ineffective retrieval during performance may not necessarily occur because initial teaching was ineffective. Another step—memory building—may be necessary.

Remembering is about retrieval

"Retrieval practice" is the process of recalling into working memory things you have learned but have begun to forget. This idea is captured in the following graph—an example of what is known as a forgetting curve.

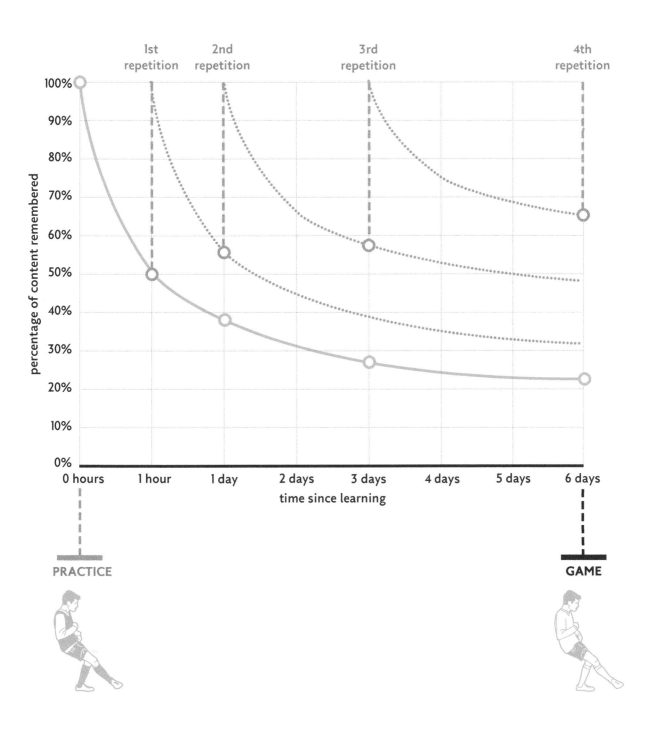

The first forgetting curve, meticulously plotted in the 1880s by Hermann Ebbinghaus, described the actual rate at which he was able to remember a series of nonsense syllables. Forgetting curves have since been recreated under a variety of conditions and demonstrate that:

- as soon as you learn something, you begin forgetting it almost immediately.

- the rate of forgetting is often shockingly high; a few hours after learning something, people routinely remember only a small fraction of it.

- each time you practice recalling what you know, the rate and amount of forgetting is reduced somewhat.

- to slow the rate of forgetting, retrieval has to come after a delay[6]—you have to begin to forget for the memory to be more deeply encoded in the brain.

- a slightly longer delay before each subsequent round of retrieval is most advantageous to memory.

That's immensely useful information, but forgetting curves can't tell us everything. Many have been derived over the years for various learning tasks, and the principles in them are broadly accepted, but forgetting curves like the one opposite are mostly hypothetical. They generalize differences across learners, content and setting. They cannot tell you exactly what the rate of retention will be for your team at time A or time B for a specific topic you've trained on, nor exactly how many times you'll have to retrieve the knowledge. Implicit memory—the physical memory of how to do something—probably encodes differently from explicit memory—the ability to recall information. And then there are individual differences and factors in the learning environment, like how much attention people are paying and how hard they are willing to work to remember. We don't know enough to predict the details of any specific single situation. Different people will forget different things at different rates. But the key idea endures: *people will forget* unless retrieval is used strategically and over time. You can cram the night before a test and do better in the short run, but you will also quickly forget what you've studied under such conditions. If you spread your studying out over a series of sessions, ideally with a good night's sleep[7] in between, you will be far more likely to remember a few months later.

Of all the unanswered questions raised by the forgetting curve, perhaps the most critical is "How many exposures to an idea do learners need to learn it?" Again, there isn't one clear number for that. Likely the required number of repetitions is influenced by the complexity of the idea and the prior knowledge of learners—experts in a given domain almost assuredly require fewer repetitions than novices to learn something.

In his book *The Hidden Lives of Learners*, Graham Nuthall proposes a useful rule of thumb based on his extensive studies of students and the resulting mastery of concepts. "We discovered that a student needed to encounter, on at least three different occasions, the complete set of the information ... to understand," he writes. "If the information was incomplete or not experienced on three different occasions, the student did not learn the concept." However, this requirement of three different exposures must take into account student attentiveness, Nuthall notes. If you teach it but students aren't fully attentive, you haven't achieved an exposure that leads to learning. Given those parameters, he and his

6. If you've used the language-learning software Duolingo, you won't be surprised to learn it's designed around retrieval practice and governed by forgetting curves.

7. Sleep, coaches should know, plays a critical role in memory formation. Scientists believe that memories are consolidated during sleep—that this is one of sleep's key biological functions—and sleep disruptions have been shown to result in memory disruptions. This is just one of many areas where recent research suggests sleeping well is even more critical to athletic success than almost anyone had realized.

colleagues found that they "could predict what students would learn—and what they would not—with an accuracy rate of 80–85%" based on the three-exposures rule.

So is three the magic number? Perhaps not. To know something and to be sufficiently expert at it to thrive under competitive conditions are very different outcomes. Understanding requires less fluency than mastery. An athlete must be able to recall her knowledge *very quickly* at a high level and under pressure. Spending a minute or two on an exam trying to recall the steps of mitosis counts as a success for a student. Spending more than a fraction of a second deciding how to exploit a flawed shape among opposing defenders is a failure for an athlete. In other words, Nuthall's rule of three exposures is almost assuredly a bare minimum.

Despite the technical questions about forgetting that science can't yet answer, there are clear takeaways that are relevant to the design of training. The first is that *by itself, even a perfect training session can almost never result in durable learning.* Coaches must plan sequences of sessions with intervals of time in between where a concept is forgotten and then retrieved to ensure mastery. Secondly, if you observe athletes at the end of a training session, you will almost certainly think they know it better than they do. Their knowledge will begin decaying from that moment on, but your recollection of their skill and proficiency will endure until the gap is exposed by contact with the opposition. Finally, spacing retrieval can make it more efficient. If you were to study 15 minutes for a test each day for three days, for a total of 45 minutes, using carefully designed retrieval practice, you'd likely do better than if you studied for 60 minutes all at once a night or two before the test. And you'd be more likely to remember what you'd learned a few weeks later.[8] Furthermore, as Matthew Walker describes in his book *Why We Sleep*, sleep is critical to memory consolidation. Much of the memory work your brain does is done while you are sleeping. Inserting three sleeps multiplies the learning effect and encodes memory more strongly.

Before we go on, let's tease out two related but separate ideas we are discussing at the moment:

- "**Retrieval practice**" is the act of recalling what you have encoded in memory in order to keep from forgetting it and to get better at recalling it.
- "**Spaced practice**" is the insertion of delays between rounds of retrieval practice to allow forgetting to begin and thus make the practice more effective. The degree of spacing is a critical variable.

It's not just quantity and timing of retrieval that matter. A bit of struggle is helpful too. "The more effortful this process is, the greater the strengthening effect," writes Peps Mccrea, "provided the retrieval attempt is actually successful." The key point here is that when you work harder to recall something, you encode the retrieval pathway more deeply. "Desirable difficulty" is a term that some cognitive scientists use when describing this phenomenon.[9] Players who are challenged when they retrieve what they know remember better and for longer. But don't miss the second point in Mccrea's observation: challenge helps when it *leads to a successful attempt at retrieval*. If the challenge is so great that the retrieval fails, memory is less likely to be facilitated.

8. As a side note, Brown and Roediger also explain that learners are not especially accurate in their perceptions of how much they are learning as they study. For this reason, people persist in engaging in lower value activities—such as rereading—instead of higher value activities, such as self-quizzing. Our athletes cannot very accurately tell whether they are learning most of the time, which is important to remember.

9. "Memory is the residue of thought"—Daniel Willingham

10. Success is rewarding. It likely provides a tiny dopamine rush that causes participants to want to continue engaging in cognitive activities. Willingham explains, "Working on problems that are at the right level of difficulty is rewarding, but working on problems that are too easy or too difficult is unpleasant." In fact, Willingham defines problem-solving as "any cognitive work that succeeds."

11. The "correct path" is different for different athletes, obviously, but one key rule to remember is that experts and novices learn differently. Experts learn from struggle; novices are often confused by it. Experiential situations—putting players in a situation with constraints and letting them figure out solutions—are generally found to be more effective with expert learners.

12. Consider this problem: in a game, a player dribbling a ball must respond to defenders approaching from every conceivable angle. If players only practice dribbling directly at a defender in training, the knowledge is less likely to emerge when circumstances in the game vary unpredictably.

So we want our athletes to frequently recall what they know in situations that challenge them to the right degree. When learners[10] aren't challenged, they don't learn optimally; but, Daniel Willingham tells us, the same can be said when the challenge is too great. Then working memory is overloaded and learning is not encoded in long-term memory. Coaches have to observe carefully for both the level of challenge and the rate of success. As far as I know, there is no reliable rule for what rate of success—that is, the rate of learners successfully executing the task or retrieving the information—is ideal, and this is probably one area where important differences exist between novice and expert learners. Experts are far more likely to be able to learn from mistakes because they understand them better and because they see fundamental principles at work rather than superficial details. Novices, less so. But it may be useful to observe that the more players learn, the greater the level of complexity and challenge they can productively learn from. Novices at a task might benefit most from a success rate of 80%, while experts might thrive at a 50% success rate. Again, those numbers are absolute conjecture. What we do know is that whatever their proficiency, we probably want athletes to experience *consistent* but not *constant* success.[11] This applies to retrieval and memory-building but also presumably to other tasks.

One other concept that can be used in coordination with retrieval is **elaboration**. In *Make It Stick*, Brown, Roediger and McDaniel describe this as the process of connecting material you are retrieving to other things you know. Making connections turns isolated single points of knowledge into connected webs of understanding, what cognitive psychologists call "schemas." The more connections you have to an idea in your memory, the more potential cues that can cause you to retrieve it and the more likely you are to remember it later, the authors write. So retrieval in varied settings and contexts with different examples or details will be most valuable. Elaboration, for an athlete, might include being asked to recall information—using different words ("Tell me what we mean by half spaces but do it without using the phrase 'between the lines'") or under different settings ("OK fine, but what if there were two defenders here?"). When it is interwoven with details and connections, a single memory becomes something stronger and more useful because it is more comprehensive. Variety in the retrieval setting—different places on the field, different spacings, different actions by the opposition—makes athletes more adaptable while making their memories more accessible.[12]

But what effective retrieval requires most is delay and therefore time. The work of overcoming forgetting is what prevents it in the long run. Put more simply, the best time to remember something is when you have begun to forget it. Combine that with the fact that retrieval should involve recalling and applying concepts in varying settings with the right amount of difficulty, and installing knowledge in long-term memory now implies building a schedule of retrieval where the spaces between retrieval gradually lengthen, and where variation and unpredictability are gradually added to the settings in which athletes are required to recall what they are learning. (And as discussed in chapter 1, this process should occur as much as possible in the right perceptive environment.)

Another concept that's critical to understand when designing training for long-term understanding is "interleaving." Switching topics during training accelerates forgetting of the original topic and thus allows a coach to create the same effect as spacing—making remembering more difficult—in less time. You draw athletes' focus away from an initial activity and then shift back to it. The original task is now harder to remember. Critically, this allows coaches to begin using retrieval within a single session. "Interleaving works by putting knowledge 'out of our mind' and so creates productive opportunities to retrieve it again," writes Peps Mccrea in *Memorable Teaching.*

One of the key themes in Brown, Roediger and McDaniel's book, *Make it Stick*, is that we are poor judges of learning because it's hard to see it when it happens, and our intuition about it is often wrong. We believe—I did for years—that sustained, unbroken focus leads to maximum learning. In a way, it does. It leads to fewer errors in training and that's what makes it look effective, but this initially high success rate flatters to deceive because it also leads to a faster rate of forgetting. So while "**blocked practice**"—practicing a topic in a steady unbroken fashion—is useful in some situations, it will be rapidly undone by forgetting unless we combine it with something called "**serial practice**," (sometimes "interleaved practice") which is the process of interleaving multiple activities during training.

I should note that some people argue based on the research that blocked practice is never optimal and should be avoided. I don't agree. I think blocked practice is beneficial until a skill or concept is stable in the mind of the learner. That is, until they are able to do it or understand it reliably. In what you might call the "initial teaching phase," a deep, Zenlike focus on a single task can help ensure understanding. Once athletes arrive at this understanding or can execute a skill correctly, then the rationale for maximizing the memory benefits of interleaving carries the day and coaches should intentionally use serial practice. It's worth noting that interleaving is not only about memory; new aspects of a concept are still being learned. Athletes are committing a core concept to long-term memory but also "elaborating" learning connections and applications in new contexts, so this portion of the learning process may be significantly longer than the amount of time spent in blocked practice.

Building it back up

Dave Love is a shooting coach who's worked with three NBA teams in addition to athletes at other levels of competition over the years. He's often brought in to change a player's mechanics. They're doing something that stands in the way of their long-term progress—their wrist is not flexing enough or, as was the case with one player Dave coached, they lean to one side without realizing it when they shoot—and Dave's job will be to break the habit and replace it with a new one that shows up in the game. Here he describes how he applies the idea of interleaved practice and how his thinking about it has changed.

DAVE
LOVE

When a player is working on a new skill or changing an existing habit, they put on blinders. Everything is very internal. It's necessary to start there with a bit of blocked practice to allow them to think about their body and what they want it to do. And, from a psychological point of view, to help them feel successful. It's sometimes important to do easy things early to change the athlete's perception that, say, they're a weak shooter. The best way to change that is often to show them results. Simple things early often show them that.

But if they get put into a game at this point it can be trouble, because the world is totally different from how they've been training. The training is too easy, and in a real game there's too much uncertainty that they're not ready for. It's hard for them to accept that they're not able to use the new skill so early in the process, but you can't rush it. The constant challenge for coaches is determining the appropriate level of challenge for players as they learn the new skill.

Early on in my career, I did too much blocked practice. I waited too long to bring in uncertainty and there were no decisions being made by the athlete, so the struggle to begin translating the skill to the game persisted and I would get frustrated when players could not apply what they were doing in practice.

What I try to do now is to find the point when the athlete is internally aware of what their body is doing and they are able to become aware of the environment in which they might execute the skill. At that point, I start making the practice more complex and working in variability and avoiding predetermination—situations where the athlete knows exactly how they're going to be asked to execute.

I have six different "layers" that I use to add variability: I can add distance; I can add speed; I can add movement; I can add dribbles and catches; I can add defenders; and I can add decisions.

If it's too variable early on, you're not going to change anything in the movement, but that period is actually fairly short and I now try to move more quickly to a more variable environment.

Let's say the player needs to get their wrist bent back when shooting. The player has to be able to perceive that flaw, so I will strip away as many layers as needed in the beginning to let a player concentrate on coordinating a movement differently. I'll let them get close to the hoop to recoordinate and then slowly add in those six layers as they improve at the new movement. A couple of years ago, I would have been more predictable and linear—*If you can't do it from 12 feet, don't try 13*—but now I'm trying to challenge myself to introduce more variability. More apparent progress in the moment right away might not lead to meaningful results. It feels scary as a coach because you feel in less control, but the control that made it feel less scary—10 feet, then 11 feet then 12 feet—was fake anyway.

Here's a very simple example. If I wanted to teach young players the Cruyff turn, I might start with blocked practice. We might do 20 or 30 Cruyff turns in a row. My goal during this time would be to refine the skill so that players encoded a highly proficient version of the move. But after I had encoded the turn in a correct and stable way so that players are doing it correctly, I'd want to transition to serial practice. Perhaps I'd ask them to do a Cruyff turn and then a step over and then a drag back. Or perhaps I'd have them work on their passing for a bit. Then I would ask them to do ball work, including the Cruyff turn, once again. Each time they changed to a new task, they would be distracted by the cognitive focus demanded by the *other* skill. This would cause forgetting and require them to work harder to execute their Cruyff turn when they came back to it, ultimately aiding encoding and recall. But if I moved to serial practice before my young athletes were executing an effective Cruyff turn—if it was wrong or flawed or ineffective—I would of course risk encoding those flaws in memory via interleaving as well.

THE CRUYFF TURN

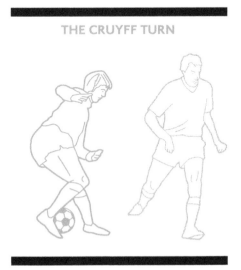

If I wanted to see my players' use of a skill like a Cruyff turn, or a concept like a high press, show up in the game, however, I would need to go further. As discussed earlier in this chapter, I would want my players to practice in an environment that recreated the perceptive cues and conditions that told them when to use their new skill turn. They would need to practice reacting to and reading situational cues—*How far from the defender should I be when I try that move?*—but this would also be critical from a memory-building perspective, and as such is an example of a third type of retrieval practice, "**randomized practice.**"

Randomized practice takes the concept of interleaving a step further, making the pattern and timing *unpredictable and ideally context driven*. Eliminating predictability at some point in the training sequence is necessary to success. Without doing that, training will always be cognitively easier than the game; and if training doesn't lead to sessions that aren't more taxing than competition, it won't fully prepare players—a point the legendary New Zealand All Blacks coach Wayne Smith makes in James Kerr's book *Legacy*. "The training, decision-making wise, should be harder than the game," he notes, and so the team employs the "overlying principle of throwing problems" at players and "randomizing situations," especially in the final training before matches. But the challenges of randomizing are about more than preparation for immediate competition. Smith also notes that "We found we were getting better long-term learning" as a result. Interestingly, when asking athletes to respond to "unexpected events" and "forcing them to solve the problems," we often imagine new and unexpected problems, but the most worthwhile problems are probably those that require what they know how to do at an unexpected time and context when they have to identify the cue. They are applying and adapting known solutions as much or more than they are deriving or discovering them, but this is not necessarily a problem. If you have a clear game model, your end goal may be the coordinated ability to execute a known solution at the right time and adapted to context. Coordination in team sports is underrated as a form of problem-solving. If your fly half solves a problem by going left and your inside center by going right, you have no solution at all.

Of course, a game situation is the ultimate randomizer. But in a purely random game, on the other hand, there is rarely enough opportunity to apply a skill you are learning to sufficiently master it. Games are too random for optimal learning so a coach would want to introduce randomness strategically—"controlled randomness."[13] This is one reason constraints-based games can be so effective for advanced learners. Their goal is often to strategically distort the game to cause more frequent recurrence of desired learning situations.

13. Strictly speaking, of course, none of this alleged randomness is random at all—it's just unpredictable; but with apologies to mathematicians, we'll stick with the term.

NICK
WINKELMAN

Nick Winkelman and randomizing BP

I recently observed Nick Winkelman, Head of Athletic Performance and Science for the Irish Rugby Union, present on this topic to coaches at a Major League Baseball club. He used a very simple example: in the batting cage, blocked practice would involve having a batter hit fastball after fastball after fastball. This is generally what clubs did for training for years. Perhaps if you were trying to learn or change some new aspect of a swing, you might use this approach to groove the basic motion you desired from the player; but once that base mastery was achieved, the blocked practice would begin to lose its effectiveness.

Serializing practice would mean going from fastball to changeup to curveball. This would be better once you were trying to build in adaptation and the ability to use the changed swing in the real world. Get the swing right, adapt it to a new setting or perhaps use a different swing as a new setting demands. Begin to forget. Now here comes another fastball. Recalling the new swing now will be more challenging but create a more durable memory.

Random practice would mean something like fastball to curveball to slider to fastball to fastball to slider in an unpredictable pattern and in situations where the player has to practice linking the new skill to the perceptive cues that tell him he should use it. Perhaps this might even be a simulated game situation where certain patterns are more likely in different settings—e.g. more fastballs with a man on first and second base open. This is important. It would be entirely plausible to learn a new swing but revert to an older one under pressure if the cues experienced under game conditions weren't associated with the new swing. So the randomizing would increase the likelihood that the player would use the skill in performance because he could use it in reaction to an unpredictable situation. It's also worth noting that the randomizing isn't purely random here. It's unpredictable. Would the coach probably have the batter face at first more than one-third fastballs and then slightly fewer later on? Quite possibly. On a related note, cognitive scientists often point out that learning is hard to see. What looks less productive in training can often yield better long-term results and this is especially true, research suggests, of blocked practice. Players perform better during training, but the long-term learning brought about by adding serial and random practice will be stronger even if athletes don't look as smooth at the moment. Coaches must steel themselves.

But as Winkelman pointed out, serializing can happen both within and between activities in a training session. It could also mean batting practice, then fielding practice and then back to batting practice. The most significant way we "block" our practice is in doing a session-long focus on something. It would be better, Nick suggested, to spend a total of 80 minutes on a skill but break it up into four 20-minute segments spread across five days than to spent 90 minutes on the activity all at once one day and then move on to something else or to begin working on it in a session, move away from it and then come back to it.

I discussed the application of some of these ideas recently with Russell Payne, Army West Point head men's soccer coach, after I observed a training session. His players were working on passing patterns. In the first sequence, a player received and turned to play on to a teammate. In the second, he played back to the passer at an angle and the passer played on to the teammate. In the third sequence, the player passed back to the original passer and broke forward to create a 2 v 1 with his teammate.

It looked a bit like this:

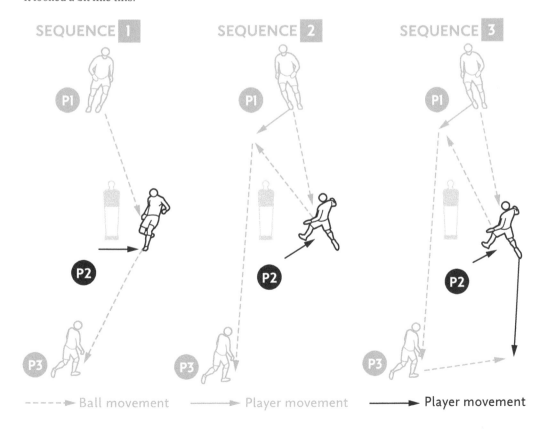

The team practiced this in rounds of a few minutes each, interspersed with feedback. The feedback was precise and technical. The exercise was dynamic as well, as Russell guided his players through questions about when and why they would use each approach. And the culture was intense and focused. Afterwards, we discussed ways to potentially use interleaving to get even more out of the activity.

The first lay in transitioning from blocked to serial and then randomized practice as soon as players demonstrated stable proficiency with the sequences he was teaching. Serializing the activity would have meant alternating patterns, thus causing players to have to work harder to remember how to execute each variation. The next step would be to randomize, making the sequence of patterns unpredictable and causing players to have to work hard and react quickly to the requirements of the situation. We brainstormed ideas for how to do that. The simplest solution would be for the coach to use verbal commands called to players before each round, but we preferred the idea of making players choose based on a visual cue that replicated what they might see under performance conditions. Russell proposed inserting a defender just off the shoulder of the player who received the first pass. This defender would play a limited role at first—merely positioning as if to mark tightly or loosely to signal which passing pattern his teammates should use but reinforcing perception (as discussed in chapter 1). Over time, the defender could add increasing pressure.

The second way to potentially improve the exercise would be to come back to this a day, two days, and then perhaps four days later. Fortunately, the data on retrieval practice does not appear to suggest that a long duration of retrieval is needed to achieve the desired result. Coming back to an activity like this one for five minutes on three occasions might be more efficient than 20 minutes on one occasion. Of course you might stretch the amount of time if you were trying to connect and elaborate on the concept—that is, to expand players' understanding—but mere retrieval can be powerful in short bursts. It doesn't have to be scheduled into next week's training but can be dropped in as sort of a punctuation mark. *Twenty minutes of rondos. A quick water break. Five minutes of our patterns from last week (you remind me how they went). Back to rondos.* In fact, thinking of retrieval practice as a sort of pop quiz can be productive. One of the most consistent findings of cognitive psychology is that frequent low-stakes assessment is one of the most productive learning tools there is. In the classroom, this means that the test isn't the end of the learning cycle but a constant and reoccurring part of it. In such cases, the quizzes might be scored—*Here's how you did*—but not graded—there was no consequence and no recording of the grade other than the consequence of each learner understanding how well they were learning.

MARC
MANNELLA

Making time for self-study

Marc Mannella is a former school leader who works with professional sports franchises to optimize learning within their organizations. One of the biggest challenges faced by baseball franchises, he finds, is schedule. How do you practice and develop players when there are 162 games played over 187 days?

How do you balance the different types of development players need and space them for learning when time is tight? Marc describes one solution.

The daily grind of a baseball season makes finding an ideal planning interval trickier, but not impossible. In professional baseball, it is typical to play games every day or night for a week or more, without any time off. When the schedule provides for a merciful break from game play, it is not just a day without a game but a true day off. So baseball teams that want to create intentional learning opportunities during the season need to find creative ways to work those into a tight schedule. One minor league manager I worked with found a novel cadence to address both the short-term need of debriefing the previous game and the long-term need to focus on the long-term development of his players.

"When I started managing, I tried different approaches to tackling the mental side of the learning," he said. "When I was a player, I hated meetings and thought they were a waste of time. One of our coaches would get up in front of the clubhouse and tell us everything we were doing wrong while we sat there looking at him, waiting for it to be over. When I retired from playing and became a manager, I could see the need to teach, to get everyone on the same page, but wanted to find a better way to do it."

The system he created looked like this. On game day, the pitching coach would meet with the entire pitching staff and the catchers for a ten-minute meeting to debrief the game from the night before. It has to be short, and in order to be short, the coach needs to know exactly what he wants guys to take away from the night before. The coach can't just say "So, last night: what do you think?" The questions have to be pointed. But that needs to be balanced with making sure it is a conversation with the guys, not the coach just talking at the guys. The guys need to think if they're going to learn. The trade is higher intensity for a shorter and more productive time together. The hitters attend a similar meeting with the hitting coach shortly thereafter (allowing the catchers to attend both).

Since those meetings are designed to review actual game events, however, the manager could never predict what topics would be discussed more than a day in advance, and they didn't provide a setting in which he could teach the topics that led to players' longer-term development and achievement of organizational objectives, so he knew he needed a second type of meeting. One less reactive and more proactive. He could choose a topic that was important well in advance and plan for it. After playing around with different intervals, he settled on meeting every 7–10 days, often at the end of every three three-game series. This interval allowed him to gather relevant video clips to support his teaching, to space concepts so they didn't feel like a blur, and to spiral back to key content.

This design, with the two disparate parts, allows athletes to learn from their game performance but also continue developing their broader knowledge—both of which are necessary if they want to progress toward the major leagues.

PART 1: THE TIME IT TAKES TO LEARN

If the key to durable learning is spacing practice out to allow memory to decay in between iterations, this implies that *there is almost nothing players can master in a single exposure.* One session on a topic may allow athletes to perform differently for a brief period of time, but those changes will soon evaporate. And if one session will never be sufficient, *coaches who want durable mastery and long-term development will have to plan across longer intervals of time.* Planning one session at a time won't do.

But how long? There's no sure right answer, but I can provide some useful parameters based on my work in schools. For example, I am confident that if long-term learning is the goal, the ideal planning interval is longer than a week. This is important because one-week intervals are the time frame I suspect many coaches use to plan their training. I could be wrong, but there are very strong incentives to plan one week at a time.

First, coaches use matches to gauge progress and set goals. Win, lose or draw, coaches sit down afterwards to consider what their team needs to work on so things look better next time around. You struggle on Saturday because your team's first touch is weak, or you aren't able to possess the ball when pressed, so you decide to work on those things during the week. Logically, next Saturday, you look for evidence of improvement. It's important to realize that the improvement you see is as likely to be performance as it is to be learning—the beginning of something that will become long-term mastery only if the training environment causes players to continue retrieving it at intervals, perhaps with an increasing degree of challenge and complexity over the coming weeks.

If the topic is a skill like redirecting one's first touch, the ongoing retrieval may occur with enough natural frequency to allow players to improve, but if it is a topic that will not naturally occur over and over (switching the field of play, say) or a skill where there is a significant risk that it may be done incorrectly or without coordination among players (*missed* opportunities to change the point of attack; first touch *insufficiently* redirected away from pressure; etc.), the first steps of learning may erode quickly. Ironically, it might be better for players if a coach was disappointed by their progress after the next match. A coach who says "They still don't have it. We're going to come back to that again on Monday and Wednesday" is a coach who is likely to take steps to increase progress in the long run, though ideally there would also be coaches saying "That was great. So much better than last week. Now I've got to stay on it over the coming weeks so I can rely on their ability to switch the point of attack permanently."

Another incentive to plan in week-long intervals is the tactical challenge of an upcoming match. Coaches think, "Right, we play Crosstown United on Saturday. What will we need to train on to beat them?" This may work to some degree, but much of the change will likely be short-term performance rather than long-term mastery. On Saturday, there will still be some recollection of what the team did on Thursday. Doubly so if they also did it on Tuesday. But the forgetting will continue afterwards. This exposes conflicts between short- and long-term outcomes (a topic I discuss further in chapter 6). It's not a simple conflict. Coaches *should* make tactical adjustments for upcoming opponents. Doing so surely builds player understanding. Changes in performance can help us win in the short term, and depending on how important winning a given match is, that's not irrelevant. But it's still a short-run game. The Saturday after your players learn to adapt their pressing to beat

Crosstown United, Underhill FC presents a different challenge. There's a decent chance that what players began for the Crosstown match will quickly decay unless it is part of a longer dialogue with the team. You may find yourself surprised by how little your players remember when you play Crosstown next season. The ideal might be to spend a few weeks on a few core tactical approaches at the beginning of the season and circle back to them before a match to retrieve and make small adaptations. Either way, the trade-off between the win over Crosstown (which performance improvements can help you accomplish) and the long-term development of your athletes (which the short-term performance changes are unlikely to help you achieve) is worth considering. *Is it possible that development for many players stalls at exactly the time they enter the most competitive environment of their lives precisely because the learning suddenly tips more steeply to short-term goals?*

The third reason why planning in one-week intervals is common is periodization. Coaches rightly worry about training loads on athletes and plan in weekly cycles as a result: recovery on Monday, high intensity on Tuesday, lighter on Wednesday and high intensity again on Thursday. It's hard to sketch out the training load without imagining the specific activities, though, so you sketch in the things you intend to cover at the same time. And you're unlikely to have a second planning process that causes you to look at learning in longer intervals of time.

And that's exactly the problem. The science of memory suggests that what appear to be improvements after a week of training are likely to fade quickly unless athletes retrieve and apply the concepts involved periodically over the coming weeks. Match-driven week-to-week planning is insufficient for long-term development. While this is especially critical to consider with younger learners, it is relevant everywhere and easier to overlook later in an athlete's career. Should some weekly planning based on short-term goals be happening? Sure, especially at the elite level—professional and college teams, perhaps even some high school as well—where the purpose is to achieve success for the institution via immediate results. Perhaps even for a youth club there are a few key matches per year where winning is a big deal—a high-profile tournament, say. But more broadly, the incentives are far too strong for coaches to continually invest in learning that fades quickly. In many ways, doing so is rational: they are likely to be evaluated, if not by the club, then by parents, players and possibly even themselves, based on wins or the readily apparent signs of improvement. The cards are heavily stacked in favor of short-run coaching, and it's possible that the majority of athletes at most levels of the game spend the majority of their time learning in environments that are heavily weighted towards short-run incentives, usually without coaches even realizing it, and where little attention is paid to the steps necessary to build long-term durable learning and development. I cannot tell you how many coaches of professional teams tell me they are stunned by the things their players have never learned. Sadly they tend to blame this on the athlete. "The response is not 'We need to teach that guy'; it's 'We can't run that play with him in there,'" a colleague told me.

One question a coach might reasonably ask is whether retrieval practice doesn't happen naturally during free play and therefore whether simply adding a lot of it to training would be sufficient to build long-term expertise. After all, the best players in the world—emerging from *favelas*, say, or some other neighborhood where their primary learning tool is intensely competitive unstructured daily play—seem to learn pretty well via this model.

It is true that simply playing frequently is likely to cause *some* knowledge to be transferred to long-term memory for players, and it is also true that a certain amount of free play is a valuable part of training. But some knowledge and skills are more likely to be transferred to long-term memory than others and the reinforcement will be random—free play will likely teach touch and guile and general principles of movement, but what else gets reinforced is impossible to predict and skills that require coordination and tactics may be lowest on the list. And of course the development will also be asymmetrical in terms of which players learn what—and most. So, if we want shared knowledge across a team, we're not likely to get it. Further, there's a data problem with free play. The players that coaches are referring to when they refer to its successes are the winners—a few exceptional players—and even those lucky few emerging from an unknown street with precocious skill must still then go somewhere and attempt to learn the game of positional responsibility, coordinated pressing and how to break down a well-coordinated low block. You don't go from the *favela* to the first team; you go from the *favela* to the academy. Are there prodigiously talented players who emerge from neighborhoods around the world and then fail? Absolutely. There will be lucky winners from the model, but also thousands of losers from that model and a coach is a teacher and seeks the maximum learning of all topics for all players. Free play is useful, but it is not likely to be sufficient for a coach who is committed to optimizing learning for everyone.

PART 2: WHAT TO DO ABOUT IT

So what steps could a club take if it wanted to begin planning for forgetting and focus more on long-term memory and lasting expertise? In the section that follows, I'll offer some suggestions, starting with an idea called unit planning—planning mastery of a series of concepts over a roughly six-week interval. After that, I'll describe some simpler steps clubs and coaches could take to begin leveraging the power of spaced practice—or experimenting with it to see if they think it makes a difference—without redesigning many of their existing processes. My goal is to allow you to begin applying the science of long-term memory-formation no matter the context of your club or team.

The (six-week) unit plan

Another common form of planning involves updating a club's curriculum. Once a year, the color-coded spreadsheet is tracked into the deepest recesses of some computer drive. A lively discussion about what it's really important to teach ensues before the document is returned to lonely solitude and people pretty much return to doing what they did. A one-week planning interval is too short, but a year is far too long.

What's the right planning interval if we want to build long-term memory, then? Something in the order of four to six weeks, I'd guess. That's an estimate, based in large part on experience in schools—an inexact analogy. The right length of time might be slightly more or slightly less, but four to six weeks is well suited to memory formation.[14] Ideas can appear, lie dormant for a few days, come back again for study, be combined with other ideas, and come back a few days later. Within a unit focusing on several goals at once, topics can be interleaved. Four to six weeks is also an interval of time that is manageable from a planning perspective. I still remember being a young English teacher and being asked to turn in my calendar of lesson objectives for the year. I was overwhelmed to the point of paralysis by

14. "If we want that knowledge to become rapidly and easily usable in a way that minimizes the burden on mental capacity, then we need to facilitate regular practice over a sustained period of months or even years," writes Mccrea.

this task. The more I glanced ahead and claimed that we'd be on chapter 17 of *The Grapes of Wrath* on March 11, the less reality-based I thought I was being. Perhaps this helps to explain why so many artfully planned curriculum documents so rarely get used. A year is too long to operationalize for most people. As a teacher, I found it more feasible—and frankly a helpful form of self-discipline—to map out the topics we'd hit each day over the next month in our unit on Greek drama. I'd do this six or eight times a year, watch how things played out—never strictly according to plan, by the way—and get gradually better at thinking through progressions of content, spacing of quizzes and the like.

Four to six weeks is also an interval that allows for change and newness from both the athlete's and the coach's perspective. I'm a believer in consistency and enduring principles, but it also shouldn't feel to learners like they are just repeating the same conversations all year. Seeing themselves making progress and taking on new ideas is motivating for learners. New learning goals and new topics to study are helpful—especially if we achieve mastery of some aspect of a topic one year and return to it to expand our knowledge the next year. This might influence whether you choose slightly shorter or longer units. Perhaps three-week units work better for younger players, whose attention spans are shorter and topics simpler. More senior players might require an even longer interval to master elements of play that require coordination and reaction to their opposition's approach.

Within a four- to six-week unit, you might choose several important topics to focus on: depending on the scale of the topics, perhaps two on the offensive side of the ball, two on the defensive side and one in transition, plus a few technical skills as well. With four or six weeks, you could include enough diversity of concepts for training to feel familiar but not too predictable. Bonus points if tactical concepts are what Steve Freeman of Black Watch Premier calls "corresponding topics": *What I am working on defensively is what the opposition would do to defend that and vice versa*—pressing and building out of the back, say. This makes it so it is easier to go back and forth, and the training environment adapts naturally and progressively: *My defense is getting better at pressing so it's harder for my offense to build, but my offense is getting better at building so there are new details to master in pressing*. During the first few days, perhaps you'd want to introduce concepts using a more "blocked" approach, paying attention to cognitive load and phasing in information so players successfully begin transferring to long-term memory. You'd take your time teaching them details over a number of sessions. You don't have to rush. In fact, you may move faster by going slower. Once players understand what they are trying to do and what their roles are, you'd begin interleaving, changing topics and coming back to concepts, adding manageable new bits of complexity and challenge each time you return so players elaborate on their knowledge as they retrieve it.

So perhaps day 1 is pressing. Day 2 is building out of the back with occasional reminders to defenders about what they would be doing if they were pressing—or questions about what hypothetical defenders might be doing. Day 3, it's back to pressing. Day 4: building out of the back. Then perhaps a second new topic—let's say we're working on getting wide and crossing on the offensive side and on defending crosses and transitioning on the defensive side. We spend much of the tactical session on crossing, but cycle back to a ten-minute review of pressing in the midst of it. Perhaps the primary focus is on crossing (and defending the cross) for three out of the next five sessions and pressing (and building out of the back) for two. But there are still opportunities for retrieval of the concepts that aren't the primary focus of a session. Maybe you pause the crossing exercise and suddenly say, "OK. Keeper has the ball. Yellows, you're going to try to build. Oranges, you're pressing. What are the key things you need to do? Play!" This is classic retrieval practice. Not only does it cause players to have to suddenly struggle to remember their roles when they press or build but when you are done with it and come back to crossing, their learning of those roles too will benefit from interleaving. The two minutes of distraction will cause them to have to work harder to remember. Perhaps the sessions start with a skill focus and we are doing something similar. We work on driving the ball or first touches or receiving with the chest, first in blocked then in serial fashion.

One other thing is important to add to this sketch of a unit plan: a "retrieval list." This is a list of what's been learned over the past year or so. Having a tidy list prompts me to find occasional opportunities to retrieve concepts from not only the current unit but also older ones. Just because a unit is done does not mean forgetting has stopped, so once players have mastered an idea, there's no reason to leave their retention of it to chance. Investing effort in keeping what we know alive is generally underrated in its value, and fortunately it can often be done quickly. My retrieval list might include things we learned in previous units that we could cycle back to, even if briefly. One simple way to do this might be to use the list of what's "in the curriculum" for a given year. If nothing else, it's a good way to get a curriculum out of its dormant state and keep it alive and in the consciousness of coaches. Adding a place on the list where I could note the dates on which I reviewed each given topic would allow me to keep track of my spacing and retrieval more strategically. I could see at a glance that I hadn't worked on or talked about up-back-through in five weeks. "If I'm a professional coach and I have a staff," coaching consultant Marc Mannella told me, "that's the first thing going up on the whiteboard. We're all managing it together."

How—and how often—should topics off a retrieval list make appearances within a unit? First, I'd avoid "retrieval gone wild." Skipping haphazardly from one thing to another will likely lead to distraction and attention residue more than carefully encoded long-term memory. But what about one or two regular times in your schedule when your goal is to reinforce two things previously studied through retrieval practice? Perhaps a ten-minute band of time in every practice or twice a week dedicated to retrieval. Or perhaps you shift objectives temporarily during free play or scrimmage. So two or three times you give the ball to the keeper and say, "OK. Keeper has the ball. Yellows, you're going to try to build. Greens, you're pressing. We'll pause afterwards and I'll ask you how we did." You could of course just wait for those things to occur naturally, but there are benefits to the intentional and visible shift to the topic you want to focus retrieval practice on. It causes players to attend to their actions more carefully and become more aware of what they're doing. It disciplines you to watch more carefully. And if you pause and say, "Greens, our pressing was good there but not quite great. Tell me what worked and what didn't" it won't feel like a gotcha. Players will likely have more to say because they were more aware of the fact that they were suddenly trying to press. Implicit in this example is the fact that retrieval doesn't require a lot of time to be effective, so there are a variety of ways you can use it without a massive reallocation of time. And retrieval could also mean reviewing via questioning or feedback during an exercise on a different topic without actually changing the exercise. "Pause. Girls, we've just won the ball. Quickly, when we win the ball in transition and the defense is disorganized, what do we want to do?" Or perhaps "Pause. We just won the ball in transition and the defense was disorganized.

This is something we have studied. What should we have done better there? Yes. Let's roll the ball back to Sophie. She'll turn the ball over to the yellows again and you'll show me what that should look like." You could also use game-based activities as platforms for retrieval: "During our 5 v 5, I want us to practice playing in, back out and changing the point of attack. I'll give you two points if I see a great example." There are a variety of ways to embed retrieval practice, in other words; the key is to delineate specific times when you will be accountable to yourself for using it and during which you plan what you retrieve intentionally and watch carefully for progress. In the end, this will save you time as encoding what players learn in long-term memory will help you avoid having to reteach it from the beginning next year.

No matter how you approach it, I recommend keeping a retrieval list as a starting point. Tracking what you retrieve and how often you do it will cause you to become more aware of it and you'll rapidly gain insights about what works and what doesn't. Perhaps you'd start with a goal: *We're going to review these three concepts at least four times.* As you do so, you can start to make notes about when and if they start to show up in the game. Over time, you could get more technical and note the date each time you review a concept, seeking to gradually increase the length of time between rounds of retrieval. Or perhaps you'd want to add a place to take notes: *Still strong or We struggled with this; review again soon; or Next time, focus on the importance of the entry pass.* There's nothing wrong with starting simple, in other words, and a retrieval list doesn't require you to change all of your other familiar systems and routines. You can try it out before you make massive changes. But long-term success in the battle against forgetting will likely require designated times when ideas unrelated to the session's major focus can come up for review.

Activity design

Understanding retrieval practice can help coaches ensure that athletes remember. Similarly, understanding working memory can help coaches refine individual activities within a single training session to achieve better results for learners. Remember, working memory is the part of the brain where conscious thinking—thinking you're aware you're doing—happens. Its ability to understand and solve complex problems is what differentiates us from every other species on earth. But despite its "superpower" of higher order thinking, it has clear limitations. It can only focus on one or two things at a time, and it struggles with duration—it can lose track of a concept quickly, especially if its focus is distracted by something else. Thus one of the most important things to consider in any learning environment is the "load" on working memory—essentially how near to capacity it is and how hard it is straining to think about the ideas it is consciously processing.

Let's briefly consider a typical situation in which working memory is heavily taxed—I am driving to an unfamiliar destination and receive a call from my wife, who needs to discuss a planned renovation to a bathroom in our house. There are tough decisions to be made. As we talk, I become less attentive to my driving. The person behind me starts to notice that I veer a bit in my lane and react slowly to traffic signals. I miss a turn I wanted to make. My perception is degraded. Working memory helps me interpret the rate of oncoming cars and whether I can turn left safely. Suddenly those calculations are less precise because my working memory is used up by the conversation with my wife. The chances of my having an accident increase.

Pushing my working memory to process so many things at once has had three distinct effects in this example:

- It reduces the quality with which I execute both tasks. I drive poorly and I don't think as clearly about the issue my wife and I are discussing.

- It causes me to struggle to remember new knowledge. I don't encode the route to my destination in long-term memory and will have to start at a blank slate next time I drive there.

- It decreases the accuracy of my perception of the world around me.

I've mentioned several of these effects elsewhere in this book but it's important to look at them together as we consider designing training activities because, as this example shows, managing the load on working memory strongly influences learning in multiple ways.

Managing loads on working memory goes two ways. We don't want to overload working memory but we also don't want to underload it. People are curious by nature. They *like* to be challenged, and that challenge is critical to both learning and motivation. The brain is drawn to solving puzzles, for example, because it is a source of pleasure. But to sustain interest in the puzzles, they must be of the right difficulty level. "Curiosity prompts people to explore new ideas and problems," writes Daniel Willingham in *Why Don't Students Like School?* "But when we do, we quickly evaluate how much mental work it will take to solve the problem. If it's too much or too little, we stop working on the problem."

Ensuring sufficient challenge in the training environment without overloading working memory is one of the most important things a coach can do, in other words. The cognitive psychologist Robert Bjork calls this "desirable difficulty." A bored learner is a poor learner—and possibly prone to distractions. Making sure the training environment sustains the brain's interest in the challenge is critical to effective activity design.

One common misconception about challenge, however, is that it requires novelty, but the brain's need for challenge doesn't mean coaches should seek to constantly introduce new activities. In fact, one of the challenges of training is often to introduce challenge when introducing distraction. Consider Matt Lawrey's training sessions at Atlanta United's academy—among the most engaging I've seen. Matt's sessions start every day with rondos. In fact the rondos start before the training session. The routine is as follows: you show up, greet your teammates and when there are six guys ready, you form a group and start playing. The rondo spaces are set up in advance. By the time Matt walks onto the field, players are already hard at it, chattering away and playing happily and competitively. This is in part because of the familiarity of the rondo. They know how to play the game so they can dive right in and get to the part they love quickly. No long explanations or quibbling about rules. Let's call that idea "knowing the ropes." It's underrated.

As soon as practice officially begins, Matt again capitalizes on his players' knowing the ropes right away. "Rondos," he calls out. "Game starts on my whistle. Don't lose!" Bang! Training is officially underway, and on Matt's whistle, the players snap to life. They are using a platform they know—rondos—but each round, there's a slight variation. "Round 2,"

Matt announces. "Count your passes. Ten passes means burpees for the defenders. Go!" Again they snap joyfully to it, in part because they know the ropes, but there's always a tiny variation to keep the challenge. "Round 3," Matt announces. "Defenders, if you win the ball, you must keep it for three seconds. If you do, the burpees go to the offensive players. Go!" Using a familiar format or platform allows players to focus on the changes in the activity with minimal load on working memory—or with their working memory focused entirely on "keeping the ball" rather than learning the rules of a new activity. They can do a rondo in their sleep but constant small variations shift their focus to different aspects of technique or tactics and add challenge. This gives Matt the best of both worlds. You could write a book about the array of variations he comes up with for his rondos and the things they reinforce. "Pause. Round 4," Matt announces. "Defenders, this time if you win the ball, you can take a risk. If you complete a pass to your partner, you earn his way out of the middle too. Or you can just keep the ball. Don't be foolish but don't be selfish. Play!" There's little limit to the range of challenges you can build on top of a flexible platform. And a familiar setting is often the best place to introduce variety and challenge.

Matt's activity design demonstrates a key concept in cognitive load theory, an area of cognitive psychology developed by Australian psychologist John Sweller. Understanding it can help educators maximize learning by managing loads on working memory. There are two types of loads on working memory in most learning situations, Sweller notes. One, intrinsic cognitive load, involves demands resulting directly from students thinking about the thing they are trying to learn. The other, extrinsic cognitive load, involves demands on working memory resulting from things students are not actively trying to learn but which they have to think about while learning. You introduce a training activity to your players that you hope will teach them to shield the ball and exploit space. When they are thinking about space and position and body shape, they are dealing with intrinsic load. When they are figuring out how to play the game so they can learn those things, they are dealing with extrinsic load. And the more figuring out how to play the game places demands on working memory, the less working memory is left over to think about learning space and movement. Extrinsic tasks can place demands on working memory greater than the intrinsic task.

Let's say that Matt woke in the middle of the night and thought of a new training activity that would be the ultimate tool to teach players to press and respond to pressure. He calls it "The Pressing Game." He arrives at training the next day and explains it to players. There are four pairs of cones, two each of two different colors. First the orange team has the ball. If they play the ball through the first set of (green) cones, they score a point. If the black team can cause them to play back through the first set of (yellow) cones, they get a point. If they can get the orange team to play between the second set of yellow cones, they earn the ball and the sides switch. Also, there are four players in each zone and two who can go anywhere.

Are your eyes glazing over? Right now, you're experiencing an exaggerated version of what Matt's players might feel the first time he used the Pressing Game: high extrinsic cognitive load. Tons of working memory used to figure out how to *do the activity* rather than how to learn the intrinsic tasks that are its ultimate purpose. No matter how perfect the Pressing Game is, teaching it to players causes them to use more of their working memory for extrinsic tasks. Learning will be temporarily reduced. How should Matt respond? There are several possibilities. Perhaps he could simplify some of the extrinsic demands of the exercise and thus increase the amount of working memory available for intrinsic demands. Does he need four sets of cones and zones where players can and cannot go? Or perhaps he could phase in the rules of the drill so players master a simple form and then the complexity grows? He also might ask himself whether he could achieve much of the benefit by teaching pressing from the rondo setting his players know so well. If the answer is "no"—it may well be—his goal should be then to ensure that the Pressing Game yields enduring results. If he uses it 25 times and it's great, the investment in getting up to speed and learning the ropes was worth it.

But much of the power of Matt's session comes from the fact that he is using an activity players know well and do every day, thus there is almost no extrinsic load. All of their working memory is available to focus on intrinsic tasks. The message is not to avoid new exercises or to only use simple ones but simply to be aware of the tradeoffs between extrinsic and intrinsic load. Yes, players should be thinking hard, but about what? We will of course need new settings to teach new things but we should remember that there is an installation cost to learning for each new activity and the cost varies based on its complexity.

For me, the ideal training activity is a platform: a basic set-up that players can master into which a coach can introduce simple variations to shift the learning focus. Such exercises preserve flexibility but reduce the need to allocate working memory on extrinsic tasks. And of course the balance of intrinsic and extrinsic loads has an effect on player engagement and motivation. A lot of extrinsic cognitive load means downtime and learning things different from how to play the game you love. Novelty—the newness of the activity—and challenge—the difficulty of the task—are different and, ironically, a lot of novelty can reduce the level of positive engaging and constructive challenge that players feel. Even once Matt's players understood the Pressing Game, the first 20 minutes they played it, they would mostly still be figuring out how it worked in a practical sense.

Cognitive load theory has other important applications for coaches. If we know that working memory struggles to hold onto more than one idea at a time, it means training exercises should phase in complexity and learning in stages, introducing players to one idea and letting them apply it right away, then adding another. As they start to execute more fluidly and with less strain on working memory, a new challenge or a new idea can be added. This keeps challenge at a level that engages players and helps them enjoy learning but that avoids asking them to do too many things at once. As my experience driving while talking on the phone revealed, people who try to do too many things at once fail to encode those things in long-term memory, degrade their perceptive capacity and often see their overall performance at other skills dip. So, learning will often go faster if coaches go one step at a time. Rather than giving players five things to try to do at the outset of an exercise, give them the same five in sequence spread out across the activity.

If you were working on building out of the back, say, and wanted to players to do the following:

1. Circulate the ball quickly with crisp passes on the ground.
2. Receiving players—snap open to receive the ball across body and see field of play.
3. Pass to the front foot or into space.
4. Look for diagonal passes first.

rather than listing all of these things at the outset and asking them to master all of them, it would be far more productive to say, "We're going to start by concentrating on weight of pass. We want the ball to move, so passes must be crisp and fast but also easy to handle, so on the ground. Let's work on that now." After perhaps five minutes, you might stop players and say, "Yes, we're really starting to get it. Let's keep the crispness of our passes but also think about where we pass. We want to strike balls to the front foot so our teammates can receive across their body. If there's space ahead, we can put the ball ahead of them and let them run into it. Let's see that now..." and so on.

Not only would this manage loads on working memory but it would also be more interesting for players: by differentiating each of the elements and giving players the chance to practice, you'd make an exercise seem like it was constantly changing and evolving, with new but manageable challenges constantly being framed. More learning and happier, more engaged players.

Another key takeaway from cognitive load theory is that novices and experts learn differently. Experts can execute most of a task with little load on the working memory and can therefore more easily and more rapidly incorporate new ideas. They may be able to handle more than one new concept at a time. Experts are generally more aware of their own strengths and weaknesses—one of the curses of being a novice is that you are unaware of the skills you lack and tend to overrate your own performance. You might be able to give experts three things to think about as they build out of the back. Each expert might choose the right one to focus on for their own learning needs or be able to focus on different topics at different times, but novices could not. They would not understand their own performance and the context enough to be able to shift their focus rapidly and judiciously among topics

The most important difference between novices and experts, however, is how they respond to low-guidance learning environments, like discovery learning situations where a coach does not explain what to do or how to do it but where athletes are supposed to derive knowledge from a situation— for example, a game where constraints are placed on the attacking third to make it extremely narrow and players are expected to learn how to adapt. Research suggests that these settings are far more productive for experts than for novices, who often don't know enough to distinguish effective solutions from poor ones. The things they learn are more likely to be wrong or random.

Experts faced with a complex problem, Paul Kirschner and Carl Hendrick write, look at the problem and see "deep principles" that help them "categorise and solve" it effectively. Novices, on the other hand, see "superficial features." Everyone is noticing things in discovery environments, in other words, but the value of what people notice correlates to their level of their prior knowledge. In a study involving physics problems, for example, novice problem-solvers often noticed the wrong things: two problems both involved motion of a ball so the novice assumed they must be solved the same way. But in fact one was an acceleration problem and one was a velocity problem. They were not

> Research...shows that the difference is not only quantitative (i.e. that experts know more) but also qualitative (i.e. their knowledge is also organized differently).

PAUL
KIRSCHNER

CARL
HENDRICK

solved the same way. "Research ... shows that the difference is not only quantitative [i.e. that experts know more]," write Kirschner and Hendrick, "but also qualitative [i.e. their knowledge is also organized differently]."

Sweller calls the tendency of novices to benefit from more direct guidance and experts to get more from problem-solving situations the "guidance fading effect": "Students should initially be given lots of explicit guidance to reduce their working memory load, which assists in transferring knowledge to long-term memory," he writes. "Once students are more knowledgeable, that guidance is unnecessary and ... should be faded out and replaced by problem-solving." Kirschner and Hendrick stress the benefits of an incremental "fading" where the process is gradual. As learners develop more mastery, guidance becomes less verbal and direct and players are allowed to glean their insights from experience and perhaps more open-ended questioning (of the sort you will read about in the last section of chapter 3).

It makes perfect sense, then, that Toronto FC head coach Greg Vanney[15] relies on a series of sophisticated constraints-based exercises where subtle changes in the rules force his professional-level players to calibrate fine distinctions between situations as an opposition seeks to draw them out of their defensive shape. The guidance fading effect would suggest that this type of training would be ideal for experts, but it also tells us it would be less ideal for novices. The flaw is the assumption that what works for Michael Bradley et al. should also work for youth players who don't understand the nuances of positioning and coordination and who are less likely to accurately perceive the important signals from the environment.

However, it's also worth remembering that whether learners are experts or novices is not fixed and can depend on the task at hand. Experts can revert to a novice state when they are learning something new. So even if a constraints-based coach like Vanney wanted to install something new—a set piece, perhaps, or an attacking pattern for an upcoming opponent—he might find that that his players suddenly and temporarily revert to a more novice status for a given task, and he thus might need to adapt his teaching in response, perhaps by creating what Sweller calls a "worked example": a careful demonstration of the ideal solution with key terms and decisions explained. He might then expect his players to rapidly progress back to a problem-solving environment. Across the facility at the youth academy, this progression would likely happen more slowly. Across town at a club developing U14 players unfamiliar with the idea of playing between the lines, it would be more productive to recognize that players would be novices at the task for a sustained period of time and that direct guidance was preferable.

There is, in other words, no one best approach. This is, I hope, a theme to this book. Discussion about learning methods often attempts to extrapolate what works for the best players in the most elite environments—i.e. professionals—to other environments. There is an immense amount to be learned from watching experts train, but it is easy to apply it hastily and erroneously to novices.

15. Greg generously and patiently explained a series of brilliant constraints-based activities and variations to me one Saturday in Toronto when, given his schedule, I am sure he would much rather have been home with his family. Ironically, my working memory was filled to bursting trying to understand the nuances of what he was saying and diagram it in my notebook at the same time. Afterwards, I could remember only bits and pieces. It was a parable of the failure of a novice's working memory. His observations about how to force a defender to choose whom to mark during build-up play would surely have made this a better book.

What prevents skill transfer?

One of coaching's biggest challenges is skill (or knowledge) transfer: the idea that concepts that seem to have been mastered in practice often do not show up in or "transfer" to the game. In chapter 1, I discussed being able to establish order over chaos—a team's ability to successfully get to a place where it can apply a given concept. It's a similar concept to something Sefu Bernard, Director of Player Development for the WNBA's Washington Mystics, calls being able to "build the concept." It's one of the keys to concept transfer and he discusses that here.

Basketball is evolving to a shared understanding that the game is about advantage and disadvantage—that's what it comes down to. Offensively, can you find it, use it, create it, and share it? Defensively, can you neutralize it, disrupt it, deny it, and get it back? That's the game in a nutshell.

The most effective way to develop an individual's ability at, and a team's cohesiveness in, recognizing and exploiting advantage-disadvantage is to do things with as much context as possible. Once I accepted that the keystone habit came down to the thinking side of the game, the next questions for me were: How do our practice planning and our drill design match up to that? *How well do we prioritize perception-action (i.e. vision-anticipation-decision-execution) versus technique training?*

One of the things I started to do was take our practice plans and make notations in the margins. I differentiated drills by "phases." (A framework I picked up while working with the Canadian women's national team programs) The phases are A, B, C and D. Phase A refers to "on air." There's no defense. It's unopposed. Phase B means we add guides—opposition that has a job to provide a kind of constraint that leads players towards a certain solution or decision. For example, maybe I want to make a player use their non-dominant hand so I put them against a defender whose job is to guide them toward using their left. Phase C is small-sided games: 2-on-2, 3-on-3 or maybe a 3-on-2 or 4-on-3 advantage or disadvantage. Phase D activities are game-like: 5-on-5 and often allowing for flow between offense and defense with less interruption.

Ultimately, by marking up our practice plans, I want to know over the course of the week how much time we were spending in phase A and B drills. Because A and B lack context. You don't have the game-like cues; you're not forced to make decisions without defenders. As coaches, we can spend a lot of time in phase A and B drills and then wonder why players can't decide and execute in the real game. My feeling is that they haven't spent enough time in phase C and D activities. Sometimes it's uncomfortable being in phase C and D as a coach. It doesn't look as clean. You can structure A and B so they look neat and precise. But the skills break down under pressure. I am looking for whether the athletes can "build the concept" we've been working on within the chaos and strains of the game. If they can't, then that falls to me as a coach in how I've designed the training environment and structured what we do.

If I teach my offense with half-court drills where everybody is already in their spots and then, when the game starts, they can't get to those spots, there's an issue with my teaching. Where did it break down? Well, in the game, the players suddenly have to inbound the ball, then bring it up court while being pressured, and are faced with the limitations of a shot clock; and, perhaps, we always started by giving them an advantage in our phase C work rather than requiring them to create it or work their way out of a disadvantage. Or, similarly, perhaps I run separate drills for inbounding, for full-court pressure, for half-court defense, for offense...but they haven't learned to flow into or out of any of those moments. That's on me as the coach.

We spent time working on it but we didn't connect the dots and require them to build into the concept. We're not ready until we can build into the concepts. And, if they're unable to apply what was done in practice to the game, there's been no retention and transfer.

Coaching great John Wooden said, "You haven't taught until they've learned." So if they're not able to do the thing that we want them to, that's on us. We plan the practice.

I love how sprint coach Stuart McMillan puts it: "Context shapes content. Content shapes context."

There is no secret sauce, but I will say that planning and design is where the magic is found!

Activity design rules of thumb

Intentionally managing loads on working memory is critical to accelerating learning, but there are other useful design principles for an effective training activity as well. I close this chapter describing a few "rules of thumb" that I think learning research clearly supports. A list like this can be to help you envision the activities in your training sessions or also review them. Checklists, I will discuss in the next chapter, are underrated planning tools and they help you keep from missing something important in your planning process. This is not to say that every rule of thumb below should be included in every training activity. The list is a list of questions you should ask yourself. These design elements should frequently be present in much of what you do; if there's an easy way to tweak an activity to make it jibe with one of these rules, it may be worth considering strongly. That said, any list of principles deserves the reminder about the nature of principles: they are generally but not always right and tend to need adaptation and application to the specific situation.

FIRST RULE OF THUMB: Have a targeted goal

In *Peak*, Anders Ericsson summarizes the findings of his career researching the science of deliberate practice. He writes that successful practice requires well-defined goals "not aimed at some vague, overall improvement," but targeted to the most specific outcome possible, ideally one that can be accomplished within a single session. The challenge is that this is more specific than what most people are naturally inclined to do. Almost everyone mistakenly thinks they already do it because they have a purpose in mind—usually something like "We are working on changing the point of attack" or "I want to show them the roles of the backs in a 3-5-2" or "I want us to play forward more aggressively." For younger players in a skill training, it might be "I want to work on foot skills" or even "I want to teach them the Cruyff turn."

These purposes are too general to be effective. For a coach with a general purpose ("We want to work on changing the point of attack" or even "Get better at changing the point of attack"), an upgrade would be to choose something more specific, ideally both observable and manageable. The result might be something like "We want to improve our ability to change the point of attack by accelerating the rate of our passes and positioning ourselves to handle the ball more quickly." With a more specific goal like that, you can start to imagine what practice will look like. We'll work on rapid passing, adjusting body shape in receiving the ball, simplifying and directing our first touch and playing with our heads up, possibly moving decisively after our passes. As a coach, this helps me decide what focus to bring to the individual rounds of practice within the activity, what Ericsson calls "a series of small changes that will add up to the desired larger change." Since goals are so often vaguely applied, I will call what we're talking about here a "targeted goal" to distinguish it from the less precise but more frequently used type of goal.

SECOND RULE OF THUMB: Practice in rounds

As we discussed above, working memory is most effective in encoding concepts in long-term memory and noticing key perceptual details the load placed on it by other tasks is minimal. Generally, we want athletes trying to do one new thing at a time. So design activities in rounds. Introduce a single teaching point. Let athletes try it. As they show progress, stop them and add another teaching point or, if they struggle, explain a key misconception and send them back to try again. It seems slower but in the end it's far faster than frontloading all of your teaching points at once. If you do that nobody will learn everything, most will learn little or nothing, you won't know who's mastered what and you'll be back at square one tomorrow.

THIRD RULE OF THUMB: Isolate then integrate

A good activity progresses over time. It gets more challenging and more complex. It edges closer and closer to game conditions. In many cases it surpasses them, creating a training environment that's faster and more demanding than the performance environment so that the game itself seems easy by comparison. In *Practice Perfect*, Erica Woolway, Katie Yezzi and I described a progression: begin by isolating a skill, then integrate it over time. Practicing in rounds—that is, adding one new idea at a time and giving athletes the chance to use it right away before adding more—makes implementing this relatively easy; but, you might ask, integrate what? Make more challenging and complex how? Here are several axes along which a training can develop:

- Simple to complex. Progress from blocked to serial to random practice. Start with small positional groups and make them larger. Start with a single movement off the ball. Then add another and another. Or slow to fast to faster. Simple things done fast and with precision are often mistaken for complexity.

- Easy to hard. Start working on speed of ball circulation in midfield play with numbers up. Then numbers even. Then numbers down. If you can do that, you'll be ready for the game. Or start with plenty of space and try to execute as the space gradually gets smaller and smaller.

- Order to disorder. The first time you practice attacking with two forwards, let your midfielder start with the ball and let everyone begin in position. But then have the opposition play the ball out to the attacking team so they have to reconstruct their shape in a new place on the field. Or require your players to start out of position. End by having the opposition start with the ball and your attacking team having to first win it. Having done so, they will be out of position and disorganized. They will struggle to get back into position and possess the ball. Attacking from this position will be much more challenging and much more realistic than starting with all the pieces in place. It will force players to exert order over the game. Only when players can do that are they truly ready.

FOURTH RULE OF THUMB: Mix in mix-ins

Imagine your basic high-end ice cream shop. You order your flavor but a lot of the value is in the endless variety and richness of the mix-ins: chocolate chunks today; gummy bears tomorrow. Look for opportunities to mix in ideas from your "retrieval list." The sudden inclusion of a previously mastered idea helps encode in long-term memory, and short retrieval periods are often as effective as longer ones.

FIFTH RULE OF THUMB: Manage extrinsic load

Don't forget the gift of the familiar. It lets athletes focus their conscious thinking on the thing they're learning, not the procedures for the activity. If you can't reuse a familiar platform, try to phase in exercises over time. And if you're going to invest in installing it, consider whether it's adaptable enough to teach multiple topics.

SIXTH RULE OF THUMB: Adapt to level of expertise

All learners don't learn the same, so an activity should be adapted to your athletes' level of expertise—generally and on the specific topic in question. The more novice, the more explicit the instruction. For experts doing things they are familiar with, discovery-based methods are often more useful, but keep an eye out. If players struggle—either to master or because they seem under-challenged—it may make sense to consider whether you've read their level of expertise correctly.

The challenge coda: how hard is hard enough?

The third rule of thumb describes a process in which things get increasingly more challenging over time. And this raises the question: how hard should they get? "The training, decision-making wise, should be harder than the game," New Zealand All Blacks rugby coach Wayne Smith reminds us. At least that's the ideal answer. If you can get to that point productively—with players still executing well and with the difficulty still manageable—the game will be comparatively easy. What could a training activity that is harder than the game look like? It could mean faster than the game, or "numbers down," with more opposition or more pressure. And it should be sure to incorporate Christian Lavers's lesson from chapter 1. The final version of an activity must transition from the previous phase of play. Otherwise players will not be ready.

CHAPTER 3

GETTING MORE OUT OF
FEEDBACK AND QUESTIONING

Perhaps the single most common tool we use in coaching is feedback. We give it constantly: to an individual athlete and to groups of athletes; during training and during a match; while athletes are training or when they've paused for a break—not to mention afterwards: in the car, in the locker room, or on a corner of the field. We give feedback to colleagues and teammates as well. Feedback is everywhere, and that makes it rich in both opportunity and challenge: we use it so frequently that getting even marginally better at it could transform the results of our teaching. But what we do constantly, we often do with least reflection. Familiar things easily become a habit and it's hard to change what you're not paying attention to. What's more, feedback is so familiar, it can feel too mundane to be worth sustained attention. If a colleague sent you a video on tactics, you'd watch it, but a video on feedback? Perhaps not.

FEEDBACK

The goal of this chapter is to help you be more productive with feedback so you can help athletes learn more and grow faster. To do that, we'll need a working definition: *Feedback is guidance provided to athletes after an initial effort at execution.* The term implies reaction. You explain something and you're teaching. When your athletes try it and you tell them how they did, you have feedback.

Most coaches give feedback in two situations: during stoppages and during live play.[1] Feedback during stoppages tends to be addressed to groups. We stop the team and make an observation—"We were too compact," say—then we describe an alternative or ask players questions until they have arrived at one. Live feedback is often more likely to be addressed to individuals—the ball is in play but we shout, "Check to the ball, Marco!"— though we also use it with the group, too: "Yes, better pressing, guys!"

There are benefits to both. If the comment about checking to the ball applies only to Marco, letting everyone else keep playing means they are learning more—and are probably happier. Why should they stand around while Marco gets told to adjust his movement? And perhaps Marco will be more open to the comment if it isn't made in front of others. For these reasons, some coaches believe in giving live feedback exclusively. But that's probably idealistic. After all, Marco is in the middle of playing. It's an open question whether it's possible to both play and listen well at the same time. Marco may

1. Arguably a third type of feedback is that which players give themselves and which coaches try to maximize when they use constraints-based approaches. This is most applicable to expert learners and I'll come to it later.

not even hear you. If he does, he may nod to appear as if he's listening and tell you yes, he understands, using a little polite deception so he can get back into it: *Yes, Coach. Got it. Yes, yes, yes.* There's a good chance he doesn't get it, though, or if he does, he'll soon forget. And there's a decent chance that what he means by *Yes, Coach* is *Please stop talking to me, Coach—I am trying to play.* So there is a larger risk—more important than whether he checks to the ball—that over time he will practice ignoring you, learning that only half-listening to your words is how to respond to your coaching.

I was thinking about this recently while observing a session run by Matt Lawrey, of Atlanta United's academy. He wanted to help the #9 understand an opportunity to time his run differently. "Darren," he called, and Darren turned his head briefly but continued to play. After all, receiving shouted instructions while you are playing is normal for athletes. But what Matt did next was different.

"Look at me," Matt said. "Ignore the game for a minute." Darren still seemed unsure of whether to stop playing completely. "It's OK," Matt said, smiling. "Just stop." Slowly, Darren locked in on Matt. Now the feedback: "When you're checking back to the ball, wait half a second. Disguise the run slightly and then: bang! Like this." He demonstrated. Then released Darren back into the flow of play.

Tiny changes can have immense influence not only on our success in communicating a message in a given interaction but also on culture more broadly. Instead of tacitly asking Darren to divide his attention, Matt signaled that the feedback was the priority. He was framing the culture he wanted, one that starts with full attention. There is an implicit question asked of every team: *What do we do with the things a coach tells us on this team?* On some teams, the answer is: We nod and half-listen. On Matt's team, the answer is: *We give our full attention.*

Would Matt use this approach in every situation? No. Is it possible that the rest of the team could have benefitted from the guidance? Or that Matt could have created an opportunity for Darren to immediately use his feedback? Or could Matt have pushed Darren to figure the idea out for himself? Sure. Maybe. A hundred maybes. But that too is part of the point. Every simple iteration of feedback involves a number of choices and decisions. Getting better at feedback means developing operating principles and shared vocabulary so we can study and discuss those decisions.

OVERVIEW

This chapter describes operating principles for feedback. They're organized into three levels. Think of them as 101, 201 and 301. Each is organized around a theme.

Level 101 describes fundamentals: core things to get right. A coach never outgrows fundamentals, and just because they're fundamentals does not mean that they are easy or that most coaches—even at the elite levels—get them right. The simplest things are the most easily overlooked. One of my favorite practice videos is this one of Hall of Fame basketball player Dwyane Wade practicing dribbling. He's one of the best point guards in the world and what does he work on to elevate his game? Fundamentals. Coaches, too, should always be attentive to the basics of their trade.

Watch "Dwyane Wade practicing dribbling" at www.coachguidetoteaching.com

Level 201 focuses on what happens *after* you give athletes feedback—specifically whether and how they apply the guidance you've given. After all, just giving feedback causes no learning by itself. It's the effort to apply it afterwards that causes learning. If feedback gets ignored, there's no afterwards to speak of. A coach must build a culture where athletes not only attend to feedback but also use it in seeking to learn.

Level 301 focuses on using feedback to foster decision-making and therefore providing feedback through questions or by creating situations that cause players to problem-solve. In the long run, we want athletes to ask themselves questions, to engage in constant self-reflection. We teach them to do that by modeling those processes for them and, in ensuring that they help players succeed, convincing them of their benefits.

Before I share these operating principles, here are some things to note.

First, they are rules of thumb. They are usually right and frequently helpful, but not always right or most important in every situation. Feedback is used by a wide variety of coaches with a wide variety of styles to help diverse learners in different contexts master a dizzying variety of skills and knowledge. Under such conditions, principles will always require judgment and discretion. Even the truest principle has a wrong time and place. As Christian Lavers reminded me: "The answer is, 'It depends.'"

Second, a story about a visit to a Major League Baseball franchise. I had been invited to present to their major and minor league coaches. I asked, "What are the biggest teaching challenges you face?" and the first coach to speak said, "They don't *want* to take our feedback. They say yes, but they're trying to ignore most of it." Everyone in the room nodded. I hadn't seen that coming.

"Why?" I asked.

"A lot of times, they just don't think we're right," the coach said. "They think they're the exception. That they know what works for them."

"And even if they believe you when you tell them 'Shorten your swing,'" added another, "they know that if they take that advice, they will go through a period where everything will fall apart. Changing their swing *might* get them closer to the majors eventually, but it will for sure make them hit .220 for the next six weeks. A player has to really trust you to take that risk." Players weren't sure coaches really knew them, were truly out to improve them, and wouldn't judge the ensuing struggle harshly. They had to believe in and trust the relationship to embrace taking the risk walking through the valley of the shortened swing.

Feedback exists within a broader relationship and a larger culture, and those things are often just as important as the details of the teaching. Each iteration of feedback both shapes and reflects culture; it teaches something but also reinforces—or erodes—relationships, and this is true whether or not the coach realizes it. As the coaches I was visiting had found, if a culture of trust does not exist then the operating principles only matter so much. But don't forget the converse: giving feedback that helps players improve is one of the most important ways to build trust. Trust is an outcome of feedback as much as a prerequisite.

FEEDBACK 101

Focused feedback

Here's an example of feedback a coach might give during a typical soccer training. Let's say it's a group of U16 girls working on changing the point of attack. Stopping the girls as they pass the ball across the back four, the coach says:

> *Pause! Girls, when we switch the point of attack, we must strike firm passes at pace! They must be on the ground and struck with authority. Remember, we are trying to make our opponents move quickly side to side! And when you receive a pass you must be attentive to body shape— open your hips and receive across your body so you have options and can see the field but are prepared to make the next pass quickly. Also, some of us are panicking a little if we are pressed as Ashley was here. Two things must happen if we're to overcome that. Ashley must use her first touch to create the proper angle. But Shannon on the far side must adjust her angle too. She's high if she can be, but if Ashley's under pressure she has to drop deeper to give her a clear pass. Show me that now, Shannon. Good. OK, everybody got it? Play!"*

There's a lot of good advice in that stoppage. In fact, that's the problem: there's far too much of a good thing. Here are five key points the coach made:

1. *We must strike firm passes at pace!*
2. *They must be on the ground and struck with authority.*
3. *When you receive a pass, you must be attentive to body shape—open your hips and receive across your body—so you have options and can see the field.*
4. *Ashley must use her first touch to create the proper angle.*
5. *Shannon must adjust her angle in response.*

Each of these teaching points is clearly described. Several include context to help players "understand the why." One describes a perceptive cue that athletes can use to determine when and how to use the guidance. But all that good stuff may prove irrelevant. The five points the coach has made will quickly overload her players' working memory. They won't be able to remember, much less use, that much information at once. This is an extremely common trap for coaches—one we're often lured into by our best intentions. In the midst of our feedback, we think of a related point and add it on impulse to help players see a connection. Or we genuinely believe that we can accelerate their learning by adding in one more thing. Unfortunately, the result is often the opposite.

Skills and knowledge must be encoded in long-term memory to be used under performance conditions, and this means we should constantly be aware of loads on working memory. Working memory, you will recall, is incredibly small. Trying to hold too much information there will cause other cognitive processes, including the process of long-term memory formation, to slow down or stall.

Consider what's likely to happen immediately after this interaction. Since nobody can focus on five things at once, the best-case scenario is that each player chooses something—the single thing most useful to her—to focus on. But this is unlikely. The odds are better that each athlete will choose quickly and perhaps randomly one of those things to focus on. OK, that still doesn't sound so bad. It's good advice and everyone has taken some. But each athlete will have chosen a different topic and none of those choices will be clear to the coach. She won't be able to give them feedback on how they're doing at trying to use the idea. Lucia may work on opening up to receive and at the next stoppage the coach may remind her about something totally different—the pace at which passes were struck needs improving. But in fact, her mind was on receiving the ball, and instead of helping her to sustain her concentration, the new feedback will now shift her attention and dilute her focus.

And what about the next stoppage? No athlete will have mastered all five ideas, so should the coach say the same five things to them next time? How long should she dwell on those five topics, especially when she will find it difficult to observe her players' progress? Were they getting better at striking the ball at pace? Hitting it harder but leaning back, putting it in the air? Were some players improving and others not? Trying to make an assessment about the progress multiple athletes make on five different tasks will be all but impossible, and therefore so will the coach's ability react to her players' learning.

But the most likely outcome of this feedback is even simpler: in trying to remember to do so many things, they will do nothing with sufficient focus to achieve mastery. There's a decent chance the overload on working memory will cause their performance to get worse, actually. As Dave Hadfield of New Zealand Rugby put it: "When you chase five rabbits, you catch none." In the end, trying to apply more than one or perhaps two ideas at a time is unlikely to result in consistent understanding. It is more likely to foster confusion and even frustration. It will normalize a lack of accountability for using feedback. Sustained over time, these things erode faith in training.

DAVE
HADFIELD

When you chase five rabbits, you catch none.

Consider, now, how the session might have played out if this mass of feedback was broken up into smaller chunks that the coach gave in sequential rounds, each providing a single "rabbit" to chase. The first round might sound like this:

> *Girls, pause. One of the most important things for us to do is to strike our passes at pace. We're trying to make our opponents work! For the next few minutes, I want to see every pass struck at a pace like this: [demonstrates]. Challenge yourself and challenge your teammates. Go!*

Suddenly the task for players is clear and observing their execution is a manageable task for the coach. She can now give them useful feedback on the pace of their passes, reinforcing success as soon as it happens (*Yes, Brianna! Excellent pace!*) and helping them to see their progress and sustain focus. She has begun building a culture of accountability—the unspoken message is I notice *whether you use my feedback or not!*

Soon there will be a second round of feedback. Consider these different options for what that might sound like, depending on the girls' progress in their play after the first round:

> **Option 1:** *Girls, pause. Much better! We were really striking the ball with pace there. Tell me what you noticed about what it felt like and what you needed to do to succeed. [Coach takes three observations from players.] Good. Let's stay on this point for two more minutes so we can get really solid on what it feels like when the ball moves at pace. Keep pushing yourself! Go!*

Option 2: Girls, pause. Much better! We were really striking the ball with pace there. I hope you felt it. Keep doing that, but now I also want to focus on accelerating our speed of play when we receive the ball. Snap open your hips and receive across your body. [Demonstrates] This will leave you prepared to continue the movement quickly. What are we focusing on when we receive? [Takes answer] Yes, hips. Go!

Option 3: Girls, pause. That was good. I saw many of us striking firmer passes. But some of those passes were bouncing or going in the air. We've got to get them on the ground. Fortunately we know how to do that. How do we keep the ball cutting the grass and rolling crisply on the ground, Ashley? Yes! Body over the ball. Lucia, show us what that looks like. Good. Now back at it. I want to see sharp passes on the ground. Go!

Option 4: Girls, pause. What were we focused on as we were playing? Lucia? Yes, speed of passes. I saw some passes struck faster, but not enough. Let's stay locked in on this point. On every pass, you'll hear me shout "Yes!" if it's the kind of pass that you should be happy with and "No!" if it's too slow. I want to hear lots of yeses. Go!"

These four different versions of the second stoppage represent four different responses to their play:

- In option 1, players were generally successful and the coach decided to sustain their focus on the point to push for more mastery—after all, getting something right once or twice is not the end point of the journey but only the beginning!

- In option 2, players were generally successful and, with the load on working memory required to strike sharper passes reducing, the coach decided to link what they were now doing successfully to a related skill.

- In option 3, with just a single point of execution to observe for, the coach was able to observe a common technical error and has chosen to fix it.

- In option 4, again with the benefit of a single thing to look for, the coach was able to notice the inconsistency of execution, rather than a single most common error—and so was able to adapt her use of feedback to let her generate more awareness in players of their own success during subsequent live play.

I've taken the time to describe four different possible responses the coach might use because one of the primary benefits of focused feedback is that it allows the coach to observe and respond to players' needs accurately. The job of the coach is not merely to shout true things about the game but to match the true thing to the proper time and place in her players' struggle to learn.[2] *Do this now in this way and it will change what is happening to you.* Doing that requires being able to observe accurately and few coaches can accurately observe for five things at once.

Focused feedback is not without limitations, especially for expert athletes, who in many cases benefit more from the implicit feedback provided by a constraints-based problem-solving environment—something I'll discuss later—but I want to make a brief digression into some of the research that explains how and why a coaching environment characterized by focused feedback builds attentiveness, efficacy, and self-awareness—and just maybe makes players happier.

2. I call the idea of observing carefully and adapting your teaching to the results "checking for understanding," and it's the topic of the next chapter.

In any learning environment, some people develop faster and some people develop slower. One major factor in the rates at which people learn is their ability to sustain concentration and focus. To some degree, the ability to focus is something each learner brings with them—some arrive more attentive than others—but it is also something coaches and teachers can influence. We can socialize athletes to sustain focus on what they're learning and strive to make this a habit. In his book *Deep Work*, Cal Newport studies the conditions necessary to produce world-class work. He uses the example of writing computer code. If you can write it well, you're lucky, because code of high quality has never been more highly valued, but global competition is intense. Code moves freely and instantaneously around the globe; any line of it written anywhere immediately competes with yours. The competition is always coming. So, Newport writes, "you must be able to do it quickly, again and again," with "it" being your ability to master new and difficult things. Honestly it sounds a lot like the life of an athlete—a highly competitive race to learn to do what's challenging better and faster. The key to winning this race, Newport writes, is the ability to sustain states of unbroken attention and deep concentration. Those who can focus best for longest separate themselves from the crowd.

However, Newport also observes that it has never been harder to build these focused mindsets because our daily lives (which include our work and learning environments) socialize distraction, lack of concentration, and states of constant half-attention. They erode rather than build the sort of locked-in mental focus that ultimately drives so much success.

A useful term in understanding why is "attention residue."[3] When you switch from one task to another, your mind remains partially focused on the previous task. You pause during a project to check your email, and when you've returned to the project, your mind is still partially on your email even if you don't realize it. You're now less likely to do your best work. This is especially true, Newport points out, when learning new and difficult things, when concentration is most needed, but researchers have found that most working environments encourage people to operate in constant states of low-level distraction. There's no reason to think the training ground for athletes is any different. They too are at risk of letting states of semi-distracted partial attention become the norm.

One of the benefits of giving feedback on one thing at a time is that it builds habits of concentration and follow-through in training, especially if the coach sustains focus on an idea. An athlete hears an idea. There are no other ideas to distract her so she develops a clear conception of it. She applies it right away and gets further feedback on how she is progressing. *This was good; try that instead.* She tries again. *Good, now add this.* She tries a third time, her mind still focused on the task. Over time, she learns to stay with an idea rather than constantly shifting to some other thing that has popped into her head, (often because her coach put it there). When players jump from one thing to another as they seek to learn, it is often the coach who is the chief distractor. He has been talking about spacing but suddenly notices something he doesn't like about the angle of runs and stops to talk about it. Then Avery gives the ball away and he pauses impulsively to talk about not giving the ball away. Distracted coach equals distracted player. Focused coach equals focused player. And pursued consistently, a focused mindset becomes habit. When we socialize sustained attention to an idea, athletes' minds are learning to do what will be required of them at the next level—even before they get there. They will learn to focus even in situations where they will have to learn from trial and error or experimentation and no feedback is provided.

3. The phrase was coined by Sophie Leroy at the University of Minnesota based on her research into workplace productivity.

One other way focused feedback helps athletes learn is by causing them to live inside what cognitive psychologist Shawn Achor, in his book *The Happiness Advantage*, calls "The Zorro Circle." The idea is that if we "concentrate our efforts on small manageable goals, we regain the feeling of control so crucial to performance." Focusing on mastering a single defined concept helps people to see progress and build a sense of their own efficacy. "By first limiting the scope of our efforts then watching those efforts have the intended effect" we gain knowledge and confidence, Achor writes. Getting feedback and applying it in a way that improves your performance is motivating and empowering. It makes you believe in the process of getting better. "Internal locus of control" is the term psychologists use to refer to people who believe they have control over what happens to them. The opposite is having an "external locus of control" which describes people who believe that the events that happen to them are not the result of their own actions and decisions. It's not their fault, in other words. Almost every coach has worked with players of both types and won't be surprised to find that having an internal locus of control drives learning and correlates to long-run success.

The name "The Zorro Circle" refers to the results of focusing on precise manageable goals which you can see yourself accomplish. Feeling accomplishment (seeing your own progress) and engagement (losing yourself in something) are critical components of happiness—as powerful as sources of happiness as is pleasure, if less often acknowledged. There's a cycle here. Players are happy when they see themselves succeed. Happy athletes work harder and are more motivated. Over time this influences their mindset. It becomes self-belief.

Some coaches might wonder: "What about all the things I don't tell players when I am paring down my feedback to just one point at a time?" This concern is a bit of an illusion. Think of all the things a typical coach says in feedback that athletes fail to use because they can't focus on them. Giving one point of feedback at a time will likely get your athletes to mastery faster than repeating the same five points over and over. A success rate of one out of one moves you forward faster than zero out of five. And when athletes are focused on a topic, you can add live feedback more productively while they play. It's counterintuitive, but slowing down the flow of feedback can actually speed up the rate at which players learn.

Fast Feedback

At a recent meeting of coaches, I shared a video of John Burmeister teaching cello to a student named Anna. In the video, John gives Anna short bursts of precise feedback which she immediately applies, over and over. Within three or four seconds of hearing his guidance, she's working on it. You can watch the video here . This transcript will help you to see what's so exceptional about it. It begins with Anna playing a phrase of music.

Watch "John Burmeister teaching cello" at www.coachguidetoteaching.com

> **John:** Good. Now let's add the trill so it's: [demonstrates]. It's basically a turn here as well: [demonstrates ×2]. Can you echo that? My turn: [demonstrates ×3]. Try it.
>
> [Anna plays]
>
> **John:** Beautiful. Do it again.

[Anna plays]

John: Three more times, just like that.

[Anna plays ×2 and mumbles]

John: What'd you say?

Anna: Sounds bad!

John: Not to my ears. Do it again. One more time.

[Anna plays]

John: Good. Now let's put it into the speed of the actual, so it's: [demonstrates]. Don't worry about the 8th notes yet, just: [demonstrates] [sings notes]

[Anna plays]

John: Can you get two of the movements here? [demonstrates] [sings notes]

[Anna plays]

John: That's closer. Keep working.

[Anna plays]

John: That's it. Do it again.

[Anna plays]

Anna: It's slow.

John: A little bit. So just change it.

Anna: I can't.

John: Yes, you can.

[Anna plays]

John: That's it. That was beautiful. What nice ornaments! The whole phrase by yourself: vibrato, trill.

[Anna plays]

John: Beautiful. Onward. 1, 2, 7, go...

The clip highlights that *one of the most important factors in the effectiveness of the feedback is how quickly the recipient gets the chance to use it*. The speed of feedback matters, as anyone who has listened to long-winded and redundant feedback can attest. John's goal is to get Anna to use his guidance while it's fresh in her mind, as often as she can, so he avoids extraneous words and tries to say things once. The echo of his demonstration is still in her ears as she tries to replicate it. In this short clip, Anna plays the trill *11 times*. This quick back-and-forth makes the session feel fast and dynamic. Delivering feedback that shows self-discipline through crisp and efficient word choice—what I call *economy of language*— is critical to success. There's a constant sense of action and application as a result. It's surprisingly easy for feedback that takes a long time to deliver to begin to fade in a recipient's mind. They can easily lose it before they use it. But Anna is making a habit of using feedback as soon as she hears it. Think about that for a moment. It's easy to overlook how much of our feedback gets ignored. We say something and athletes nod. Maybe they even say, "Yeah, thanks. That was helpful." Occasionally, they may even mean it. In most cases, they intend to use the feedback but fail to follow through on it fully when they begin to play because it's just not prominent enough in their mind.

Imagine you're giving feedback to another coach—perhaps on this very topic. He's asked you to come watch his session and you notice that his stoppages go on and on. He says something then says it again. Sometimes, when he's really feeling it, he makes his point a third time. There's not enough time spent playing and his players tune out much of what he says. You say, "Sometimes when you give them feedback, you speak for longer than is necessary or make your point more than once. See if you can say it once and then let them try it right away. In fact, maybe try using a stopwatch and set a goal of speaking for no more than 30 seconds."

That's great feedback but your colleague says, "Yeah I know. But they just don't listen. If I say it once, they don't use it. I find I have to say it a second time to get them to really lock in on what I'm saying."

He's already begun explaining away your advice, telling you why it won't work or at least giving you a reason for why he does what he does. The more this happens, the less likely it is that he's going to use the guidance to change. *Hear the solution and explain it away* is a common dynamic in the annals of feedback. Yes, we want recipients to reflect on the feedback that we give them, but their reflection will be most useful *after they've tried to use the feedback*. The ideal sequence for recipients is *receive-try-reflect* rather than *receive-reflect-try*.

But let's also assume that it's possible that your colleague is right and you're wrong. Generally it's important for givers of feedback to presume their observations could be wrong—*will* at some point be wrong. Humility is necessary for teaching as much as learning. So how do you get beyond his skepticism short of saying No, *I'm right on this?*

One idea might be to ask him to use the feedback first and then decide. "Yeah, you might be right," you'd say. "But try it a few times and see what you think. I'll observe and can give you my two cents' worth." In fact, the ideal situation is that you are giving him this feedback at a break in his session so he can go use it right away. In that case, you'd say "For the next three stoppages, try to make your point exactly once and in 30 seconds or less. I'll time you and raise my hand slightly at 30 seconds. Then let's both talk about whether we think players are more attentive."

What you have done is delay the discussion about whether it works until after the experiment of trying it. We've all met the person who has a reason why every piece of good counsel won't work. Building a culture that says "Try it first. Right away. Then we'll see" helps make action a habit and avoids smart rationalizations becoming a handy tool for resisting feedback.

One perverse thing about feedback: the value recipients get out of it often decreases with each additional second we spend giving it. The more we say, the more the focus on each word or idea is diluted and the more the opportunity to try it right away is delayed. An economist might describe this as "diminishing marginal returns" to more time spent talking. That said, it is not always as simple as just say less: you can't always be super-fast with complex topics. What matters is the ratio of time spent to value derived, and the longer the time you invest in discussing something, the more important the follow-up actions to reinforce it afterwards become, but all things being equal—and they aren't always—faster feedback is usually better.

You can see a good clear example of feedback that's both fast and focused in a clip of James Beeston at a recent session with Black Watch Premier in Albany, NY. His session topic is on using up-back-through against a low block. In this relatively early round of feedback, James simply wants his players to make a habit of varying the weights of their passes: the first pass, into the target, must be sharp. The second layoff pass is softer to allow the player to read the options and strike the third pass, a through ball which again must be sharp. In the first round, the players executed the three passes, but the variation in pace was not decisive enough, and their ability to do this will be critical to success later on when they will be practicing reading defenders' movements and changing passing patterns accordingly.

As the clip begins, James pauses the team. His feedback is simple:

> ...And freeze! For the next minute, I want you to focus on the weight of the pass. The first ball is nicely punched through, the set is softer, and then the through ball is a little bit more punched through as well. OK? Focus on the tempo of this passing! Play!

You'll notice that James gives players one thing to work on: varying the tempo between the passes. He says it once and only once, choosing his words carefully. There's no extra verbiage and he lets them try it right away. In fact, it's a remarkable 18 seconds from "freeze!" to "play!" so a culture of single-minded focus pervades, but James emphasizes it with his last reminder to the boys. James reminds his players of where their minds should be with his last statement before he releases them back to play: "Focus on the tempo of this passing," he says. But of course a single statement like that, while useful, won't keep the boys focused. If he wants them to be focused, *he* must stay focused, and so his live feedback reinforces the one point he's made during the stoppage in consistent language. Over and again, he offers brief cues to remind players of the point he made. "Touch set and through!" he says. Or he reminds them that the focus is tempo: "Focus on this passing." It's an exercise in maintaining attention.

(As an interesting side note, you can see James set his watch at about six seconds in. He's timing himself to help understand and improve the pace of his feedback.)

Finally, you'll also notice that he uses consistent verbal commands. It's part of the routine of training with James. He says "freeze!" and "play!", and the response is instant and universal. Not only is no time wasted but no focus is lost in transitions where minds wander or players chat about distractions. Having strong routinized procedures like this is a topic I will discuss further in chapter 5 on culture, but it's critical to keeping the feedback environment focused and this acts as a sort of flywheel that sustains momentum. Players are focused so stoppages are lightning quick, which preserves energy and focus while they play, which carries over into the next stoppage, which is fast enough to transfer the energy back to playing.

Watch "James Beeston fast and focused feedback" at www.coachguidetoteaching.com

That sounds simple, but simple things are often hard to do. Recently I showed the video of John Burmeister's cello lesson and James Beeston's training session to coaches. A club director raised his hand. "I agree with you," he said. "But how do I get my coaches to stop talking so much? It's the biggest problem we have. I watch them and they're talking and talking and the kids aren't listening anymore and they're still talking."

One effective way to improve "economy of language"—the skill of saying something in the fewest possible words—is to plan better. We say things in too many words when we're not clear on what we want to say. Trying to think of what to tell players about their execution in the moment, as we are coaching, is a recipe for imprecise language, and because we were thinking it up while we were saying it (and therefore distracted), we are more likely to repeat it two or three times, hoping to refine it or make sure it sinks in. And we're more likely to say too many things when we're not sure of what the most important thing to say is. Solution: for each activity in a training session, write down in advance the most important things you want to see players execute. Draft some talking points that you can use to cover the key ideas you want to address during training so your language is halfway there already. James, working on the rhythm of up-back-through, might jot down something like: "Punch, set, punch" or "Take a little off the set" or "The set touch should lure them in; the through touch should punish them." This would help him use precise language in the moment and by helping him remember his key points, also help him to be patient. Often we keep talking because we remember something important at a certain moment and don't want to lose it. Taking notes as you observe—"Remember to stress 'eyes up'"—can also help overcome the worry that you'll forget and therefore ensure more self-discipline in what you say when.

A second useful tool to improve speed and focus is a smartphone equipped with a stopwatch and a voice recording app. Time your feedback as you see James doing (or ask a colleague to). Set a goal and try to get faster. Or record yourself and listen back. I guarantee it will be awkward—there will be lots of extraneous language. I've often found it helpful to transcribe what I've said in a given round of feedback and then go through and cross out every unnecessary thing I said. Do this two or three times a week for a few weeks and you will be practicing giving clear, efficient direct feedback, and your economy of language will get better.

One of my favorite words in coaching is "pause." It's especially useful to initiate a stoppage. As in: "Pause. Let's go back to what happened when Kieren had the ball." I prefer it to the word "stop," because "pause" implies that the delay is temporary and athletes will be playing again soon. It keeps their focus because the stoppage is framed in their minds as something likely to be quick. Using the phrase reminds us that players want to play—if we say "pause," we should be as quick as we can. But no matter what word you use to initiate and end your stoppages, be consistent! Using the same phrase to start and stop every time will help make players' response automatic and consistent so you can make your point right away. In fact, I think it's helpful to explain this to athletes. "When I say 'freeze,' stop as quickly as you can so we can talk briefly, right away and then get back to playing as fast as we can!" Consistent language at the end of a stoppage is just as important. Feedback gets slowed by repetition. A coach makes a point. Then he repeats it. Sometimes he makes it again. Now everyone is both dying to play and beginning to tune out. One reason for this unnecessary repetition is that there's no punctuation mark to cap the feedback crisply and show it's done. It's a rhythm problem. Making a habit of using "Go!" or "Play!" like a punctuation mark makes you better at dropping it in decisively when you are done and helps you avoid unnecessarily repeating yourself.

Solution oriented

The goal of giving feedback is to help athletes get better. Sometimes this means providing a pinch of motivation or inspiration. Sometimes it means catching an athlete getting it right and helping them understand how and why to persist in the action. But most often it means helping them to see how they can do something differently to improve the outcome. Maybe that sounds obvious, but it doesn't take much observation to know that doing that well is a constant challenge.

Consider Carlos. He's a defender and he's struggling. He's slow to react when defending the dribble. He gets off balance and lunges in a last-ditch effort to try to save the day, but this only makes things worse. As his coach, likely the first thing you notice is the glaring mistake, so the first impulse may be to narrate it. "Carlos! Don't dive in!" The language here matters because in describing what you see, you've described what *not to do*, rather than what *to do*, and it would help Carlos a lot more to tell him what actions to take instead or what to observe to make a better decision. "Keep your position, Carlos," would be slightly better—it would remind him to stay between the attacker and the goal. Saying, "Tackle only if you must," might give him a rule of thumb to use. But ideally, a good coach would go further. He would help Carlos recognize that he is standing up straight and, in the moment when the attacker throws a move, has to make two motions: first he has to crouch to load his muscles; then he has to react. If he can *start* crouched, he'll be faster in reacting. He's got to bend his knees and get his butt down. He's got to position himself slightly off center of the attacker, angle his body outside and position the inside foot slightly forward to incentivize the attacker to play wide and to reduce uncertainty. Or perhaps he needs to understand more about where to look to read his opponent's actions as reliably as possible. Maybe he needs to do several of these things, but he surely can't work on all of them at once. So which things first? Being a coach is a bit like being a doctor, looking for causes instead of symptoms. A good doctor doesn't tell patients: "Stop coughing!" or "You gotta get your blood pressure down!" So if you hear yourself telling players to eliminate their symptoms—"Don't dive in!"—try to identify the root cause and a precise action to fix it instead.

Generally speaking, specific is usually better. That is, a *precise action* that will help the recipient solve a problem is more useful than a description of a *desired outcome*. Desired outcomes describe what would come from better execution, but that rarely helps people get better.

| DESIRED OUTCOMES | | |
DESCRIPTION OF PROBLEM	DESIRED OUTCOME	PRECISE ACTION
TOO SLOW!	WE'VE GOT TO PLAY FORWARD QUICKLY	MAKE SURE YOUR FIRST TOUCH HAS FORWARD DIRECTION WHEN WE HAVE
DON'T DIVE IN, CARLOS	KEEP YOUR MAN IN FRONT OF YOU, CARLOS!	BUTT LOWER AND CHIN HIGH, CARLOS

Descriptions of the problem and desired outcomes are often true but useless. They presume that players know how to accomplish those outcomes when often they do not. To push beyond what you want to avoid—"Nobody's supporting!"—or the outcome you want to have happen—"Get open!"—coaches must seek root causes in order to explain how to solve the problem.

This could consist of a more precise example of what to do technically—"Drag the ball back at this angle so it's not under your feet"—greater clarity on how to make a decision—"If the player with the ball is not under pressure, we have to give depth"—or guidance on what to do with your eyes—"You must check your shoulder before you receive,"

I recently observed music teacher John Burmeister doing this as he worked with musicians in a youth orchestra. The piece they were playing required the entire orchestra to play a single note in exact precision, and at first they failed to do so. A lesser teacher might have said something true but useless: "We need to be in sync!" or "We've got to stay together!" But like a doctor, he had seen the symptom and sought to treat the cause. They had learned to master their individual roles by looking at the music in front of them. Now, playing as a group, they needed to adjust their eyes to focus on the conductor. Cueing them to play the section again, John said: "As the measure ends, make sure your eyes are on me. Not the music—me." Once or twice through the measure and it ended in perfect unison. He had fixed the root cause instead of merely telling his patients to make the symptom go away.

But, how do you get good at something like that? I asked several coaches and their advice focused on the importance of constant observation. Often when we watch other coaches, we're not focused on what we're looking for. Listening specifically for their feedback and the solutions they provide can be helpful, as can filming or recording yourself. One coach told me he started taping sessions or half time talks and it had been a breakthrough. "Take a second look at what you said and examine the reactions of the players," he advised. "How could you make that information more specific the next time you run a similar session?" Another coach told me it was helpful to occasionally coach players who were younger than those he was used to coaching. You could assume less and had to explain more—and more clearly—which was good practice. Another suggested observing coaches in another sport, one you know only moderately well. Which pieces of feedback would have helped you? Which would not have? One of the challenges of being a coach—and once, presumably, a player who excelled and therefore learned easily—is that what's unclear to those who know less or learn less readily is often invisible to you. The key in the end is to discipline yourself to see past symptoms and ask yourself why the issues you see are emerging. Why, why, why.

In-game coaching and feedback

Here's a pet theory: the chances that an athlete will get useful feedback decrease as the intensity of the situation in which she's getting the feedback increases. The more competitive the environment, the greater the likelihood that the coach will describe the problem or shout statements that are *true but useless*.

"Too slow!"

"Somebody's gotta mark him!"

"We can't lose the ball there!"

"We've got to be organized!"

That's ironic: the more urgent the situation, the less useful the intervention. I discuss this further in chapter 6, but here is a good rule of thumb: during competition, only using language encoded during training to describe something you've taught before is likely to improve performance. You would want to deliver such guidance at moments when the load on working memory is least: when the ball is out of bounds; when they are away from the play; etc. That's the time for tactical adjustments and reminders. During live play, feedback is mostly a distraction, and afterwards it is even less useful.

The phrase *using language encoded during training* reminds me of a very short clip of legendary FA coach Dick Bate.

The topic is closing space defensively. What has happened before this? Bate has explained how fast to close, at what angle, and when. Then he explained body position: that you must be low to be able to react quickly to the inevitable response from the opposition. In this phase of practice, players are committing the actions to long-term memory, so they do it automatically and without using working memory— all their cognitive power can go to reading the opponent's next action. But as his players do this, Dick uses the same phrase each time: "Get out and get down!" He pretty much only uses that phrase. Why, you might ask, does that matter?

He is encoding a "cue" alongside the action: a short, memorable phrase of just a few words at most that reminds players of something the coach is sure they know. There are several benefits to attaching the phrase to the action:

1. In training, Bate can use it to remind players what to focus on before they execute. You can hear him doing this in the video. Bate calls the phrase out before players need it, not after. The reminder increases the odds that they get it right and encode the correct actions. It is much more efficient to give feedback before the action, rather than trying to use it to fix it afterwards.

2. If players struggle during a training activity, the phrase allows him to question effectively and efficiently: "When I say 'get out and get down,' what

Watch "Dick Bate encoded language" at www.coachguidetoteaching.com

are the specifics I am expecting to see? What should your feet do? Your knees? etc." All those details are grouped in his players' minds under the topic "Get out and get down." It helps him fix things faster and helps them link concepts together more clearly.

3. The phrase is short and sticky enough that Bate can use it afterwards—just possibly during a match—to cue players what to do without overloading working memory. The speed of the phrase is critical—it must be merely a mnemonic device, something that reminds athletes of what they know, not something that explains something unfamiliar. Every additional word makes its success less likely—in a game, a coach might shorten it to "out and down." If it's short enough, he can use it to activate players' memory at lower risk of distraction and greater likelihood of success.

4. You can also imagine how valuable this might be across a club. If every coach in the club used that phrase, once someone had taught it, they could all activate players' knowledge for years to come with that same phrase.

I showed this video of Bate to Jim Driggs, formerly head men's basketball coach at Allegheny College, to whom it instantly made sense:

> The best coaches that I've been around create a shared language that's instrumental in their teaching. The phrases stick with players and staff. We spend hours, sometimes, thinking about our words. If you haven't planned the words/language, then what you actually do in a session will be diminished.

Everything Jim says is true. It's also one of the keys to more productive in-game coaching. Only phrases that your players already know cold are likely to help them in the game.

Watch "Pete Carroll Moneyball moment" at www.coachguidetoteaching.com

A shift to providing more solution-oriented feedback may sound to some readers like a youth sports kind of thing. The sort of thing you do until players grow up, then the "real talk" starts. That's why the video of Super Bowl-winning Seattle Seahawks coach Pete Carroll ▶ I mentioned in the introduction is so instructive: it reveals that solution-oriented feedback is a critical part of his staff's philosophy because it makes them more successful at the elite level. Here are Carroll's exact words: "We're really disciplined as coaches to always talk about what we want to see, the desired outcome, not about what went wrong or what the mistake was. We have to be disciplined and always use our language to talk about the next thing you can do right. It's always about what we want to happen, not about the other stuff."

Describing solutions is part of the team's coaching philosophy. It often has the effect of making players feel nurtured and supported, but for the Seahawks it's about maximizing human performance—even when winning is what matters most.

Positively framed

Consider two players: Alberto and Bernardo. They experience nearly identical interactions at training. Their respective coaches blow the whistle during a small-sided game and point out something they must do better. They are asked to execute again, with hips open or eyes up; or with the ball played wide instead of centrally, driven instead of chipped.

Alberto resents being criticized in front of the team. The coach's words feel like an accusation, a judgment, they imply that he has failed at something. As play resumes, part of him is thinking: "Why didn't Coach say something about the previous play when I was perfect? He is looking to catch me out."

Bernardo, on the other hand, appreciates the opportunity to improve. He perceives himself to have received valuable knowledge about how to accomplish his goals from someone who is vested in his success. The feedback suggests the coach's faith in him, even though the moment is about improving on a mistake. Play resumes and Bernardo snaps open his hips and drives the ball to the winger to start the counter. "Ah," he thinks, "that was better," and he is happy.

Now multiply this by a thousand similar interactions—each player is told: *It must be the other foot, We must press tighter here, or You must be in the passing channel sooner,* but each time Alberto feels resentful, while Bernardo relishes the chance to learn. Alberto thinks, *Why don't you tell Bernardo to get into the passing channel instead of me?* and Bernardo thinks *Thank you for helping me find the passing channel.* Imagine a team of Albertos and a team of Bernardos: one where players see their teammates listen grudgingly and mutter excuses, the other where they see them lean in to hear better and learn without defensiveness. Players new to the team observe these reactions and do as their teammates do. A culture emerges. The content of the feedback the two teams get over the course of a season could be exactly the same and the players might start equal in quality, but is there any doubt that FC Bernardo will flourish and Alberto Athletic stagnate? Soon enough, people who don't know better will talk about how FC Bernardo just gets better players to work with. Maybe they'll attribute it to some sociological characteristic: kids from that part of town are better athletes; more resilient, hungrier.

The success of the feedback you give is only partly a reflection of its technical content. It is also a factor of the attitude and mentality with which players receive it. But these qualities are not merely a function of individual personalities, the cultures and families they come from, and larger trends in society. Team and club culture can socialize players to respond productively to feedback to a much greater degree than most people realize, but this tendency must be built up through a thousand small, often unremarkable interactions. A speech in which you tell players that they must seize opportunities to get better and embrace a growth mindset may have some use, but far less, probably, than the influence of a dozen interactions in which players feel the rush of accomplishment or your faith in them during struggle. The work of building positive mindsets about learning is done through attentiveness to language in the moments of feedback when we are often focused on some other task. I call this topic "positive framing."

The phrase "positive framing" often causes coaches to assume it is about praising players more. It isn't, though coaches get enough guidance about praise that it's worth examining—and exposing the flaws therein. "Rules" for praise, and for building players' receptivity to feedback through praise, are among the most common advice that coaches—and teachers—get. People will tell you to use a *praise sandwich*: tell players a good thing, then offer criticism, then tell them something else good. People will tell you to praise five times as often as you criticize. Despite good intentions, this sort of advice is poor.

One flaw in it is the assumption that praise is the same as positivity. *Positivity in feedback is not the delivery of more good news, but the delivery of the information players need in a manner that motivates and inspires them and communicates our belief in their capacity.* And praising players more will not accomplish that; ironically, it can do the opposite. I'll take a moment here to briefly explain why.

Praise is powerful and valuable but it is also a bit like a currency within your team. Too much of it causes inflation. If you describe every play as "awesome," soon enough the word and your praise more generally become meaningless. When everything is awesome, nothing is awesome. And there's a lot to learn if you want to be a great athlete, so if you need to praise someone five times just so you can tell them how to get better, you're going to be in trouble pretty quickly.

A praise sandwich is no better. Believing you must disguise criticism with praise assumes that players do not want to know what they can do better, that it is something a coach has to trick players into hearing. It assumes players are weak, in other words. Treating players like they are weak makes them weak and besides, what most players want most is to understand the truth about how to get better. The key is not in praising more but in describing struggle differently.

Actions, Not People

When Bernardo's coach told him how to do something better, he heard an expression of faith in him as a player. That's the soul of good feedback. We want to say, "I believe in you" and "that can be better" at the same time. Happily, the two are not so hard to marry together. The first step is to frame critical comments as a judgment on an action, not a person.

Think for a moment about the phrase "You don't"—as in:

> "**You don't** work hard to regain possession when you lose the ball."

Compare it to the same statement but with *didn't* substituted for *don't*:

> "**You didn't** work hard to regain possession when you lost the ball."

The word *"don't"* judges the person. *This thing that you did is something you always do.* It globalizes a mistake and implies it is an enduring flaw. Maybe even hints at deliberateness.

The word *"didn't"* judges an action, a one-time event. It leaves open the possibility that the player usually does it correctly but failed to in this instance. It's one moment; we can fix it quickly.

But as some readers may have already noticed, even *"didn't"* focuses on the problem rather than the solution. Now compare: "You **didn't** work hard to regain possession when you lost the ball" to "You **must always** work hard to regain possession when you've lost the ball," "You must work your hardest to regain possession when you've lost the ball," or, "**We must work hard to regain possession when we've lost the ball**," or "We must work hard to regain possession **even when it's difficult**."

I've shared multiple versions of this phrase to emphasize the ways different statements subtly shape culture in different ways—group responsibility and ethos in the frequent use of "we," for example, or the importance of persistence and consistency in the use of the word "always."

Learners want to know how to get better. When we fail to show them how to do that, we fail them. The point is that if we are attentive to subtle changes in language, we can hold players accountable for the quality of their play, describe the things they must add to their skill set and set a high standard of excellence. We can help them feel that we are building them up, not tearing them down. Habits of language are the long-term tools of culture building.

Positive framing is the art of being attentive to the subtexts of language and tone. Making small adjustments—turning *you don't* into *you didn't*—can shift the feelings our feedback creates in the moment and over the long run can remind players that *the reason we are giving them critical feedback is that we want them to succeed*—their goals are also ours. When you are able to offer critical feedback—*Here is what you did wrong; here is what you must do better*—in a way that feels respectful, motivating and inspiring, players learn more and relationships are reinforced. Once this begins to happen, there is a secondary effect: praise is set free. Its primary role is no longer to "balance" critical feedback and make players feel better. You can begin to use it for its most valuable application: helping players know what to replicate. This is a topic I will return to later.

We've talked already about focusing criticism on narrowly specific actions and not globalizing. Here are a few more themes that will prove useful in framing criticism positively:

Use challenge and talk aspirations

Athletes are by their nature competitive; they want to prove they can do things. They yearn to be great and to accomplish things. Turning a point of criticism into a challenge or tapping into their aspirations to succeed are easy ways to harness that spirit productively.

A simple way to **add challenge** in your feedback might be to add the phrase, "See if you can." As in "Now, see if you can do it in one touch," instead of "That must be done in one touch." Or you might go with a question: "Can you do it in one touch?"

To **talk aspirations**, you might turn it into "A player of your quality should play that with one touch." Or "You're good enough now to play that with one touch" or even "At the level you're at now, you can start trying to play with one touch." Or you could make the aspiration relevant to team goals: "We're going to become the kind of team that plays comfortably with one touch."

As you can see, there are plenty of variations, and while aspirations sound very different with younger versus older players, it's a concept that applies to all age groups.

U10: Now let's see if we can be like Messi and play that ball with one touch.

Professional athletes: This weekend, they will press us hard and we'll have to play quicker. Let's try that again and see if we can play at a faster tempo with every touch.

The theme in each of these cases is that the coach's language draws on players' desire to win and succeed and connect those larger goals to the change they're being asked to make.

I am not arguing that every phrase needs to be done this way. It's great if you can say, "See if you can do it in one touch" sometimes instead of "Do that in one touch." Certainly "You must do that in one touch" is better than "You never play one-touch" or "Why are you afraid of playing one-touch?" But such phrases can be overused, and what counts as overuse depends upon the athletes you're talking to. Is there a time to be blunt, no coddling? Yes, but the two ideas do not operate in opposition. They work in synergy. You build a culture of *I am here to support you* and the moments when you are blunt are more effective thanks to the larger relationship you've built.

Here are a few more examples. I've added some discussion to help point out the subtext of some of the phrases so you can adapt or apply them to your own style and setting.

"Now, Allie, can you do it quicker?"

- "Now" subtly credits Allie with things she's already doing right. Because of that, we are ready for more.

- "Can you?" turns the technical feedback into a challenge, a question she answers with her play.

- The –er ending on "quicker" implies that Allie was at least a little bit quick the first time around. Compare "Can you do it quicker?" to "Can you do it quickly?": the latter implies lack of quickness; the former simply focuses on being ever better.

"Clean that touch up, John."

- I learned the phrase "Clean that up" from watching Kelvin Jones of Columbus Crew's youth academy and I find it powerful. It reminds John that he's on the way to success, that he has the concept right and now needs to hone the details.

"Now, Maddy. Can you take it up a level and cut in on your left and shoot?"

- "Can you take it up a level?" gives Maddy credit for her work and rewards her with the goal of reaching a higher level. It implies accomplishment.

- "Cut in on your left foot and shoot" is important too—don't forget to be solution oriented. Players are counting on us to help them see precise actions to solve challenges.

"Now, Maddy. I want you to be able to do what Christen Press does and cut in and shoot with your weaker foot."

- The language here connects Maddy to a player that she wants to be like and implies that the task she's being asked to do is something a world-class player would think about.

"That's fine, Sean. But when you get to the first team, you'll have to do that quicker, so let's start doing that now."

- "That's fine" implies this is not about being wrong so much as being better.

- "When you get to the first team": this is a skill for first-team players. I assume you are good enough to get there some day.

"That's fine, Sean. But if you are going to play on the first team, you'll have to do that quicker, so let's start doing that now."

- Puts a bit more accountability on Sean. It's more of a challenge to make the first team vs a statement of faith he will make it, but states that this is the kind of skill that will make a difference.

"That's fine, boys. But if some of you are going to play on the first team someday, you'll have to do that quicker, so let's start doing that now."

- Reuses elements of "fine" and "if you're going to make the first team" but globalizes the statements to refer to the whole team.

"Boys, some of you are going to play on the first team some day and will have to do that quicker. Show me that now."

- Reuses expression of faith—some of you will make the first team. Who doesn't want to be one of those players? Executing the skill is now the first step in getting there.
- "Show me that now" adds in the challenge to do it right away.

"You've done well to tackle, Devin. The next level is to also connect to a teammate afterwards to keep the ball."

- This feedback combines acknowledgement for a play done well with the idea that there is something Devin can do to use that skill to be more successful.

Socializing your players to relish challenge and providing aspiration has the added benefit of encouraging them to not be afraid of making mistakes.

We're in it together

I mentioned watching Kelvin Jones at work. To me, he's a master of positive framing, and many of the phrases above are stolen or adapted from his coaching, so I want to share a video of his coaching and some of his own thoughts on his coaching language. This video **was shot several years ago, just after I first saw him coach for the first time, and he agreed to be taped working with a group of boys in Virginia. Now, years later, he's the Academy Director at Columbus Crew, working with elite players. But I played the old video for Kelvin and asked him what he noticed about his language and approach with players.**

The phrase "can we," for me, reflecting back on it, reinforces the idea that you're not in this by yourself. We're in it together. I'm here with you so you should feel comfortable taking risks. Don't be afraid. And you're not the only one who's having issues with some of these things. That's important.

Tone and how you phrase things is also important. They're there to have fun but they're also there to learn how to compete, and "can we," I hope, reminds them that they are competing not just with each other but also within themselves. Can you do this faster? It reminds them: test your limits; see what faster is for you.

KELVIN JONES

Watch "Kelvin Jones positive framing" at www.coachguidetoteaching.com

Going back to the ratio of positive to negative feedback, I see myself more times than not giving corrective feedback. I mean if the pass wasn't good, the pass wasn't good. They need to recognize that. But also, saying "You can do this better; I know you can do this better," makes it not blaming or negative.

When I use the phrase "fix it," I want it to come across as a reminder: *It's under your control. It's a fixable thing.*

Economy of language helps. You can start to lose players the more you talk, so being clear about what you want in the exact language that you want makes things more seamless.

At a break, I might go into more detail; but coaching (live), I want to be really clear on what I want from them and have them be thinking about how to fix it in the moment. Just fix the first touch or fix the pass. I want them focused on what they control and believing they can do it.

I see some emotional constancy too. I'm not saying it doesn't sometimes sound different with my 19s. There are two sides of it. This has been part of my reflection process in thinking about myself on the sidelines, getting mad at them and yelling at them because they've messed up. Mostly that isn't going to help them. It's going to make them more stressed and their quality of play may even continue to drop. It's about finding the right moments when you need to be hard or stern. Those moments need to be far apart and not very common. There are things you can do or say that bring out the level of intensity and engagement that you want without yelling.

We have a brand-new group of 14s, for example, who are truly just learning how to train. We were playing a rondo and they were taking it with the wrong part of their foot, passing it with their toe, trying blind backheels. The quality just wasn't good. And so I went in and I started asking them questions: *What part of the foot do we need to use? Why? What surface should we use for the pass? Why?* They knew the answers. So then I said: "So, make this better. It's not good enough." But I wasn't yelling. I'm trying not to be harsh. I want them to understand and think not that their coach is mad but that *this isn't good enough. For me. As a player. Given my goals.*

When I first got into coaching when I was done playing, I was often an assistant with the older age kids, and in those roles you get to know the players a little bit more, and you often understand their reaction to the head coach more than the head coach does. It made me realize: you always have to be able to put yourself in the player's shoes, to know who they are and where they are in their journey.

Assume the best

Earlier I discussed how important it is to distinguish the person from the action when giving feedback. It's fine to tell Johan he must close down a shot more quickly; it's less productive to tell Johan he is lazy if he fails to do so. Coaches should describe solutions, not imply character flaws. As teachers we want to communicate as consistently as possible that our expectations are high and we require excellence and effort everyday but also that we believe deeply in the individuals we coach: we see their best side; our faith in them does not waver when they struggle. This not only builds relationships but also encourages players to take the sorts of risks that learning requires. *If you try it and it goes poorly a few times, I will not judge you or give up on you. I will ask you to try it again.* The more you expect from athletes, the more you should also remind them that you think they are capable; when they struggle, your first instinct is to assume that this is normal and they will soon succeed. Coaching requires you to deliver complex messages including ideas others may find contradictory and to express them at the same time and in a single moment. It's a difficult challenge but it remains one of the secrets to successfully establishing a culture that demands the best from athletes.

As we've already studied, talking aspirations to an athlete who has gotten something wrong is one effective way to do this: "A player of your quality must be able to drive that ball instead of lofting it. Try it again." Assuming the best is another useful way to show your faith in athletes when you are teaching them how to be better. At minimum, it involves avoiding the unnecessary attribution of negative intentions to mistakes. I hope this is obvious: telling Johan, who is slow to come out and close down a shot-taker at the edge of the box, that he is "lazy" is a big assumption to make. Certainly Johan won't soon forget it. And besides, perhaps the reason was more complex. Perhaps he wasn't sure of what to do, or whose responsibility the shot-taker was, or didn't understand just how quickly you wanted him to close. In fact, if you think about it, some of the possible reasons for Johan's failure to close could be indicative of mindsets or concerns that make someone a good player in the first place. Perhaps Johan is slow to close because he takes positioning and defensive shape seriously and always wants to be careful about abandoning the middle. Or perhaps he's worried about overcommitting and being exposed to a cut-back. Yes, he should have closed. Tell him in no uncertain terms to "get out and get down," but also recognize that his mistake might have come about from an excess of diligence, responsibility or some other trait you want your players to embody.

The game is full of wrong things done for good reasons. There are sins of diligence—players don't do something well because they are worried about being out of position. There are sins of enthusiasm—players take an idea you give them and want to use it too often or too aggressively. In a complex game, there are mistakes that come about through selflessness, coachability—trying too hard to do exactly what you asked—and responsibility passing on an opportunity to make sure you don't neglect your duty.

So imagine if the feedback Johan gets occasionally acknowledges that complexity. "I know you want to protect the middle, Johan, but at the top of the box you've got to close him down faster." Or: "I appreciate that you're always trying to keep our shape in the back, but here you've got to be absolutely decisive in closing." Assuming the best means acknowledging legitimate reasons why an athlete might have *done something* you want to correct and describing it in your feedback.

Here are a few more examples:

- I can see why you'd want to play wide there, Allie, but this is a situation to play centrally.
- I can see why you'd want to play wide there, Allie. That's often right, but here there's an opportunity to play centrally. Why is that better? [Or what tells you that?]

- I'm glad that you want to play forward, guys, but there are cues here that tell us it's not the right decision.

- Playing to D'Andre is fine—you're thinking about retaining possession—but there's an even better option I want you to consider.

- I appreciate your instinct to avoid risks in the back, but this is a case where giving space hurts us.

- OK, I'm glad you're thinking about switching the field, but let's look at where we have numbers up in this situation.

- OK, your touch let you down, but I like that you were trying to find the entry pass there.

In each case, the coach shows appreciation to individuals or groups for actions that reflect a thinking player trying to incorporate the ideas the team values. Coaches should want that and appreciating it will help ensure it continues. Each of these corrections is also a sort of investment in relationships with players. As you correct them, you remind them that when they get it wrong your first instinct is to think, *Well there must be a good reason for it* as opposed to *Here we go again* or *That kid*. You build trust in acknowledging legitimate reasons for a mistake. And defensiveness—explaining away your mistakes, even internally to yourself—uses working memory. Reducing it can help players listen more attentively.

One other benefit you might notice is that these examples often tell players what factors they *should* have been considering, whether all of them were or not. You tell Johan you are glad he's always thinking about protecting the center of the field when defending even though he must get out decisively now, and you offer a two-sided reminder to the rest of the team. As much as you'd like Johan to be a bit more aggressive, it would also be nice if more players thought about their responsibilities as much as he does! Now you have reminded them: always balance defensive priorities like shape with aggression. Johan needed more aggression here, but shape is still important. To defend is to constantly weigh those factors.

One other benefit of assuming the best is that it causes *you* to think about the reasons why players do what they do differently. Presuming well-intentioned errors can help you see more of the positive thinking that already exists. It's a bit of a shortcut to assume that "Duh" is the reason for most mistakes. It isn't, of course, especially if you're teaching players to think. Putting ourselves in their shoes and disciplining ourselves to reflect on the factors players consider and to embrace the difficulty of their decisions makes us better coaches.

I am not arguing that all or even most corrections should involve a recognition of some good reason why it might have happened. As with any other tool, this is an approach that could easily be overused, waste time and imply that players could not discuss errors without a sprinkling of sugar on them. It could become the new praise sandwich. Of course it's also possible that Johan was a bit lazy and simply needs to work harder. I'll come to that in a moment.

How much you use it depends on your style, your players, the context. But assuming the best is powerful because it lets you show your faith in the people you teach and remind them that your first assumption is that they will do the right thing. Because the moments when athletes struggle are the moments when they are most likely to fear that people will give up on them, they are also the most powerful for reminding them of our faith in them.

In the moments when others might communicate doubt, doing the opposite builds the kind of trust that is at the core of a long-term learning relationship.

But what if, in the end, Johan is apt to cut corners and hasn't closed the man because he's just not a very hard worker? You could argue that relationships with players are like a bank account. Making regular small deposits over a sustained period of time is the key to prosperity. And if a withdrawal—a moment of honest and potentially hard-to-hear straight talk—proves necessary, the higher the initial balance, the greater the honesty it can sustain. It allows you to pull Johan aside because you think he actually is slacking in his effort over a sustained period and his success is at risk. It lets you say, "I think you're not giving me your best. I think you can play harder," and have him hear that message with openness. That sort of feedback will be successful in helping Johan, in other words, roughly proportional to the degree that your other interactions have proven that you believe in him and want him to succeed.

Plausible anonymity

A final tool that can allow you to give critical feedback in a way that creates a positive climate, builds trust and encourages self-reflection is something I call plausible anonymity. It's useful in situations when you are giving feedback to a group. You can make it clear that you observed players executing incorrectly while not naming names. This is something I noticed watching FC Dallas coach Chris Hayden. In his session he would say things like "I see some of us doing a great job of really accelerating to try to get to a spot [demonstrates ideal movement], and others of us are fairly casual in trying to get to a spot [demonstrates sub-par movement]." This feedback asks everyone to self-assess and to compare themselves to the model. In fact, that's its primary benefit. Everyone on the team is now set to try to upgrade their movements slightly to try to make sure they are in the first group—those whose movements were sufficient and those whose were not. If they were not doing their best work, it allows them to correct it privately and it encourages them to internalize a process of asking themselves, Was that my best?, without necessarily being told, You must strive to do better.

Interestingly, there are degrees of anonymity that might be used. Perhaps Ruben needs to sharpen his movements. A bit of subtle eye contact at the moment you say "some of us" can remind him that he may be especially in need of some self-assessment. But it also reminds him that you are deliberately not naming him publicly. Ideally you will build a culture where players are comfortable having their mistakes discussed in front of the team. But while you are getting there or with players who struggle to get comfortable with that approach, using plausible anonymity can be useful. Here are a couple more examples:

- "I saw a range of quality there with our defensive stance, from this [demonstrates well], which is how Mackenzie looked, to this [demonstrates poorly] which might be how some other players looked. Make sure you look like the first example. Go."

"Pause: some of us are snapping open to create space and others of us are moving into the space at a slower speed without change of pace. Attentiveness to this kind of detail is one of the ways you show me that you want minutes on Saturday. I'm not going to call anyone out. I just want you to know what I am looking at so you can make sure to check yourself and hold yourself to the highest standard."

Watch "Chris Hayden
positive framing" at
www.coachguidetoteaching.com

All together now: positive framing in Chris Hayden's training session

One of my favorite videos of great teaching on the soccer field is one of Chris Hayden of FC Dallas, which my colleagues at US Soccer shared with me in 2013. The number of elements of positive framing he uses is remarkable.

"A little sharper with your movement, David."

"David, see if you can sharpen up your movement. Quicker!"

- Chris gives constructive feedback to David twice here, so I am assuming the player's initial reaction was not sufficient. The first time, Chris assumes the best—"a little sharper"—validating his starting point and making it seem like progress is something David can achieve.

- The second time, "See if you can sharpen up your movement," employs a challenge. You can hear the subtle difference in Chris's feedback the second time when he adds "quicker" at the end. Also the use of David's name comes first. Perhaps Chris is making sure David attends to the words more carefully. Perhaps, given that his name came second in the first bit of feedback, David wasn't listening because he didn't know it was directed at him.

"Tell him, tell him. It's late, Martin. Tell him. Tell him, now! Excellent."

- This feedback to Martin is similar to the "1-2" in the first sequence: it's crisp and feels pressing in its importance but retains a focus on the solution. After he gives Martin the initial guidance, he follows up to let him know whether he's doing it successfully. When Martin gets better by using Chris's feedback, he instantly knows it. Of course, Chris is careful to protect the power of the word "excellent" by not overusing it so his praise retains his leverage.

"See if we can play a quick combination. Quick combination. Benjy, in your supporting run, make sure you're facing the next pass. Orient yourself so you face the next pass. It's easy for you."

- Another challenge framed with "we." There's a focus on body shape for Benjy that clearly describes the solution in language—"face the next pass"—that sounds like it's been thought through in advance.

- The phrase "it's easy for you" seems to be a reminder of Benjy's overall quality. A player of his quality will easily be able to make this adjustment—a bit of assuming the best.

Final thoughts: tone and modeling

We've talked a lot about language and word choice. But in listening to great coaches, I'm sure you hear what I hear when I listen to Kelvin and Chris and Matt: the tone is just right. Constructive feedback is firm and clear. There's no need for sticky-sweet, but anger and frustration aren't usually productive. Soccer is a competitive game. There may come a time when you must raise your voice with a player or snarl a bit in tone. But most coaches, in my opinion, go harsh too readily—perhaps it makes them feel like they are being more demanding and that high standards and harshness go together—but it's worth considering whether introducing strong emotions into feedback is in fact a distraction. You snarl at a player and your player thinks: "Does he shout at everyone like that? Equally? Even his favorites? Why is it always me?" You're a bit more confrontational and the player thinks: "Does he sound like my father when he shouts? Does he think I'm not trying?" All of these things are distractions that allocate small stores of attention and working memory to something other than learning—which is what you want him thinking about.

You'll also notice the other side of the coin: great coaches are careful not to judge everything to be "awesome." They use positive reinforcement liberally but lightly. "Good" or "Well done" is often more compelling than "great" or "awesome." Too much praise can make it seem like you are surprised that a player was successful.

Modeled feedback

In a simple piece of feedback—*Try it like this*—the "this" can often be expressed as (and sometimes more) easily and effectively in a demonstration or a "model" as in words. This is probably not a revelation to you: most coaches use modeling as a form of feedback frequently. There are a thousand variations:

- Try it like this.
- *More* like this.
- Notice the difference between this [demonstrates mediocre execution] and this [demonstrates elite execution].

Modeling an action for players can often circumvent the limitations of working memory. That is, there's some evidence that working memory for visual and language-based communication is additive if carefully combined.[4] Athletes can absorb more information from a picture with a few carefully placed words than just words. In fact my colleagues and I often give feedback to teachers at workshops who are practicing teaching moves such as positive framing via models. We might pause a group and say, "Now consider trying it this way...."

> **4.** The illustrator of this book, Oliver Caviglioli, is also an author of the first rate and his book *Dual Coding* is an excellent starting point.

Afterwards, we have often noticed that participants replicate multiple aspects of the model, not just the part we were trying to demonstrate. We have suggested a shift in language but suddenly our facial expressions or body language are showing up in participants' practice too. What people see during a model enters their awareness without their realizing it. And this of course is a reminder of both the power of modeling as a form of feedback and the importance of intentionality and planning. (As a side note, we now plan our models in our workshops and often rehearse them to make sure they communicate well what we want them to. This would be a great action for a coach to steal, practicing and refining a demonstration she and her assistant want to provide during a training session.)

In most cases, my discussion of feedback in this chapter *presumes* coaches are including demonstrations of desired actions as part of their verbal feedback—that is, they are communicating ideas via both visual and verbal channels. Interestingly, both John Burmeister and James Beeston model the tempo they want in the cadence of their words when they give verbal feedback. Even their words operate on several levels.

Still, modeling—a demonstration to show someone how to do something—is, like feedback, something that appears so simple that it is easily overlooked and is therefore ripe for a bit of optimizing. That's a topic Katie Yezzi, Erica Woolway and I wrote about in *Practice Perfect* and one I take up again in chapter 2 on planning and design. That said, some brief thoughts on modeling may be helpful here.

The same constraints I've discussed throughout this chapter also apply to feedback that is partially verbal and partially modeled or even majority modeled.

Being fast and focused with verbal feedback, we learned, is critical to managing the limitations placed on learning by working memory and attention. And doing those two things builds a culture that socializes action right away. It is no different with modeling actions or positioning. *Be fast and focused and let players try it right away.*

Models should focus on the solution more than the problem. As we learned in chapter 1, most of what we learn from looking we learn without realizing it. When you show players something, show them what quality looks like. We want, in the course of our coaching, to make excellence in the detail look normal. It can occasionally be helpful to compare a suboptimal move to an ideal one, but mostly the time spent showing players what poor work looks like is less productive than helping them see and imagine the goal—we want it constantly in their mind's eye.

Similarly, models can be positively or negatively framed. A coach who's not managing his or her emotions can easily make a model spiteful or sarcastic or mocking. As with our words, we want our models to show our faith in our players.

A final note: you need two things for a model to work:

1. The model has to show the right thing.
2. Players have to see it.

The second part seems automatic, but it isn't. Players stand and "look" at models without processing what's valuable all the time. They aren't paying attention. Or they are trying to, but they don't know where to focus—research tells us that focus is quite narrow and people fail to see much of what is right in front of them as a matter of habit. Thus if you are about to model defensive body position, you can increase the likelihood that your players observe what you are trying to show them if you tell them what's most important to attend to. If you say "Watch my feet as I model it for you," they will notice the way you position your feet. If not, they could be looking at any of a dozen things. It sounds so obvious that it's easy to dismiss, so I'm going to say it again. Before you model, tell players what to look for most and where to see it. This concept is called "calling your shot."

FEEDBACK 201

Using the right words is important when giving feedback, but only a tiny proportion of what athletes learn from the feedback process happens while they are listening to us talk. The learning happens when (and if) they try to use our guidance, so one of the most important characteristics of effective feedback is that it causes or allows conscientious action afterwards. Feedback that results in athletes using advice they've been offered, reflecting on it steadily, adapting it to new situations, learning to assess their own play and performance, and improving steadily as a result is good feedback. If this happens, athletes come to believe in the process of getting better through coaching. Good feedback essentially helps athletes believe in the coaching process.

A quick story about my wife, Lisa, and me may help to emphasize some of the challenges in this area. When it comes to laundry, Lisa and I have different philosophies. For her, every item of dirty clothing must go in the basket. Only an item of laundry fully within the basket counts as "in the basket." There is little, if any, gray area involved.

For me, the term "in the basket" suggests more flexibility. Items of laundry may be left in various places for an unspecified length of time while a determination is made whether they should actually go into the wash. Clothing hanging off the edge of the basket is clearly still "in" the basket under any reasonable interpretation and counts for full credit. An item of laundry that is on the floor but where *the intent was clearly to get it in the basket* deserves partial credit. In short, when it comes to laundry, Lisa is a "letter of the law" kind of gal and I am a "spirit of the law" kind of guy.

This can lead to occasional disagreement and even conflict, and the truth is that I have been on a "behavior improvement plan" for much of my married life—mostly without result. Typically, an interaction in which Lisa is attempting to improve the level of my laundry game will involve her asking me to step into the doorway to the closet in our bedroom. There she gives me feedback. "Honey," she will say, "look at the laundry basket. What do you notice?"

Her technique here is strong. She is causing me to focus on the perceptive cues that should trigger a decision that I will be able to make on my own going forward—"laundry on floor" equals "pick up and place in basket." But the truth is that I do not wish to pick up my laundry. It is much easier to leave it strewn on the floor and only pick it up when the situation grows urgent—and I quickly learned that if I wanted to keep doing that, I was going to have to use a bit of strategy. Fortunately, I realized that the key was to have a great attitude.

When my wife says, "What do you see?" I say, "It's my laundry, Babe. The way those shirts are on the floor. That's really bad! They're not even near the basket!"

"See the way your jeans are draped over the edge?" she'll ask, and I'll say, "Yeah. That's really not good. They have to be all the way in the basket. It looks messy, the basket is hard to pick up, and it's harder for me to get my stuff in the basket. I'll do better." You have to admit, few husbands are as self-critical and open to feedback as I am.

To emphasize this perception I say, "I get it, Hon. I totally get it." And then I repeat back to her the key points she's made. "Jeans have gotta be all the way in the basket. No stuff on the floor." When I do that, I look her right in the eye and nod subtly to emphasize each point. I often close with, "That's really helpful," or, "Thanks for telling me."

And then, the next day, I toss my dirty laundry on the floor all over again.

By almost any measure, I am great at taking feedback. I am not defensive; I listen carefully; I show that I am listening and understand; I say thank-you.

But this story reveals that *taking* feedback is different from using feedback, which I am terrible at. I do not change my behavior. I fail to put good advice into action. I persist in my poor habits. In fact it is by appearing to be so receptive to feedback that I make the world safer for complacency. I humbly appreciate feedback in exactly the same moment that I ignore it and opt to do nothing with it afterwards.

If it's not already obvious, athletes do this all the time as well. (So do coaches, by the way.) So when we talk about coachability, our assessment should have more to do with how people use feedback than how they take it. If we want to get better at improving people, we have to "win the after." We have to cause productive action. Feedback 201 discusses ways to do that.

Aligned feedback

One reason athletes do not give sufficient thought to feedback after hearing it is that coaches often communicate that their feedback is not very important. To be clear, very few coaches intentionally communicate that they don't think their feedback is important, but many do so accidentally. Imagine a coach who makes a stoppage during training. Players are building out of the back. He's read the first part of this chapter and knows to focus on a single point of feedback, so he stops his players and says, "Pause. The pace of our passes must be quicker when we are building out of the back. A pass like this [demonstrates] is too slow; a pass like this [demonstrates] causes the opposition to have to move quickly to defend. It will expose gaps in their shape. Let me see those passes struck hard on the ground." He's done a solid job with fast and focused feedback.

As his players resume training, however, he begins to offer comments to individual players: "Faster feet, Adam!", "Great decision, Carlos!", "Can you find the entry pass, Marco?", "Kevin, receive with the other foot there!" and so on.

Individually, much of this feedback may be useful, but as a whole it is missing something critical. Moments ago, the coach stopped the whole training to say that the weight of passes was very important. But once the stoppage ended, he was distracted by a dozen other things and no longer seemed to be thinking about it. None of his live feedback was about the pace of their passes. No one knew whether they improved or whether he saw them trying, or whether their passes were now fast enough to expose gaps in the defense. Worse, his words suggested that the stoppage was already all but forgotten; just seconds afterwards, his focus had shifted elsewhere. The short-term message was that pace of passing wasn't important enough to him to sustain his focus on it. If he did this consistently, the broader message would be that what he'd told players during stoppages was rarely that important. And if it's not important to the coach, it's unlikely to be important to the player.

But what if the live feedback the coach gave after the stoppage had sounded more like this: "Yes, that's what we want, Luis!", "Hit it even harder, David!", "Better, Danilo! I like the pace, but it can't be bouncing.", "OK, gentlemen, now we're starting to get the pace of passing that we need." In the second set of examples, the coach has disciplined himself to focus on whether and how his players are using the feedback he just gave them. He has managed to ignore for the moment most of the other things he observes.

There are two benefits to this change. The first is immediate. Players receive ongoing feedback about whether they are making the desired change effectively. This helps them to understand how they are doing at accomplishing the task: *I am trying to change but am I doing it right? Am I making progress? Have I done it enough? Too much?* Being more attentive to both the goal and their progress towards it will cause them to learn more rapidly. David strikes the ball slightly harder and thinks perhaps he's met the standard but hears the coach telling him that he has improved but must still improve more. He remains focused on execution and is now more aware of what constitutes sufficient ball speed. Similarly, Luis immediately knows that he's made a successful change. His effort made a difference visible to the coach. He can focus on making it a habit or—perhaps if the coach said, "Yes, that's what we want, Luis! Now see if you can play it so he can receive across his body"— refining something else about his passes.

More broadly, the coach has reinforced the importance of his teaching points. When he gives feedback, he notices whether athletes focus on it afterwards—whether they use it rather than just nod in understanding—and this helps them build the habit of sustaining focus. Players get feedback on their effectiveness at using feedback. The coach is building a culture of follow-through and self-awareness.

The nature of the aligned live feedback can vary. If players focus on an idea but struggle with it, the coach could refer back to the teaching points. "Faster passes, boys. We're still not there." If players seem to be forgetting the focus of the feedback, he simply reminds them as James Beeston does: "Focus on these passes!" If he sees successful implementation, he can begin to describe the next step in the process: "Yes, that's it, Luis! Now let's get it to the proper foot!" or "Now let's step a little higher!" In this case, the new idea is a consequence of mastery of the first one.

Does the coach still see things he wants to change about Adam's footwork and Marco's decision-making? Yes. Would it be OK if he mentioned one or two of these things? Yes. Not every single comment after a stoppage has to refer back to the teaching point the coach just made. And I'm not suggesting that you have to call it out every time a player makes a poor touch. If it's new and difficult, giving players some space to struggle privately is good. But a strong degree of alignment between feedback during stoppages and the live feedback that comes after them is important. It shows that what matters, what the coach is watching for, is whether the feedback gets used. It's the follow-through, the "after," that matters most in the big picture. Doubly so when execution is strong. That's the moment to tell players, *Yes that's it! I see a difference!* You're now doing what will help you succeed. If players are not using the ideas we discuss as a team, the first question we should ask is whether we have clearly shown them that we value it and expect it. Aligning live feedback to stoppage feedback is one of the fastest ways to do that.

Since one of the purposes of aligned feedback is to build a culture that values attentiveness to coaching points, it's worth sharing something John Burmeister, the music teacher, shared with me. Watching a video of himself with his youth orchestra—the one included in chapter 4, "Checking for Understanding"—he noted the moment where he stopped the orchestra to ask for a dynamic check. "Before this, we'd been working a lot on dynamics," he said. "Then we moved on to the *ritardando* but I want the message to be, *once we work on something, I am always listening for it. You are accountable.* So if we talked about it in that session and I don't hear it, I'm stopping to address it." Applying that to the idea of aligned feedback suggests an opportunity to think about aligning live feedback not just to the previous stoppage but also to any stoppage from the day's session, to the cumulative understanding we've developed in the day's training.

Here's a last tip that comes from a session I recently observed with a collegiate coach. During a water break in his session, we discussed the importance of sustaining focus on his coaching points after a stoppage, but he was finding it hard. He *intended* to reinforce his coaching points afterwards, during live play, but there was so much to observe and comment on. He would simply forget. At the next water break, we came up with an idea. He was in the habit of keeping a clipboard with him, and we decided he would briefly write down a shorthand version of his coaching point each time he stopped: *Defenders must maintain depth to avoid being split*. This would be an interesting record of what he taught the girls for later reflection, but writing it down also allowed him to track his own follow-up by giving himself a check mark each time he gave his players feedback on whether they had maintained depth. "Good depth, Allie!" was a check. So was "Stay deeper, Sidney!" He had to make five check marks on his clipboard before he could stop his players again and this helped him to develop the habit of sustaining focus.

SEFU
BERNARD

"Everyone has to know her one thing"

Washington Mystics Director of Player Development Sefu Bernard also thinks a lot about the alignment of feedback, but he sees it as something that's more coordinated even than the feedback a coach gives within a single practice.

Over the years, in tracking individual player development as well as team development, we realized that we can't work on ten things at once. It seems silly to say, but that's what tends to happen. If we've got ten things we'd like to accomplish, we have to prioritize and decide. This is where I apply the "Rule of 3." I work to whittle the list down to three things we're going to work on specifically with a player, and often there's just one thing that becomes our focus for feedback.

Every player needs to have one most important thing that they're being given consistent and timely reminders and encouragement about. And it's critical when you have multiple coaches that everyone has to know each player's one thing.

Maybe there's a player and we've been working on scoring solutions on the left side of her body. She needs to be more fluid and confident on her non-dominant side. That's her one thing. So maybe she comes in early before practice for 15 minutes of extra work on it. Then practice starts and we start by walking through a new offensive play. Next, we warm up. Then do some defensive coverages working in small groups. Followed by competing in short intervals.

Let's say she gets the ball in scoring position when we're playing 5-on-5 and fights her way to shoot off her right side even though there's an opening to the left. That was her test—and a test of our feedback as coaches. If we don't give timely feedback on her one thing, we as coaches have failed her. We should have been watching for her one thing. The intervention should have been about her one thing. That's the part that we as coaches control. We can be intentional about making sure our interventions and corrections are connected to the things that are focus areas for each athlete. That consistency of messaging is vital to the learning process.

In our training environment, team travel permitting, we meet weekly to discuss player development. That's where we align on where we are with a given player and sync up on their three things. Are we moving the needle on those things? If the answer is yes, great, let's talk about what's next in their progression. If the answer is no, we talk about how we can change our approach, or change our focus to another thing.

It's useful to go through the process of narrowing one's focus for feedback on a few things. For us, it's three or less. And, as soon as you move to a coaching environment of more than one coach, you need to have alignment (which is different than agreement)—not just within a practice, but to continually be asking, "How are we pulling this theme forward?"

Correct instead of critique

Here's an example of feedback that is probably not effective for a reason that is both common and easily remedied. A college coach stops players working in an 8 v 8 setting. Jenna, a central midfielder, has received a short lateral pass from a wide player, Katie, under pressure and, with the opportunity to open up and switch the field, has played back into pressure, squandering an opportunity and demonstrating a misunderstanding of the team's game model.

"Not back into pressure, Jenna!" the coach says. "Switch the point of attack. We've got to open up and find Chelsea." Or perhaps she takes a less directive approach and she asks Jenna questions: "What options did you have there? Where did we say we want to play in this situation?"

Whether a statement or a question, both of these pieces of feedback are, for now, examples of critique: their purpose is to tell Jenna (or cause Jenna to recognize) what she should or could have done differently in this sequence. What's necessary to make that useful is to turn that critique into correction by givingJenna and her teammates the opportunity to replay the sequence and to do it over, ideally better, right away.

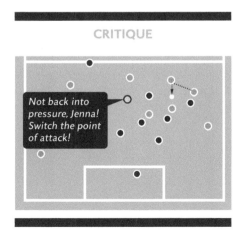

CRITIQUE

If learning is a change in long-term memory, correction allows Jenna to encode proper execution: what it feels like, what visual cues she will see while (or before) executing. It builds muscle and mental memory of the solution. Correction adds the opportunity for immediate application to the abstract concept described in the critique. It turns theory into reality.

The coach might do that by first giving Jenna feedback like "We've got to switch the point of attack there. We want to open up and find Chelsea." Then she would add: "Give the ball back to Katie and let's try switching the attack from there." Or, if she is using questions:

Coach: Jenna, pause. What options did you have there?

Jenna: I could have played laterally to Chelsea.

Coach: Yes, and that would have done what?

Jenna: Opened up the field.

Coach: Good. Ball back to Katie and let's see you try it.

Both of these situations allow Jenna to build a stronger and richer memory of correct execution. She *does the answer* rather than merely describing it and she adds to it all sorts of detail. She tries it and finds the angle at which she must open up with her first touch. She finds she can disguise her move with a feint. And her teammates practice responding too. Chelsea learns to adjust her positioning slightly as she sees Jenna receive the ball. And of course the coach now has the opportunity to provide aligned feedback to help accelerate the learning: "Yes, Jenna, that's the way. Snap open and there it is!" Or "Yes, perfect ball, Jenna" Or perhaps "Good, Jenna, but let's try it one more time and let's see if you can disguise the move a little."

Turning critique into correction lets players learn by doing, encoding stronger and deeper recollections of what "right" looks and feels like. It builds a culture where words are turned into actions. I suspect this seems obvious to many coaches and that few would take issue with it on principle, so it's worth asking why we don't do it more often. Two reasons come to mind. The first is time pressure. There's so much to teach, so much to get done, that it's tempting to try to cover more: say it and move on to the next thing. And rightly so—we want to get players playing. But remember most of the learning accrues when athletes apply what our words describe, not when we say them. It seems slower to add the correction step, but in the end it will be faster because you will find yourself repeating yourself less. The real measure of how much time we spend on something is not the total number of seconds or minutes we use but the total number of seconds or minutes we use *divided by the amount of learning that results*. Yes, you want a faster stoppage, but also one that results in memory building.

A second challenge that causes us to skip the "Now do it" step is impulsiveness: giving feedback without intentionality. We see something that bothers us in practice and impulsively stop to narrate what we've seen back to players. We're still processing it as we're talking and haven't thought through the action we want. Interestingly, a lot of research on impulsive decisions suggests that a tiny delay of just a second or two can allow you to be more strategic. If that's true, a notebook in which you write down things you observe during training and want to talk to your team about might help. Lots of times,

I suspect we verbalize a coaching point because we are worried we will forget it, so we stop to talk about it right away. At least if we verbalize it, we can convince ourselves we've addressed it. Writing things down can reduce the anxiety that we'll forget and provide the self-discipline to say fewer things with more consistent application. The delay of a second or two to jot down the note can be just enough to slow down the process and let intention replace impulse.

With younger players, you might break the correction down into a sequence: "OK. Let's bring the ball back to Katie. Jenna, as you receive, open up your hips so the ball starts to roll past you. [Jenna does this.] OK, can you see that your first touch allows you to be able to play on to Chelsea? So let me see a pass to Chelsea's feet on the second touch. [Jenna does this.] Good. Now try it at full speed. Ball back to Katie. Defense, you're frozen until Jenna's first touch!" This allows Jenna to rehearse that base action slowly under simpler circumstances and then to do it in a slightly more challenging setting after she's had the opportunity to rehearse what she's going to do successfully.

Using Binary Feedback (by James Beeston)

JAMES
BEESTON

In discussing training, Doug and I decided to test the potential of an idea from David Eagleman's book Incognito: *The Secret Lives of the Brain* that we called "binary feedback."

The idea originates from World War II, when, as Eagleman tells it, England had a very small number of people who could listen to planes approaching across the English Channel and tell, based on the sound of their engines and before they could see them, whether they were British or German. Obviously, the value of this information was high and they wanted more such people. But the spotters were unable to describe to others what they were hearing. They couldn't explain it, they could just do it. How do you train someone to do something like that?

What worked was something very simple: a spotter would stand next to a trainee, and as the sound of an engine became audible, the trainee would guess: British or German. The spotter would simply say "Yes" or "No." The result perhaps foreshadowed some of the ideas that drive AI today. A high volume of binary data—whether something was or wasn't right—was sufficient over time to help the brain learn to do something it could not explain.

As coaches, we often ask players to do things that are hard to perceive, particularly in the area of motor learning. We want to build the habit of efficient movements but a player is taking an extra step without being aware of it. What if a coach merely stood next to the player and said "Yes" if they executed correctly or "No" if they added the step? Might they learn quickly and efficiently without interruptions and stoppages? I decided to try binary feedback with some of the players I was training.

I tested it in three situations, all involving complex movements made at high speed that were challenging to describe and difficult for a player to recognize whether they'd done them or not: a footwork pattern, a "drop step" in defending, and an awareness drill that focused on when to scan.

With many players when you show them footwork, their first thought is to execute it as quickly as they can, with little attention paid to the precision and technical detail that will ultimately cause it to be successful. They learn it but not at a level that makes it effective in a match. In one case, a player often failed to put his foot down between a pull back and a sole roll, resulting in him being off-balance for the rest of the move. Simply telling him to try not to put his foot down in the middle of the movement was not especially effective. One afternoon, I told him I would focus my feedback exclusively on whether he put his foot down between the pull back and the roll by saying "Yes" or "No." There were a lot of nos in the first round and struggling to change a habit that seemed so simple was frustrating, so I started asking him to execute the first part more slowly: "If you roll the ball back more slowly, it will allow you more time to put your foot down for balance. Slower roll, faster overall movement." Suddenly the nos began turning to yeses and there was something about the quantifiable nature of the progress that was motivating. Each "yes" reinforced that he was getting it, and as they became steady, his speed of execution started to increase. He was quickly able to rebuild his habits in a movement that was largely unconscious by reacting to this simple yes/no data stream.

In the second case, I wanted to help break the habit of adding an unnecessary step as an athlete turned and ran backwards under pressure when defending. The player's extra movement slowed his momentum in reacting and pushed his body in the wrong direction—a tiny but critical flaw for a defender, and another unconscious and subtle habit in the middle of a complex movement. I wondered if binary feedback could help. Again we started slow. I would watch carefully for the extra step and simply tell him yes or no whether he had executed correctly. "Yes" meant "You succeeded in removing the step." Even when the answer was "No," I was careful to keep my own tone judgment free. We both knew that breaking a habit would mean a lot of nos. Sometimes I would just smile at the nos to show him I understood how hard it was to break a habit. Progress was slow then fast; he struggled at first and then something clicked and he began to make rapid progress. I began to test him under more complex conditions. Soon the new streamlined movement became a habit.

For the third drill, I wanted to try to use binary feedback to improve the timing of a player's "scanning"—his ability to check over his shoulder for opponents before receiving the ball. It's hard to get players to scan reliably and with the right timing, but it's even more difficult to assess if the player actually processed what he saw during the scan. It's easy to coach a head swivel; it's hard to teach the perception and cognition that comes with it.

I put an iPad on a tripod that flashed blue, red, yellow, or green in three- or four-second intervals behind a player. The player would scan for the iPad before receiving the ball and call out the color he saw. This would allow me to assess whether the player was actually processing what was behind him in a meaningful way or just making a show of moving his head. The binary feedback came in response to this—

correct color meant "yes"; incorrect meant "no." However, I soon realized that in this case the feedback was less effective because it simply affirmed whether the player had seen the light correctly. This highlighted something important about binary feedback: *it works best when it helps a player perceive something they cannot otherwise perceive.* There was no associated change in his actions he needed to make in response to my feedback and he already knew whether he had perceived the light correctly. My feedback wasn't changing his understanding of his own movements.

On reflection, there are benefits of binary feedback to accelerate skill acquisition, especially early in the process when you want to increase awareness of something unconscious, but it requires high volume and rapid sequence of feedback—and an almost Zenlike focus on an action over and over. It's also best in short intense doses. I suggest interleaving it: a few intense minutes to refine a movement, then on to something else and back to it for a few minutes after a period of forgetting.

Time to apply

When we give feedback, the teaching happens as we talk, but most of the learning comes as and if athletes attempt to apply the ideas we've described. This implies shifting more of our attention to what happens after we stop talking, ensuring we provide opportunities for athletes to correct, apply and expand their understanding as play resumes after the stoppage. We want application with as much variation and game-like context as players can sustain. That seems obvious, but it's challenging to create time and space for application. It's hard to engineer an environment where opportunities to apply feedback reoccur reliably, and sometimes we are so busy teaching we fail to allow for the learning.

I recently watched a coach make an outstanding stoppage during training. Girls were playing in a three-part grid 3 v 3 + 1, black vs green. Each of the players on the black and green teams were tied to one of the thirds but the +1 could go anywhere. Like this:

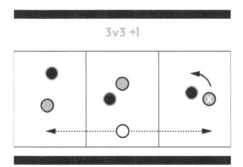

3v3 +1

The set-up caused players to have to create space and separation from their defenders. If they did, they would reliably be rewarded with the ball. At one point, with the neutral player holding the ball and green in possession, the player marked with the X tried to get open by making a looping run behind her defender (arrow). The defender easily covered it and she was unsuccessful.

The coach paused play. "To get open in a situation like this," he explained, "you often have to make two runs: one for the defender and one for the ball." He then showed her how to take a few steps as if making the original run (the run "for the defender") and then reverse direction back into the space she'd vacated (the run "for the ball"). He then had her try this. Even though the defender knew it was coming, the unpredictability of the timing and the fact that he had shown her how to make the move in the defender's blind spot made the run successful. Light bulb. She received the ball and away they went.

It was, from my (teaching) perspective, an almost perfect stoppage. The skill he highlighted was sophisticated, important and applicable across settings. It guided play *off the ball* which is far less coached than (but at *least* as important as) what players do on the ball.

Second, the fundamentals of a good stoppage were all there:

- It was fast—about 25 seconds from pause to resume.
- It was focused on one single idea only—no overload to working memory.
- It used correction, instead of just critique. The object player had the chance to rehearse the required action, not just hear about it.
- Players applied the idea right away.
- It used clear, concise, memorable language: "Two runs: one for the defender and one for the ball." Perfect.

And not just memorable to me. Memorable to them. After the coach said "Play," you could see the girls using the idea, applying and adapting it. You could see the change in their movements. It was powerful.

But only for a little while. That was the Achilles heel and, for me, the lesson.

Less than a minute later, the coach made another stoppage on a different topic from the "two runs" idea. The second stoppage was also well done in terms of teaching and of topic but *it had the result of erasing the first one from players' working memory*. The girls were now thinking of the second stoppage as they played and *they stopped making the movements they'd been making off the ball after the first stoppage*. The exploration and learning that had begun never fully took root. They needed more time to build the habit of two runs, to understand it, and to encode it lastingly in memory.

They could have spent more time experimenting with the idea of getting in their defender's blind spot and unbalancing her with a false run, realizing that sometimes you really have to sell the first run with a quick change of body language, for example, or that sometimes it's actually three runs: fake run/fake check back/continue initial run, etc.

Time to use and apply an idea is necessary to learning. The goal, if we want to increase learning, must be to maintain focus on an idea—and if we really want to accelerate learning, to focus on it, let players begin to forget about it and then come back to it. *The teaching happens in the stoppage, but the learning happens only when there is a sustained opportunity to use the ideas we discuss afterwards.* Maintaining focus on ideas sometimes means not moving on to the next idea when we've taught something well. In a perfect world, there would be a more sustained focus on changing pace and direction off the ball.

The practical actions for coaches to consider here are as follows:

- Extend the amount of play time after each stoppage to ensure that players get to use the idea.

- Remind athletes of what they're working on—"Unbalance your defender, girls; change pace and change direction"—while they are playing so they continue to seek opportunities to use it.

- Have multiple stoppages focus on the same topic (or some new variation thereon) for a significant stretch of time (10, 12, 15 minutes).

- Come back to the topic later in the session for retrieval practice and again during the next session or two, perhaps, even if briefly, to drive the nascent habit into long-term memory.

That requires self-discipline. A good coach can teach more in 90 minutes than players can absorb. We have to pick and choose what we talk about. We have to know what it's most important to coach and focus on coaching those things well.

It can also help if we take steps to make players themselves more aware of opportunities to put feedback to use so they don't miss them. Later, I will discuss constraints-based coaching—the idea that the rules and structure of a game can be designed to cause certain types of events to happen more frequently and thus allow players to learn from the experience of playing with far less explicit teaching or feedback. Such an approach is most likely to be productive with expert learners, but an adaptation of it can allow coaches to make better use of feedback with learners at earlier stages of mastery as well. During an exercise, a coach could add a rule in response to the feedback she just gave and make this new rule transparent to athletes so that they would be more alert to the opportunities it created for them to apply the feedback. For example, let's go back to Jenna for a moment, playing the ball back into pressure instead of switching the point of attack. After correcting Jenna during the stoppage, her coach might make a rule change: "For the next five minutes, all defenders except one must be on the same side of the field as the ball," or "For the next five minutes, goals scored when we change the point of attack count double," or "For the next five minutes, the ball must go from one side of the field to the other before we can score."

These changes would cause there to be more opportunity and/or reward for switching the field. Coaches could surely propose more sophisticated examples of constraints than I have used here, but the idea is that temporarily changing game rules to incentivize athletes to use your feedback can increase the rate of application.

Similarly, introducing a verbal cue that you can use during the ensuing period of play to make players aware of opportunities to apply your feedback can also be useful. For example, Jenna's coach could say, "For the next five minutes, I am going to shout 'Yes!' if an opportunity to switch play out of pressure is on. If you hear me say 'Yes!', you'll know to look for the opportunity to change the point of attack." Or "I'm going to shout, 'Pressure!' when you have the ball in tight space with numbers down. When you hear that, I want you to look to change the point of attack." Jenna's coach has increased the likelihood that players will recognize opportunities to use the idea she's discussed in feedback when they naturally occur, but without changing the rules of the game. The assumption in the first case is that opportunities to apply a new idea might not naturally occur frequently enough for players to get sufficient chances to try it after the stoppage. The assumption in the second case is that opportunities might occur but players might fail to recognize them. What both have in common is the effort to try to *manage the after* to make it more likely that athletes benefit from opportunities to apply something they're discussed—to move it from theory to reality more consistently.

One common dissent from this sort of coaching practice is that it distorts decision-making by over-controlling it. Perhaps switching the point of attack is not the best way to play out of pressure in a given situation. Can adding a verbal cue or a specific constraint (e.g. "You must switch the field before scoring") distort decisions and cause players to over use an idea? Of course. The idea of the constraint is to teach players how to solve a problem a certain way, to give them experience doing it, not to cause them to always do it. As long as you remain alert to that, the risks are manageable. If a few minutes of reinforcing an idea causes your athletes to constantly and obsessively seek to use it in every available situation, you're certainly getting high levels of attention and follow-through from your team and are definitely doing something right. It would be easy to teach players other responses to pressure and then discuss with them—or allow them to choose—which is best in a given setting.

A second way to help learners see and understand authentic opportunities to apply feedback is to ask learners to reflect on them at the next stoppage. Let's say Jenna's coach tries the approach where she calls out "Pressure!" when she wants them to recognize the opportunity to change the point of attack. At the next stoppage, she might begin by saying, "OK, guys. There were three or four occasions there when I called 'Pressure!'" and then start peppering them with questions: *Were you able to switch the field? Why did we struggle sometimes? What is difficult about it? When it worked, what did we do to make it successful?* Asking athletes to reflect in this way keeps the learning at the forefront of their consciousness and reminds them that the goal is for them to be attentive to opportunities to try the feedback, to seek them out.

Another way to get more out of opportunities to apply feedback in a more authentic setting is to begin applying the concepts of spacing and interleaving from the science of retrieval practice we studied in the introduction. Perhaps if Jenna's coach wants her team to continue seeking out and maximizing opportunities to change the point of attack, she would go on to other topics and then return to the idea 15 minutes later: "Let's go back to playing away from pressure and make sure we've still got that down." Or perhaps in the next day's training she suddenly calls out "Pressure!" during play and asks players how effective they were. The short delay and the distraction of other topics will make them work harder to remember what to do and how to do it. An easy way to apply this idea more systematically across training would be to keep notes of your most important stoppage topics and coaching points. If you have a list of topics at easy access, it will be easier to circle back to them and sprinkle them back into your teaching to ensure long-term memory.

Shorten the loop

In *Practice Perfect*, Katie Yezzi, Erica Woolway and I discussed a surprising challenge from the world of medicine:[5] radiologists often get worse over time, not better, at reading X-rays and other scans. You'd think the accumulated experience of reading thousands of such scans would be hugely beneficial but there's one thing missing: after reading a typical mammogram and making an assessment, a typical radiologist usually finds out whether he or she was right only days or even weeks or months later, when they hardly remember the details of the case and why they analyzed it as they did. *Because the delay between decision and feedback is so long, they operate in darkness and stop getting better.*

5. See Joshua Foer, *Moonwalking with Einstein*

With feedback, it turns out, speed is a critical factor. The closer it is to a stimulus you are seeking to shape, the more influential it is. In fact, the speed of a response can often be far more significant than its strength. If you intervene quickly and say "Not that way; this way; try again," you can save yourself having to talk or shout to make your point later. If the ball rolls out of bounds at a training and you find yourself saying with perhaps a bit of frustration something like "Guys, we had the ball at midfield but we played back into pressure. Again. I keep saying that we need to...", one solution might be to not wait for the ball to roll out of bounds. Instead, give the feedback closer to the initial event.

Jenna's coach in the example from the previous section might *shorten the loop* by putting her reflection questions closer to the moment in which athletes apply the feedback. So, perhaps the first time she calls "Pressure!" and players try to change to point of attack, she would stop them immediately after so they could study the challenges and problems it creates together (see "Show the problem" in "Feedback 301," later in this chapter) or make small adaptations. She'd ask some of her questions then, in the midst of the action: "What's challenging here? What do you have to do to overcome it? Yes. Keep going. Keep listening for the word 'Pressure.' Play!" Then perhaps she'd let them try to switch out of pressure a few times on their own before asking for a broader analysis of their learnings. If they were successful, she might give them multiple opportunities at a time to apply, but if they were struggling she might again attempt to get her feedback closer to the initial action: "Pause, girls. I shouted 'Pressure!' there but we were unable to get the ball out of the area we were playing in. One reason is because of our technique in receiving the ball...."

There's some good news here; a tie-in to the concept of *fast feedback*. Getting the feedback closer to the root action that causes it will change actions faster than giving more extensive feedback later on. We could let the mistakes happen three or four times, get frustrated and then try to emphasize how important the issue is by stating it three times in a row while players begin to lose focus and the opportunity to apply immediately ebbs away; or we could catch it the first time right away, make a quick suggestion, say "See if that helps" and get players back into action focused on doing things slightly differently. The speed with which we step in can often help ensure the speed with which we step back out.

I'm reminded here that some coaches divide stoppages into two categories: natural stoppages (the ball going out of bounds) and those the coach initiates ("Pause there, guys"). The distinction isn't that useful unless it means telling coaches not to use the latter type on the basis that it's unnatural and disruptive. To me, that premise is flawed. I think people make the argument because they see training where stoppages are too frequent. In that case, the solution is to reduce frequency, but if it's worth taking the time to talk about, the timing matters. Getting the feedback closer to the event that causes it when players can still study the perceptive cues is important. If you wait for the ball to go out of bounds, it's less likely that players will remember the details of the moment. They will be less likely to connect the fix to the initial event. And it will be harder for you to recreate the scene. As I'll discuss in the next section, this is perhaps the single most important reason to shorten the feedback loop. Recreating the original situation visually allows your athletes to *look at the problem* and make connections between perception and action. If you want problem-solving, you have to be looking at a problem. Getting in quickly with feedback allows you to recreate the situation simply and easily.

When possible, getting the response closer to the stimulus is a good rule of thumb, but shortening the loop is not a hard-and-fast rule but rather one best balanced with other factors. Reacting right away demands that you frame your language quickly, for example. Might it be worth taking the time to get the language right? Might you want to gather more data? Might you want to discuss how you'll talk about or demonstrate the solution with an assistant coach? Yes. Of course planning for and thinking through likely errors before training (see chapter 4) is critical, but even on-the-spot feedback is often still better if you take a few moments to plan it.

Another risk of shortening the loop is that it may make you more impulsive, more inclined to see something and step in to stop training for every little thing, instead of the most important things, or too frequently. Research on perception tells us that planning is key. The best way to manage what we see is to think through in advance the most important things we want to see and the most likely errors that could erode performance, to have our priorities mostly set out ahead of time. Having familiar and consistent routines for stoppages is also important. A coach should be able to say "Pause" or "Stop" or "Freeze" in the moment but also have players stop right away so the team can move quickly and seamlessly into feedback. If you have to reposition players and remind them to come back to where they were, you will not only waste time and cause the feedback to be further from the antecedent moment but also likely distract yourself as you tell Kelly to be more central and Carla to stand, deeper and your language and clarity in giving feedback will suffer. Finally, in a few pages, you'll read about the guidance fading effect—the idea that in the later stages of learning, experts can be disrupted by too much feedback, and in some settings with elite athletes, it's better to let an error occur multiple times before you address it.

So getting the feedback as close as possible to the action that caused it is preferred, but it may be outweighed by other factors. That said, its benefits may be most pronounced[6] with skill acquisition—when there are actions we want the body to acquire, the benefits of speed are most pronounced, and in that case, it might even be worth considering binary feedback.

6. I want to be transparent: this is outright speculation on my part as I have not been able to find research on the matter.

"Coaching hard" and "Finding a win"

Dan McFarland is the head coach of Ulster Rugby, based in Belfast, Northern Ireland—one of the top professional rugby teams in Europe and a frequent participant in the European Champions Cup. He describes two parallel approaches he and his staff use to develop players that allow them to balance the demands of coaching groups and the needs of individuals.

DAN
McFARLAND

A lot of our training involves a games-based approach. The main focus of each game is usually on either attack or defence. Depending on which, one coach will run the game and coach the objective. Let's say it's defence coach Jared Payne, for example, and he wants to work on improving spacings around the ruck and then line-speed to induce change in the attack. Any "pause moments" [i.e. stoppages for coaching points] are run by Jared; all coaching of the team as a group is done by Jared. It's his session and he has priority. They need to focus on his points.

However, the nature of rugby means that while one team is defending, the other team is attacking, often for longish periods, and we want to make sure players are developing whenever they are playing, even if they are the opposition to the unit that we're focusing on. We call our philosophy "Coach Hard," and here it means that the other coaches focus on spotting opportunities to coach individuals as *the game is going on*. This requires a lot of movement and awareness from the coaches.

Here's an example. Forwards coach Roddy Grant might focus during Jared's session on watching the offence in the breakdown/ruck. Roddy then moves behind the attack as they play. Let's say he spots Kevin, who is a little slow to arrive at the breakdown because he does not react early to the cue or accelerate to get there. Roddy might call out "Kevin—speed to contact." This phrase is one we use consistently in training. It implies that Kevin was too slow to the last ruck but focuses on the action we trained on. The solution to being slow to the ruck is "speed to contact".

The details and timing of the intervention are very important:

- First, it must be immediate but neither interfere with the player's ability to "stay with the game" nor disrupt Jared's coaching, which has priority, so the coach has to read the moment.

- Second, it must clearly use the player's name. Otherwise Kevin may not know it refers to him. Often Kevin will only turn his head for a second to connect with Roddy on this feedback.

- Third, the language must be precise and brief. The key to this is having a coaching lexicon specific to our team; in this instance it is the use of "speed to contact" which the players know means *react to tackle cue* and *accelerate to win the race* against the defender to the breakdown. If the intervention is immediate, the coach doesn't need to say, "Too slow to your last ruck", as it is implicit in the language of the solution.

- Last, but perhaps most critical, Roddy now must set out to "Find a win" as soon after the intervention as possible. As he coaches, he's specifically looking for Kevin demonstrating good "speed to contact". As soon as he sees it, he affirms, "Kevin—yes, good speed to contact." This finishes the feedback loop. It both helps Kevin know his work was better and signals that when I ask you to work on something, I notice whether you do it. In my experience, this process has a broad effect. Even if coaching is directed at an individual, the intervention is overheard by other players nearby and reinforces the importance of "speed to contact."

Coaching in the moment like this while another coach is teaching a different element of the game is a difficult skill for the coaches. It's a lot like playing, really. They have to read the playing environment for cues like whether Jared is about to say something and whether the player will be distracted in that moment. It requires attuning to the ability of the players to take small interventions whilst playing a complex sport. In that sense, it's also demanding of athletes too. They have to be able to play fluidly within a system whilst also attending to small details upon which they are getting feedback. It's demanding, but that's what it means to be an elite athlete.

Replicable praise

Most people assume that praise is most powerful as a tool to motivate people, to make them feel better about themselves and encourage them to work harder. At least that seems to be how they use it. Listening to a coach during training, you might hear something like, "Good, Sarah. Yes, Asia. Good. Good, guys! I like it!"

7. It's also true that its overuse can dilute this benefit.

It's true that positive reinforcement—telling someone they did well—can have that effect on athletes,[7] but it is even more powerful as a teaching tool because it helps athletes know what to replicate, and this application of positive reinforcement is under-utilized. Athletes get things right all the time and then fail to keep doing those things because they don't recognize that they've done them well. Or they don't see the difference between *this time* and *all the other times* they've tried something. In fact, sometimes they don't even know they've done something at all. An observant coach can change this dynamic through specific positive reinforcement at the right moment. This might start very simply with a statement describing the initial success to athletes so they understand it and can replicate it: "Yes, that's it, Lucy," versus "Good, Lucy," makes it clear you are observing a specific action, not praising her effort—a small but important difference, and one you could build on by helping her know what she got right: "Yes, Lucy. Good first touch!" Or perhaps you want to help her see even more specifically what was right: "Yes, Lucy. Love that first touch away from pressure!" Perhaps you even want to make a stoppage out of it: "Pause. Guys, what Lucy did there was really sharp. The first touch had to be almost directly behind her, but she opened up like we've been working on [demonstrates] and it allowed her to protect the ball. Let's see if we can do it a few more times, all of us, as we're playing." Or perhaps you could pause and ask some questions, perhaps not even revealing yet whether you were asking athletes to analyze a success or an opportunity to improve:

Lucy, *what did you do with your first touch there?*

Played it backwards.

Why?

Kaya was coming.

And did playing your first touch back allow you to protect that ball?

I think so.

Yes, it absolutely did. It was perfect, and you kept the ball for us at a time when we have often lost it in the past. That was very well done and I wanted us to all make sure we saw it.

Success, especially in its first instances, is an important coaching opportunity: by calling it out, helping players themselves to see it and understand it, you've increased the likelihood that it will happen again. After all, if you had made an opposite stoppage—for example, if you had seen Lucy receive the ball and allow her first touch to fall into the range of the onrushing defender and said, "Pause. Lucy, that first touch was solid but now see if you can rotate your body so your first touch falls behind you and you can protect it"— Lucy might be skeptical that she could do what you were suggesting. But here, she's done it already. Her task is merely to replicate and perhaps adapt. She already knows she can.

Another hidden benefit is that occasionally using stoppages to study success with as much attentiveness as we study struggle can change players' affective response to the stoppage itself. When players hear the whistle or the word "pause" or whatever signal we use to stop play, they experience a flicker of emotion that lingers during the stoppage. Surely there are teams on which players hear the signal to stop and brace themselves for negativity. Perhaps it's because they want to play without interruption, but perhaps it's also because they know whoever's on the ball is going to find out they did something wrong. Even with the best positive framing and normalizing of error, using stoppages to point out excellence and success when it happens can be a game changer in shifting players' affective response to feedback.

Some keys to replicable praise:

- It's a good gut check to ask whether the athlete understands what "it" or "that" is referring to when you say, "Love it!" or "That was fantastic!" If you're certain Lucy knows you're referring to her first touch, OK. If not, a word like *because* or *when* after it is critical.

- It's easy to get carried away with the praise and forget that the point is to tell an athlete what to replicate. In fact, sometimes you can say it more directly with more muted praise, as in a phrase like, "That's it. Just like that," without six layers of *awesome awesomeness* thrown in. Relatedly, if you overuse your praise words, they become less meaningful for marking true success. The 24th "awesome" thing in your training session may not feel that memorable to your athletes.

- You want them to repeat it. Earlier I showed you a video of John Burmeister teaching cello to his student Anna. If you watch it again, you'll notice his reaction when Anna gets her trill right:

John: Beautiful. Do it again.

[Anna plays]

John: Three more times, just like that.

[Anna plays ×2 and mumbles]

The phrase, "Do it again. Three more times, just like that" is powerful because it reminds us that *getting it right is the mid-point of mastery*. We assume sometimes that if athletes get something right once, it will suddenly become part of their repertoire, but really, they have to do it over and over for that to happen. Why not add an immediate opportunity to feel the success again if you can?

- Occasionally add some teaching detail if you can do it quickly. In addition to your "Yes, that's it" and possibly your "Now do it again," you can add technical guidance: "Yes. That's it. You were able to do that because of your body position. Like this [demonstration]; see if you can do it again."

- Keep it short and sweet. One of the biggest challenges of positive feedback is that we get carried away telling people how great they did because it feels good or because we want them to sense how excited we are so we over-talk it or repeat it. This dilutes our words in ways that our study of fast and focused feedback should make us alert to. And we risk sounding disingenuous when we overpraise. So be fast and sharp, simple and quick, and go easy on the "awesome."

The signal and the noise: Kerr and Curry

Watch "Signal and noise: Kerr and Curry" at www.coachguidetoteaching.com

Stopping to point out success to replicate seems like a kids thing, but it's critical at all levels. You can see Golden State Warriors head coach Steve Kerr do this with Steph Curry in this video . What's happening here is that Curry is struggling. But Kerr wants Curry to be aware of the things he is doing right, so he persists in doing them. In the long run, they will cause Curry and the team to succeed. Athletes at all levels tend to oversteer based on emotional responses that are an inevitable part of playing. I miss a shot, even the right shot, and it shapes my perception of the whole game. Or on the flip side: I take a shot I should not take and it goes in and suddenly I am the guy taking crazy shots from terrible angles. As a coach, you want me to see the long view: if I can get open like that and take the first shot, it's going in eight times out of ten. It's nice that my off-balance shot went in, but I should not be fooled.

Every action is part signal (quality of decision-making or execution) part noise (the randomness of a single situation). One of the most important things a coach can do is to help players attend to the signal and not the noise. *What are the actions that will cause me to be successful over the long run, regardless of the outcome of this single moment?* That's what Kerr does here. He's helping Curry—yes, even Steph Curry—see the signal: when he is on the floor and plays up-tempo, great things that he is not fully aware of (because his experience and perception are more subjective) are happening and will continue to happen. This will help an athlete who takes pride in his play manage the emotions of what feels like an off game and focus on the path forward. That's one more reason why coaches should have a clear game model that is about more than just the scoreboard. Being able to say *This is how we play* (especially when the approach is based on deep understanding of the game) allows you to attend to a steadier signal. Players often resent it when a coach praises an action when they're winning and criticizes the same action when they get behind, and in many cases they're right. It's confusing to play in a system where the only determinant of whether you are doing things right is the scoreboard.

FEEDBACK 301

The long-term goal of giving feedback is to make it less necessary in the future. We want athletes to learn to make strong decisions *without our telling them to*. We want them to understand the game rather than just play it, *even when no coach is there*. We want them to make those around them better through their understanding. The third stage of feedback is about causing players to do the thinking themselves so they develop understanding and autonomy. As a result, it focuses heavily on asking questions.

Asking the right questions can cause players to come up with their own answers, and can make sure that their brains are "on" whenever they set foot on the pitch, field, court or rink. But asking questions as a coach is one of the hardest things to get right. What's more, making players think is not as simple as just asking questions of them.

Using questions as a form of feedback—asking rather than telling—can be highly beneficial, but this does not mean they don't have downsides or that they are always the best way to teach. In fact, misusing them—pretending to ask a question when you really just want to tell an athlete to do something a different way, say, or asking rhetorical questions that no one really answers—is one of the fastest ways to cause players to tune questions out and reduce their effectiveness. Questions can also be time consuming. They can result in "crickets" (i.e. no answers at all) or in players guessing, in long-winded answers that slow the pace, in awkwardly way-off-the-mark answers, in poor questions that must be rephrased. This makes them potentially expensive from a time allocation point of view. Choosing the right situation, maintaining awareness of pacing, and most of all ensuring strong question design will all be critical to your success with questions. You're going to give a lot of feedback if you're a coach, for example. Being simple, fast and directive with feedback in one situation might buy you more time to ask open-ended questions the next time. It's not either/or.

The cognitive scientist John Sweller tells us that novices and experts learn differently and suggests teachers consider something called the guidance fading effect. When athletes are novices at something—and that could be newer to the game generally or *newer to the concept they are learning*—their working memory is easily overloaded, and this can cause them to fail to transfer what they learn in long-term memory. Experts process more quickly and in chunks, so their working memory is less easily overloaded. They require more challenge. This means the way we teach novices and experts should be different. "Students," Sweller says, "should initially [i.e. when they are in a more novice state] be given lots of explicit guidance." This might mean fewer questions and more directive

8. Interview in *Teacher* magazine [Australia] 8.5.2019.

feedback. Once students are more knowledgeable, more explicit guidance is less effective and too much of it can even interfere with further development of expertise, so it should gradually be "faded out and replaced by problem-solving,"[8] which would presumably involve more open-ended questions and more constraints-based learning where players try to problem-solve. Generally, then, we should be more directive earlier in the learning process and more interrogative later. First the coach should explain the principles the team is trying to execute in detail via feedback. That's directive. Then she should start to ask players how and why and which possible adaptations to use and when. At the most elite levels, you might expect to see fewer questions and more situations of pure problem-solving where the rules or design of the game—its "constraints"—are designed to shape the problems players encounter.

NOVICE TO EXPERT CONTINUUM

DIRECTIVE FEEDBACK/EXPLICIT GUIDANCE

When we press we need to press together as a unit. It should look like this: [demonstrates]. The midfield line needs to recognise it quickly. Let's play through losing the ball again and try to press better as a unit.

QUESTIONING/GUIDED PROBLEM SOLVING

What needs to improve to make our pressure more effective?

QUESTIONING/GUIDED PROBLEM SOLVING

What are the principles we are following when

QUESTIONING/GUIDED PROBLEM SOLVING

How effective was our press there?

QUESTIONING/GUIDED PROBLEM SOLVING

What do we need to look at to make sure we are in sync when we press?

CONSTRAINTS-BASED

The game is going to cause us to press in various settings. After a few minutes I'm going to ask what we've learned.

NOVICE
NEW TO THE CONCEPT
YOU ARE TEACHING

EXPERT
ELITE LEVEL EXECUTION OF THE
CONCEPT YOU ARE TEACHING

Watch "Pep Guardiola coaching Raheem Sterling" at www.coachguidetoteaching.com

Of course, these are broad trends. Good coaches absolutely still ask rank novices questions—"What could go wrong when we're trying to press?"—and give the most elite experts direct guidance (here's a brilliant video ▶ of Pep Guardiola doing that with Raheem Sterling. This is especially important to consider because while an athlete can be an expert, generally there can still be areas of knowledge where he or she is a novice.

If there is one simple way to improve your questioning on the field, it's probably getting in the habit of planning out important questions in advance. Of course, you may or may not use them exactly as you planned them. But it will make it more likely that you ask high-quality questions about important topics if you're not trying to think of them on the spur of the moment. Nothing wastes time and saps momentum like a poor question for which there is no clear answer.

Emphasize perception

One of the most powerful ways to accelerate the quality of athletes' decision-making is to ask questions that shape their perception. As I discussed in chapter 1, where an athlete's eyes go and what he or she looks at are often the core of strong decision-making. Sometimes, for all intents and purposes, they are the decision. When you don't gather the right information, you make the wrong decision. When we use a phrase like "I see" to mean "I understand," we are closer to the truth than we realize.

The challenges of seeing correctly are multiplied when athletes are required to see quickly. "Decisions" made in less than six-tenths of a second generally happen before the brain can have a conscious thought and require an almost direct coupling of perception and action. Major league hitters read visual cues from the pitcher as he delivers the ball: *Where is his arm channel? How fast are his hips rotating?* The perception—*slider*—becomes the action—*swing*—before the conscious mind can engage. If his eyes aren't attending to arm channel and hip rotation, the decision is going to be poor. Interestingly, however, most hitters appear to have no idea they are doing this.

In a match, you receive a ball under pressure and flick it into the space just beyond a defender before you even realize you've done so. You can do this because you have to have seen a lot of similar situations in the past and you know—unconsciously—where to look for the space to open up. You can read the visual field quickly and instantly react. *You succeed not only because of what you see in that moment but also because of what you have seen and paid attention to over the course of years—the aggregation of a thousand mundane decisions about where to look and what to focus on.*

Some important things to know about perception as a coach:

- What we see is subjective and we fail to see a great deal that is right in front of our eyes.
- Alternatively, we can see something and react to it and not realize that we have seen it.
- We are unaware of the great majority of our own actions and habits regarding perception. We are rarely conscious of where we are looking when we play, for example.
- Surprisingly, experts look at fewer things during performance than novices. In many ways, the definition of their expertise is that they know where to look.
- What we think of as poor decisions are often failures of perception instead.
- Perception for an athlete is heavily visual but not exclusively so; auditory and sensory perception are also relevant.

If expertise is, in many ways, knowing what to pay attention to, using our questions to guide players to know which things to look at, with what purpose and when gives them the tools to gather better information and thus make better decisions. That said, talking about how to train the eyes necessarily includes guesswork: can coaches teach athletes unconscious behaviors by making them conscious? As far as I can tell, no one knows for sure.

Happily, we can now study and understand what elite athletes do with their eyes while they perform. There is a revealing video of Cristiano Ronaldo dribbling up on a defender

Watch "Cristiano Ronaldo vision-tracking" at www.coachguidetoteaching.com

with eye tracking glasses on, for example . The glasses show how his glance scans from the defender's hip to knee to foot to knee. This is his process for reading a defender. There are similar studies showing where shooters in basketball look when releasing the ball. But whether it will work to tell athletes "Look at your opponent's hip, knee and foot" or "Look at the back of the rim" is another question. Possibly we could make athletes better by wiring their looking correctly. Possibly we could make an unconscious process conscious and merely disrupt the brain's systems and slow them down.

I think it's worth trying. If nothing else, the upside is immense. What made almost every elite athlete elite was the happenstance that something or someone in their learning journey caused them to be in the habit of looking in the right place at the right time during all those years of development. Could we take out the happenstance and help all athletes be that lucky? Can we make athletes see more by asking more perception-based questions during training? I think we can.

There are four questions in particular I'd like to propose. I'm sure coaches will come up with more and better on their own.

What do you see?

This question—used during a stoppage or perhaps film study—asks a player to describe the visual field. Since they can't describe everything, they must prioritize, and this tells you what they are conscious of, what seems important to them.

Consider Caleb, a center back, who has failed to drop off his man when a player with the ball attacked in the middle third of the field. You stop and ask him: "Caleb, what do you see?" Perhaps an ideal answer is "There's no pressure on the ball." If you get that answer, your job is easy. Caleb knows what he should be looking for. Now you can reinforce the perception-action coupling: "So what should you do?"

If you ask "Caleb, what do you see?" and get a reply of, "We're out of position," "The midfield isn't helping" or "I don't know," you now know the problem is that Caleb does not understand the cues to read. Now you know you have to help him find the signal. "The important things for a center back to notice in this situation are..." or "Watching his hips to see if he draws back his leg will tell you first that he is striking a longer pass...." Asking "What do you see?" is diagnostic, in other words: it helps you to understand what players think is important in the visual field. It's worth remembering that in many cases, coaches reveal important perceptive cues in their question. As in: "Stewart has space and time and can play forward. What should you do?" A player who can answer this question knows the solution if the coach identifies the problem. This is different from being able to identify the problem himself. To make Caleb truly independent, you must help him to see for himself.

Where should your eyes go? and What should you look at?

These questions also remind Caleb of the importance of looking actively and assess his understanding of what to look at. However, they are more focused than "What do you see?" because they ask him to generalize to specific cues or principles (and are best if we have actually discussed those cues as a team). They also could have multiple answers because Caleb might have to be attending to multiple things. A decent answer to "What should you look at?" might be "The player with the ball and the one I'm marking to see what he does. Also I am scanning to see if any other players are trying to separate me and the other center back." Perhaps that allows me to talk about when or help him be efficient. "Glance quickly to gauge pressure on the ball then you can scan for...".

What will tell you...?

This question is a more explicit effort to discuss cues. You might ask, "What will tell you whether to drop or press?" or "What will tell you how to shape your run?" Answers like "How the defender is facing" or "Whether the second defender is too loose" are signs of a player who has learned to watch the inner game. In many cases, asking these kinds of questions of Caleb is at least as good as asking him, "What should you do?" They start with the eyes and work to the decision. They are most useful when a coach has taught players various preferred options and is asking them to decide which one to use or how to adapt them. On a good team, the principles of play and the game model are shared knowledge. Perception questions ask players to learn how to decide among and adapt them.

There's a flip side of the coin here. If you are thinking about and teaching visual cues, you can also train your players to use them to deceive the opposition. Once you start asking "What will tell you which way to play?" and the answer is "The way the defender is facing," your players know what good opposition will see, and you can train them to exploit that. Your defenders can manipulate cues; your forwards disguise runs to look like they are resting and then suddenly snap into action, pretend to be looking away when in fact they are waiting for the defense's eyes to drift.

JOE
MAZZULLA

Perception, self-awareness and feedback

Joe Mazzulla is an assistant coach with the NBA's Boston Celtics. He believes that the long-term goal of giving feedback is to make it less necessary in the future, so self-awareness, which is yet another key form of perception, is part of almost everything he does. This is relevant even to technical execution. "In a game," he told me, **"the player is going to have to make adjustments to his shot and I can't help him."**

Once the purpose of working together is established, it's important to show athletes what the finished product looks like. My first step is to get as much film as possible. A key here is to find examples that the player will directly relate to. Maybe it is his favorite player or someone that models how he wants to play. It is important to find film of times when a player should have used the move we are introducing. *Here are four or five examples of where a player could have used this move.* That's why we want to work on this move. That will increase awareness and attention. Once we've watched the film, finding a key word or phrase to name it is next. It allows me to quickly apply it to a drill and shorten feedback.

If I want to be more technical, I might take video of some of the best shooters and say: *Here's how they keep their guide hand straight and do not turn it on release of the shot.* It's important to build awareness of what to pay attention to in trying to develop oneself.

I often first tell a player, We are not worried about makes or misses or results. *We are worried about making sure your guide hand stays straight towards the basket through your shot progression.*

I also try to help them know how to self-assess. In one case, I tied a ping-pong paddle to a player's guide hand to make sure it stayed straight. Then I said: *Here is the feedback the ping pong paddle will give. If you keep your hand straight, you will not see the inside of the paddle. If you see the inside of the paddle, you did not execute our objective.* I wanted him to know what to look for even with that constraint. The goal is always to grow self-awareness. He has to know what he did and what he needs to adjust for the next shot.

I try to help players understand the feedback they will see. I say, "Your feedback will come from your misses." If we're talking about hand placement, I might say, "A miss right or left means your hand was not on the middle of the ball. A long or short miss is acceptable right now as long as it is straight. Yes, we want to make every shot, but let's manage our misses by eliminating the right and left and shooting every shot straight." Or with follow-through: "If your misses quickly hit the ground and leave the painted area, your shots have a low trajectory. If your misses go straight up and bounce around the painted area, they have a good trajectory." Players have to understand that idea: "Your feedback will come from your misses."

I often use the idea of binary feedback to help hone self-awareness. *Now that we have the concept of your shot, we are just going to shoot. I will say yes or no. "Yes" and "no" do not refer to a make or a miss. Whether the shot goes in or not does not matter. "Yes" means all mechanics were correct. "No" means they weren't. Let's shoot ten "yes" from each spot.*

I also give him space to self-correct, which I think speeds teaching and development. By the end, I want him to spot it for himself. Sometimes I'll do something called "feel-good shooting." I say, "Take as many as you want from each spot, building awareness of what perfect form feels like for you. Once you are comfortable, move to the next spot."

Finally, I try to film constantly. At the end, I want to have substantial film of the player performing the skill, making the right read and executing the skill in a game-like situation so they can see it. It is also a great time to circle back and make an edit combining the player's clips with the initial player that we were studying so they can see the similarities.

Showing the problem

Recently I watched a training session at an MLS academy with a group of coaches taking a high-level license course. The goal of the session was to *create and exploit numerical advantages*, a topic that required sophisticated decision-making. Players were directed to try to create overloads but they weren't doing so successfully, and every so often the coach would gather them in a circle and ask a question like, "How did we do there?" But what "there" meant was unclear. Which moment or moments from the previous four or five minutes of play was he referring to? Even if the coach was able to clearly identify a moment and cause everyone to remember it reliably, they would all remember it from a different perspective and with different levels of accuracy and objectivity. Christian might have failed to spot an opportunity when Claudio was in space and the opposition might have been unbalanced, but in retrospect it was all but impossible to describe to Christian what he had failed to perceive.

What was missing? What needed to happen for group problem-solving to work? In most cases, feedback that begins, "Christian, a few minutes ago you had the ball and Claudio was to your right, in a channel between the midfielders, and…" might as well start, "Christian, I had a dream that you had the ball and…" They are both about equally useful to Christian.

The important thing that must be present to help players problem-solve is the problem itself. The details matter. If you want to solve a problem, it has to be clearly visible—to everyone and in the same way so they can understand it and analyze it. So, the most important thing a coach who wants to teach problem-solving can do in training is to recreate the situation he or she is discussing so players can see it. This becomes even more important as we begin to understand the critical role of perception. It's hard to make good use of perception-based questions, for example, if we don't have a specific situation to perceive. But if a coach can pause in the moment and recreate the scene, Christian with the ball and Claudio in the channel, suddenly the coach can say, "Christian, what do you see?" and everything is different. Now there can be a real conversation about the why and when of decisions.

Showing the problem also helps reinforce player accountability and precision. Let's say Jose has the ball under pressure and his midfield partners Dylan and Sal are in poor supporting positions. Jose is on an island. He loses the ball and the counter is on. This is an ongoing issue for Dylan and Sal. They allow themselves to be hidden too frequently and don't provide effective support. "Pause," you say. "When Jose had the ball there, where were his midfield partners in terms of support?"

"I was open," says Dylan, though in fact he was hidden behind a defender. From a teaching perspective, you are now stuck. He remembers—or chooses to remember—differently. Stuck, that is, unless you have recreated the situation. This will help him see that his movement leaves something to be desired. You could then ask, "Jose, can you get Dylan the ball?" or "Dylan, how would Jose get the ball to you where you are standing now?" In this way, showing the problem helps with accountability as much as perception—Dylan cannot convince himself he was better positioned than he was.

Unlike Dylan, Sal is not defensive. He wants to know what to do. But telling him, "You gotta get out from behind the defender" is pretty abstract. How? To where exactly? It will help him more if you can show him where and how to decide. The key to making progress with both players is to recreate the scene. *Jose was here. Defenders were here. You were here, Sal. Now let's talk about how we could change the outcome.*

One key to being able to do this is mundane but critical: having a consistent cue that tells your players to stop exactly where they were. For it to work, they will most likely need to be in on the reasons you use it. You'll want to explain that when you say "Pause," they should try to hold their position. Something like: *It's a small but key part of how we'll all get better. We'll make stoppages more useful and faster so we can learn more and play more and be more successful. Stop as quickly as you can. Don't try to cover for yourself and correct your position a little. It's important to look at it exactly as it was.*

So use a simple consistent signal to freeze play and practice the task of responding to the signal a few times to make sure the follow-through is sharp. Give feedback on it to show it's important: "Yes, good. Everyone stopped quickly there. Thank you." Or, "Remember: when you hear the signal, stop right away. We've got to be a little better at that." This might seem mundane, a step that's easily skipped, but taking the time to get this system right will pay you back a hundredfold in time and focus.

There will also be times when, to show the problem, you must recreate a situation that is no longer there. Consider using an idea Steve Freeman, director of Black Watch Premier, uses. "If I have to rebuild it, I make the players do it," Steve told me. "I ask them, 'OK, where'd the ball come from? Where was the second defender? Where was your support?' It forces them to be aware and to watch as they are playing. Otherwise they can't rebuild the scene." One key to being able to use Steve's idea is another theme of this book: shared vocabulary—everyone has to know what first and second defenders are for you to ask where they were. In fact, the whole process of looking at a problem together will be accelerated by shared technical vocabulary. When you say, "Pause, what do you see here?", ideally players will know the concepts you've taught them and answers that describe those concepts will help other players to see and use those ideas: *Esteban is between the lines. We have an overload on the wing.* If the only tactical concept players can describe is that it's helpful to create width when attacking, the discussion will be less replicable.

A final note: the two methods I have just described—asking perception-based questions and showing the problem—work especially well in synergy. There's power in recreating the problem and asking athletes: *What do you see?* This is especially true when trying to get players to look farther away. I had a discussion with the coaching staff of Scotland's national rugby team, who had realized that players often made poor decisions when they did not see things farther away than their immediate field of vision. What looked like the right decision if you only looked at the opposition's forwards was revealed to be less effective than another choice if you looked at their backs. But the backs were 20 yards away and the forwards were 8. Some version of this is true of so many players. What they attend to is what falls within a small circle of light, centered on them and with a radius of 10 or 12 yards. Everything else exists in darkness. One solution that the Scotland Rugby coaches came up with was to respond to an initial answer to "What do you see?" with "Look farther." That is, to socialize players to make a habit of looking farther away. But this only works, of course, if you have recreated the full scene and every player retains their position.

Means of participation

Recently I observed coach James Beeston working with a group of U19 boys. The session focused on up-back-through and James wanted players "locked in": focused, attentive and with a level of mental effort equivalent to the level of their physical effort. After an initial activity in which they spent 15 minutes or so on the basics of the pattern, James questioned his players to assess their initial understanding.

Typically when I watch coaches question athletes, I ask myself where on the "ratio spectrum" (below) they would fall. The term "ratio" refers to the proportion of cognitive work done by the players versus the coach. Understanding it requires defining two types of ratio: "participation ratio" and "think ratio."

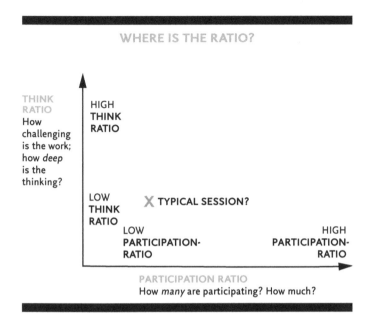

WHERE IS THE RATIO?

THINK RATIO
How challenging is the work; how *deep* is the thinking?

HIGH THINK RATIO

LOW THINK RATIO

X TYPICAL SESSION?

LOW PARTICIPATION-RATIO

HIGH PARTICIPATION-RATIO

PARTICIPATION RATIO
How *many* are participating? How much?

If the great majority of players listening carefully to a question think actively about the answer with the expectation that they might answer and are willing to answer out loud, and this happens throughout the training, then you have a high participation ratio. Everyone is actively thinking all through the session. If players barely offer only a few halfhearted answers, or if just two or three players answer all the questions, if questions hang in the air unanswered, the session has a low participation ratio. Participation ratio is represented by the X-axis in the diagram above.

Think ratio is represented on the Y-axis. If the questions are relevant, challenging, and cause players to apply important concepts, the questioning would have a high think ratio. If players are asked yes or no questions or questions with obvious answers, or if players answer questions with the first idea they come up with without pausing to think, the think ratio would be low.

An ideal session would be on the upper part of the right-hand side of the graph.[9] It would have a high participation ratio and a high think ratio. Unfortunately, I have seen a far larger number of sessions that were closer to the lower left. The coach might pause to ask his players "What do we want to do here?" or "What are our options?" Two or three players—perhaps they are highly verbal and like to talk; perhaps they are pleasers and want to eliminate the awkwardness of a question that might or might not be rhetorical—call out half-thought-through answers. Thank goodness someone said something. But 14 players don't answer and know they're not going to have to. They stand there, gazing into the distance or fooling idly with a ball at their feet, waiting for a chance to play again. They are learning that despite everything their coach says, it's not much of a thinking game after all.

James's session falls into the upper-right-hand corner of the graph. The clip starts with him asking, "On the previous activity, we focused on the up-back-through. What I want you to think about is how you can use this in a game." A typical coach might have simply said, "Who can think of some ways you might use this in the game?" but James wants

9. I originally wrote that it should be as high in the upper-right-hand corner as possible, but there are probably sessions where we actually want players to recall key principles of play very quickly from memory. In those cases, the think ratio might be slightly lower on the Y-axis.

Watch "James Beeston high ratio" at www.coachguidetoteaching.com

players to understand that the first idea that comes to them is not always the best. He says: "Turn and talk with your partner. I'll give you 30 seconds and then I'm going to be looking for answers." Suddenly the circle of players crackles to life. Every single player is answering the question, in part because James's phrase "I'll be looking for answers" is a subtle cue that he'll be cold calling—asking a player to answer the question regardless of whether he volunteers. They have to be ready.

As the turn and talk ends, no one has had time to raise a hand before James looks at Matteo (#22) and asks what he discussed. It's the first of several cold calls. The tone isn't harsh. James has given players time to think and now, in a thoughtful way, he is both asking for their ideas and holding them accountable for thinking.

Matteo answers. "Midfielders can play up to strikers, back to the midfielder and through to another forward player." It's an acceptable answer, if not especially specific or tactical, and Matteo doesn't talk about why and when. So James keeps going. "What else?" he asks. If you look carefully, you can see that another player, Quinn, has raised his hand. James calls on him. He describes how a forward player can use the pattern to pull a defender forward, then play back quickly and get into the space vacated by the defender. The fact that Quinn has raised his hand is important. Hand raising is an established signal—familiar to the classroom but rare to the training ground—that does three important things:

1. It allows James to regulate the speed at which players answer, which would not happen if Quinn simply called out his answer. As a result, James can slow thinking down and cause the team to be more thoughtful. The first answer off the top of a player's head is rarely the best answer, but it is surely the one most often heard in training. A coach must be able to cause players to hold their answers or he cannot socialize deeper thinking.

2. It allows James to distribute opportunity or responsibility across the team so it's not the same players answering over and over. James can choose among hand raisers or choose players who are not hand raisers and cold call. Perhaps James wants to hear from his central midfielder on this question. Perhaps he has a player whose first language isn't English and who needs a bit more time to formulate the words in his second language. Constraining the impulsive answers means he can route opportunities to these players as well. When answers are habitually called out, the same few players will race to answer. Both think ratio and participation ratio on the whole will be low.

3. It allows players—potentially more of them than can actually answer any question due to time constraints—to indicate their desire to participate and to signal they think they know. A sea of energetic hands helps build positive culture, but more importantly the number of hands is a form of data: only one or two suggests players may not understand the concept well.

Quinn's answer is strong but it also suggests a possible problem: players who volunteer to answer commonly understand more than players who do not—that's why they raise their hands. This means that hearing only from players who volunteer can give you a false positive. A coach might hear Quinn's answer and think *Oh, great, they already get how to use this idea to draw a defender out of a compact space*, but in fact "they" as a whole don't know this. Quinn does. Is he typical or an outlier in his understanding?

James's next move helps to answer that question. He cold calls again: "What else? Garrett?" James is getting better data on the team than if he relied on volunteers, which would give him an inaccurate sample of player knowledge. Calling on Garrett here is a sort of sample taking: what does the average player think right now?

His cold call of Garrett is also slightly different from the one he used with Matteo in that it is a "follow-on" and requires Garrett to have listened carefully to the two previous answers so as not to repeat them. In using a follow-on, James is showing that listening is at least as important as talking. It is the foundation of a thinking culture. As he continues to build a culture in further sessions, he might use follow-ons that stress listening even more, such as: "Garrett, develop that..." or perhaps "Garrett, say more about what we'd need to do technically if we wanted to draw a defender out like Quinn is suggesting."

Notice the rest of the players as Garrett is talking. They're locked in. They look at him. They're not playing with a soccer ball or talking about *American Idol*. Impressively this video is from James's first session with this team. We're 25 minutes in and they've gotten the message pretty quickly about what it means to participate mentally when James is coaching.

James now shifts his questions to technical rather than tactical aspects of the up-back-through. One of his major teaching points in the activity was to have players vary the weight of their passes, and he wants to make sure they understood that. He asks: "What about the movement and the pass needs to be good for this to happen? Caden?" Another cold call. Caden describes the need for a strong pass forward into the feet of the first player and a softer lay-off pass. This is what James discussed in the session—a good sign. But notice that Caden also adds, "to make that defender bite." He is applying what he knows to Quinn's observation. The listening and thinking are already paying dividends.

James persists in his questioning, seeking to know more about what his players understand and to build expectations for mental engagement. "Keegan, what else?" he asks. Another follow-on cold call. Keegan had to be listening to his teammates to answer. There's no other way to answer a question like "What else?" When Keegan finishes, James, armed with a clearer sense of what players understand and where they need more detail, is ready to move on. It's worth noticing the energy level as James wraps up. His questioning has been fast and engaging with no awkward standing around waiting or hoping for someone to answer. Athletes may be resting physically but they're not resting mentally. The energy level remains high.

This is what the upper-right-hand corner of the ratio diagram looks like. When James asks a question, everybody answers it, either aloud or in their heads because they know they have to be ready to talk about it. They feel accountable in a positive way. Players answer thoughtfully. They don't rush and they are listening and thinking throughout. Compare this to sessions where questions are met with silence or mumbled answers from a handful of players. Coaches often respond to lack of energy and engagement from players by simplifying their questions, sometimes to the point of redundancy: *Should the second pass be harder or softer?* This compounds the problem. The questions hang awkwardly in the air until the coach answers his own question or a player mumbles something to break the awkwardness. Every question becomes rhetorical. No one wants to answer a question when the answer is obvious.

Coaches who want to emphasize thinking in their teaching should be able to use wait time, so players share the best answer, not the first one. They should be able to cold call—asking any player to answer at any time and steering questions to relevant players. They should be able to cause players to practice talking to one another as they will during the game. If they do this, they can build an intellectual culture where players think as dynamically as they run. But to do this, they must communicate expectations and turn them into routines. *When coaches leave the means of participation to chance, it will invariably result in low levels of mental engagement asymmetrically distributed among players.*

James accomplishes a high level of mental engagement by communicating the procedures for participating in questioning and discussion to the team in advance. Most coaches (and most teachers) don't think to do this. They never explain to athletes or students how they should participate. The means of participation—who is supposed to answer the question and how—remains unclear or ambiguous. But James gave a short "roll-out speech" at the beginning of his session so the expectations are transparent. You can see the video of it here. This transcript can help you see how clearly he explains not only what they should do but why they should do it:

Watch "James Beeston roll-out speech" at www.coachguidetoteaching.com

> The main thing from tonight's session … It's going to require intensity from both a physical and a mental standpoint. I'm going to be asking you questions throughout—just to check for understanding. Don't shout out the answer. That's a big important thing because I want you to think about the answers that you're giving. If you know the answer and I go like that [raises hand], raise your hand. If you don't know the answer, that's OK. We'll work through it; we'll problem-solve together. Sometimes I might call on you guys even if your hand isn't raised, OK, because the game requires you to be switched on at all times, so I am going to be calling on guys at times to make sure the focus is still there, alright, so we're locked in from the first minute to the last minute.

This "roll out" takes James about 45 seconds. He makes sure players are looking at him and can see him. He explains what he's going to do and why (*the game requires you to be switched on at all times*). He sets his standards high but he also makes it safe to struggle (*We'll work through it; we'll problem-solve together*). When you multiply the benefits of the level of engagement James achieves by hundreds of interactions over the course of a season, this might be the most valuable 45 seconds a coach could spend. It crafts the culture of the mental side of practice as carefully as the physical. And he immediately begins practicing what he preaches so players understand that he means it because they start building the habit right away. His approach will be part of how they roll. Is it worth mentioning that the best question in the world is still not productive if nobody answers it? And honestly, the team is happy about James's approach. Nobody enjoys being bored. It's harder work, but it's more interesting and engaging for them.

Watch "Steve Freeman questioning" at www.coachguidetoteaching.com

Before I end this section, one last video: this one of Black Watch Premier DOC Steve Freeman using similar tools to those we saw James using. Notice that Steve causes players to work in functional groups (defense and offense) to discuss an exercise. He is simulating the kind of communication they will need during matches with the players they will have to communicate with. Coaches who want players to communicate during competition and to work together effectively should ask them to practice it during training. There's no reason to think they'll be good at it if they have to figure it out during the intensity of competition. They are just likely to shout, argue or ignore one another. Steve's approach gives them practice talking through challenges in training. Like any other form of discussion, it would be easy to have this disrupt your pacing and take too much time away from training, so it's important to notice how carefully Steve manages time and builds in many of the accountability systems James uses.

MARC MANNELLA

"They need to think if they're going to learn"

In chapter 2, Marc Mannella described the experiences of a minor league baseball manager who aimed to teach both reactive and proactive sessions. The system worked on the idea that meetings would be shorter because they would be more active, intense and cognitively demanding. "The guys need to think if they're going to learn," you may recall him saying. Here, Marc describes how the manager used many of the tools in this section to achieve that higher level of involvement.

The manager sets up his team's meetings, both those he runs directly and those led by his pitching and hitting coaches, to maximize the ratio. They're highly interactive, and look more like a classroom from a high-performing school than what one would expect in a professional baseball clubhouse.

He uses several variants of the cold call technique, from the traditional ("Looking at this video, would you say we are aligned correctly here or no? Jose, what do you think?") to a less traditional "warm call," ("Tyler, I'm calling on you on this next play so get ready…"). Players also engage frequently via quick turn and talks, and in longer small group discussions. Once he included 20 seconds of silent reflection before the turn and talk began.

Another one of his favorite moves is a technique called "Show Me" in which a player is asked to demonstrate physically what he is describing verbally. A player might say, "I'm trying to lower my arm channel" or "I think I got a little lower in my stance," and the manager would just say "Show me what that looks like" and the player would get up and do the thing he was describing. The manager might then cold call someone else to observe: "What do you think of his stance, Carlos?" It's definitely accelerated the learning. In fact, he says "show me" so often that it's become a bit of a thing. He ended up having "Show Me" T-shirts printed for the team.

One outcome you might not expect from his approach is how little he and his coaches talk in a typical meeting compared to how much the players talk. It's a bit ironic. They are more "in charge"—there's much clearer accountability than on most teams; the things they want to talk about get real focus—but this allows them to let the players own the conversation much more. The thing that makes it so effective is that he uses these moves so consistently. It's totally predictable. The players walk into the room with their minds on, ready to be engaged. They know no one is going to be going to be sitting, arms folded, leaned back against the lockers. Players come in alert and ready and are more attentive even before he's asked a single question.

You can probably see why it's so critical to have someone explain to new players how it's going to work before their first meeting, so at the start of the season he gets everyone together and explains how different his meetings will look and feel and why. He just makes it transparent. And since minor league baseball experiences a lot of roster turnover during a season, he makes sure new players get a personalized version of the same speech. If guys don't show up to these meetings ready to work (cognitively speaking), they will be in for a big surprise.

By the way, his work is doubly impressive because almost half of his roster is composed of native Spanish speakers. He's an English speaker, but he worked hard to learn enough Spanish to be able to ask the majority of his questions in two languages. The message he was sending was that he cared about everyone's progress; he would engage everyone.

Intentional questioning: I frequently hear coaches advised to "ask more questions" without much further guidance. What kind of questions? When? If a session plan says, "I'll use questioning here," it's probably incomplete. Questions for what purpose? Yes, we want players to think. Yes, questioning can make them do that. But what do we want them to think *about*? A question is a means, not an end.

One implicit purpose of questioning is to engage players mentally, to make them active participants in training. But as everyone who's tried it knows, that's easier said than done. Just asking questions does not guarantee the sort of involvement James Beeston gets. Questions can hang unanswered in the air, or annoy athletes because the answer is patently obvious. If a question is unclear or vague, it can slow the pace of training so much that, even if useful thinking occurs, it takes so long and disrupts the flow so much that it's still a net loss.

Questions that get athletes to think in useful ways without wasting time require technique and planning.

First, some "phrasing fundamentals": general principles to make sure questions engage athletes and get them thinking. Then I'll discuss some types of questions to help answer the question "Think about *what*?"

Phrasing fundamentals

Avoid the obvious trap. A significant number of the questions that athletes are asked are either rhetorical—the coach doesn't really expect an answer—or, worse, so obvious that they *seem* rhetorical. Questions with obvious answers are killers of intellectual culture. They pretend to ask a question but there's no real question. Over time, this undercuts the credibility of questions more broadly. *Why are we doing this?*, players implicitly ask. And when everyone clearly knows the answer, the person who says it aloud anyway appears to be clueless or a suck-up. Athletes are reluctant to answer under those circumstances and those who do lose credibility. If you're asked to do that enough, you become skeptical of the questioner.

Yes or no questions are especially vulnerable to the obvious trap. Consider a coach who pauses his U15 players with the ball in the possession of a central midfielder and asks,

"Should we continue to play centrally?" I haven't provided enough context about the play to indicate whether the answer should be yes or no, but attentive readers, like all of the players present, know the answer already. Would you stop a session to ask, "Should we continue to play centrally?" if the answer was yes?

Even if it weren't already obvious, the word "continue" seals the deal. Why add that unless the answer were no? And even if it wasn't obvious, yes/no questions yield one-word answers. It's hard to start a conversation based on that. So avoiding the yes/no framing is a good first step: "Where do we want to play from this situation?", "What tells us where we should play?" or even "What principle of play can tell us what to do here?" will probably be more productive.

Yes or no questions are also problematic because they are especially prone to "tipping," which occurs when the questioner inflects a word to suggest the answer. A bit of emphasis on "continue" in "Should we *continue* to play centrally here?" and the answer is doubly redundant. But tipping can undercut other questions too. "Should we play centrally or wide here?" is a bit better than "Should we continue to play centrally here?", but a bit of emphasis on the word "wide" ("Should we play centrally or wide here?") and we're back to obvious. The question could be about bocce, but with the right voice inflection from the coach, I know the right response.

One reason this may happen is because a coach is trying to ask a question when he really just wants to give advice. Appearing to ask a question when you want to tell an athlete what to do wastes time and builds a culture where questions don't feel engaging and authentic but rather insipid. It's hard to build intellectual engagement from that kind of experience. Make questions better by asking them only when you need them and, since phrasing matters, jot down some good questions you might use before the session starts. Your phrasing will be stronger, and even if you adapt or change them, the time you spent reflecting in advance will make them clearer than if you'd tried to think of them on the spot.

Types of questions

If one of the goals of questioning is to more actively involve athletes in the mental side of the game, it's beneficial to think about *how* we want them involved. After all, different types of questions can encourage different types of thinking and generate different types of information.

I'm going to describe five purposes for the questions a coach asks. Are there good questions that do something different? Absolutely. Does every question have to fall neatly into one of these categories? Probably not, but it's likely that most good questions do one of these things. Further, most coaches (like most athletes) have tendencies—things they are most likely to do that are often beneficial but can also cause them to miss opportunities to make athletes think in alternative ways. Coaches benefit from having a full repertoire of moves. Categorizing them can help you to be more aware of types you don't use as naturally and therefore achieve a more ideal balance.

Discovery questions: One purpose of questions is to cause people to discover new solutions to problems: *What could we do to deal better with their pressing? What else could Carlo do in receiving the ball to ensure that he doesn't lose it?* The idea behind "discovery questions" is that learners will remember and believe in solutions better when they have discovered them for themselves, and that the process of discovering things will cause them to play with a mind always attuned to new learning. Those are worthwhile outcomes. However, some coaches think of discovery as the single purpose for asking questions and sometimes even refer to the process of asking questions as "discovery learning." While questions designed to allow players to discover new concepts are valuable, it is helpful to consider the limitations and alternatives. One limitation is that discovering things through experience is something experts do better than novices because an athlete's ability to do so correlates to his or her degree of prior knowledge (and working memory available to consider new solutions). This means that it can be an inefficient teaching tool for players who don't have strong knowledge about the game. If asked discovery questions, novices will be more likely to give poor answers, which are time-consuming to respond to and can cause players to tune out instead of tuning in. Having athletes give too many poor answers also risks players remembering them. Research suggests that when "wrong" answers are given in the classroom, students often remember the wrong answers as much as the right answers and confuse one for the other. Weaker students are more likely to do this than stronger students. This doesn't mean discovery can't still be valuable for novices, just that without strong background knowledge and with less experience to perceive the key variables accurately, novices may learn inefficiently this way.

Another limitation of discovery learning is that the range of solutions players come up with may be broader than is productive. We tend to think of innovation as something that is always positive, but it's not quite that simple. Everyone arriving at their own unique answer on what to do when faced with pressing is not ideal when we all want to respond to pressing in a coordinated way. In team endeavors, there are times when we want solutions to be predictable and reliable (i.e. less innovative) and situations when we want narrow innovation (e.g. an unexpected way of getting the ball into the space in front of the #8), so it is worth thinking about other forms of problem-solving we can encourage players to use in addition to discovering new solutions.

Application questions: Questions that ask players to wrestle with how to implement a solution they already know—"application questions"—also involve a surprising amount of critical thinking and problem-solving. The problem-solving implicit in implementing a solution once you know what it is can be easy to overlook. Even if I know what I want to do—break down a low block, say—it is still not easy to do, especially against quality opposition. In fact, it's usually a lot harder to figure out *how* to make the answer come about than to figure out *what* the answer should be. Questions that ask players how to accomplish a solution, rather than what the solution should be, are especially useful in improving play—doubly so when I want players to be able to coordinate and execute principles of play or aspects of a game model as a team. That might sound like: *We know we want to play wide here. What will we have to do to get there? Or We know we've got to get into the passing lanes here, so let's use some of the things we know about our movement off the ball to do that.* Application questions have much of the rigor of discovery questions—I suppose they are discovery questions, just framed more narrowly—but they also have the advantage of working well within a game model. U18 players in a professional academy are probably expected to figure out how to make the established principles come about under challenging conditions. *What we should do* is determined by the coach's philosophy. How we're going to get that done is the player's challenge.

Perception-based questions: As we discussed earlier, there is an unbreakable link between perception and action, one that often skips the conscious intellect and that requires players to instinctively know where to look to make the right decisions. Asking "perception-based questions" that guide players' eyes is critical if we want better decisions. *Where should your eyes go? What do you see? What should we look for?* These are often as important as—and synonymous with—*What should we do?* and *Why should we do it?* Since this was covered at length earlier, I just offer a reminder here that it is a critical category of question.

Check for understanding questions: A massive gap exists between what you have taught players and what they have learned—always, inevitably. This is the topic of chapter 4 of this book, but I note here that "check for understanding questions," those used to determine what concepts players know and where the gaps in their understanding may be, allow us to find and address misunderstandings quickly. Ask: *What do we want to do here? What's our goal in this situation? What did we say our opponents were likely to do when we have the ball in this situation?* Especially when you are sure you have already been clear. The answers you get may surprise you.

Knowledge-building questions: Given the importance of background knowledge to critical thinking and durability of learning, it's worth asking questions with the purpose of encoding key knowledge in long-term memory through retrieval practice: *What do we call this? What are our principles of play when defending in our own third? How do we want to receive a ball in open play [side on] and why?* This helps to speed athletes' access to concepts in their memory and use them as a foundation for critical thinking. Because of the simplicity of these questions, asking players to recall concepts or terminology may seem mundane, but they are important and, happily, easy to ask in lots of places and settings (e.g. before the game, on a bus ride home, on the sidelines).

Here are brief examples of the five types again; the categories are imperfect. Retrieval practice is designed to build memory but also allows you to check for understanding. The line between discovery and application is often blurry. A question could easily be both. And questions can be combined in quick succession: *1) What are we trying to do? [Check for understanding]; 2) OK, how can we do that here?* [Application].

You might ask then, why categorize? Categorization is useful when and if it helps you to be intentional about questioning, to ask why you are doing it and then design questions that help you accomplish that task. Every coach—and every teacher—has been undone by a time when he or she asked questions that just didn't work. One common reason for that is lack of clarity about why you're asking. If the purpose is merely to "use questioning," the bar isn't very high and your questions just won't be that good. If you know what you're trying to accomplish, you can evaluate your questions more rigorously. If you pursue a variety of purposes with your questions, you will ideally help athletes to think in a range of ways, and that perhaps leads to the bottom line on question types: the point is not to use the one that's "best" but to see that all five are useful and find times to use them all.

- Discovery—*What are some solutions? How can we solve this?*
- Application—*How can we accomplish what we are trying to do? Which option is probably best?*
- Perception-based—*What should you look for here? What do you see?*

- Check for understanding—*What should we/you do here? What is our goal right now?*
- Knowledge-building—*What are our keys to effective pressing? What's the first thing we do when we lose the ball?*

Data-driven questioning

During a recent training session, Kika Toulouse, a coach and coach educator with the New York Red Bulls, presented a group of players with feedback. She had been coaching players to use weak-side runs to unbalance the opposition, and told players that they were going to play uninterrupted for a few minutes, during which time, she said, "You might notice me taking notes."

"I'm going to be tracking your weak-side runs, both whether we are making them in the first place and also whether we can take advantage of them and get some points," she told them. She'd track the number of times they created scoring opportunities and the number of times they scored. They played; she tracked data. Then she paused them.

"Who do you think won?" she asked. The black team had: 5-3. But not only did Black win, she said, "they were also more efficient with their weak-side runs. I counted six opportunities and you got points on five out of those six." Now for the kicker: "Orange, you had seven opportunities. You guys were actually creating more chances. But you only capitalized on three of them. So," she asked, "why do you think we weren't able to capitalize more?" A discussion ensued in which players made sense of the data: they'd had opportunities; they'd missed them; they were playing with their heads down, always back into pressure.

Presenting athletes with a data set collected as they play is powerful. It provides objective information they can analyze. Instead of relying on the coach's opinion—"We're playing with our heads down and failing to see backside runs"—they players receive objective feedback. The coach is no longer the judge—the problem has established itself. Now she's a source of solutions and guidance.

The idea of tracking data on athletes' success at executing ideas will come up again in chapter 4, but as Kika showed, it can be a powerful way to make conversations more objective. What gets measured gets managed, the saying goes. By tracking new forms of data, Kika allowed her players to take more into consideration than just goals. And of course, it's easy to ask questions like *What solutions can we come up with?* or *How can we better find weak-side runners?* when you start with a data set like Kika's. Data almost always supports better questioning.

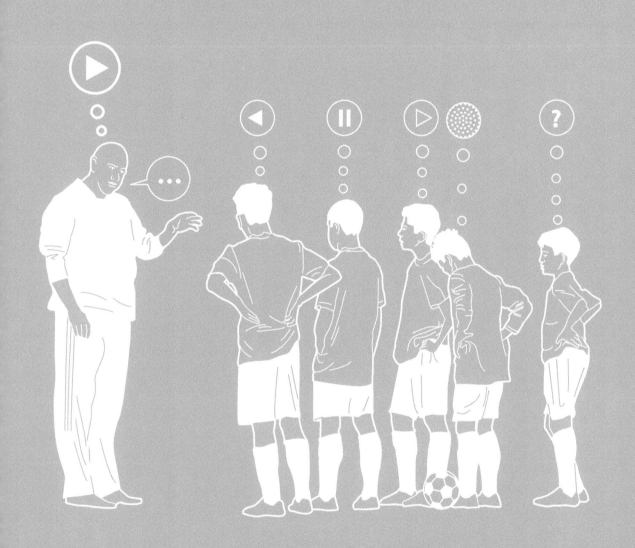

CHAPTER 4

CHECKING FOR UNDERSTANDING

"While the teacher is trying to
… discover what isn't working,
the student is in some way
trying to elude discovery,
disguising weaknesses in order
to seem better than she is."

Jeremy Denk[1]

1. www.bit.ly/33zQjQX

John Wooden was among the greatest coaches of the 20th century. No doubt he was among the winningest, but he remains among the most admired and most quoted, too. Wooden's stories, aphorisms and principles are often afforded nearly canonical status and retold like parables from the gospel:

- The story of how he began the UCLA season by instructing his players in how to put on their socks reveals that we should begin at the beginning—and perhaps that the beginning starts earlier than we think.

- The tale of his response to Bill Walton's announcement that he didn't want to cut his hair in accordance with team rules—Wooden praised Walton for standing up for his convictions before adding, "and we're sure going to miss you around here, Bill"—reminds us that the test of our principles is whether we apply them to our best players and when they result in our losing games.

Perhaps because he was a teacher before he became a coach, his wisdom about the teaching side of the craft is practical, wise and so far, mostly, timeless. Of all his adages and sayings, the one I find most useful is his definition of teaching (and coaching). Teaching, he said, is knowing the difference between "I taught it" and "They learned it." No matter the setting, bridging the gap between those two ideas is at the core of what teachers do and often the greatest challenge of the job. Certainly it is in coaching sports.

Any teacher seeks to present a concept for study as well as she can—clearly and memorably so that as many students as possible understand as much of it as possible—but no matter how good the initial instruction, learning will break down. Gaps will emerge. Often our first response is to try to establish whose fault that is, but mostly it is what happens when people try to teach and learn things, especially when they try to teach and learn things that are challenging and complex. Quite possibly the greatest insight from Wooden's adage is its calm presumption that the gap is inevitable. It is not a question of whether it exists but how we deal with it. *Teaching, he proposed, is not eliminating the gap; it is understanding it.* It is the coach's job not to offer a perfect initial explanation but to seek out and anticipate the ways athletes will struggle. To be a great coach is not just to have a deep knowledge of the zone press, not just to be able to translate it to players, but to see what goes wrong as they try to learn it. This process is called checking for understanding and is as challenging to master as it is important. Among other things, it requires coaches to shift how they prepare to teach and even how they observe when athletes are training.

THE TRIALS OF LOOKING

In chapter 1, I discussed the critical role perception plays in decision-making for athletes. To perceive well is not only necessary to good decision-making; in many cases, the line between perception and decision blurs. An athlete reads the first incipient cues that suggest how her opponent will move and is already acting on them in real time. We call it anticipation; it is as if she knows what her opponent might do—and so she succeeds. Or, alternatively, her eyes are elsewhere when the critical information—*They are pressing!*—emerges, and so she fails to react. The perception and the decision are hard to separate. Athletes can be lucky once or twice, but in the long run, their decisions can never be better than their capacity to see and understand what is happening around them.

It is the same for coaches. A coach's ability to teach and develop athletes is limited by his or her ability to perceive what they are doing during training—a task that is far from simple. We presume that seeing is all but mechanical—you direct your eyes toward an event and become aware of what is happening—but in fact this couldn't be farther from the truth. Seeing is technical, challenging, and subjective—a skill, you might argue; certainly a cognitive process far more than a physiological one. Though it is rarely acknowledged, the ability to see accurately is a coach's first skill.

Here's a tiny example of what I mean: a stoppage at a recent training led by a very good young coach. He was using passing patterns to familiarize his players with common movements in buildup play and he noticed that girls were often static when waiting to receive a pass. He paused them briefly and, standing next to a central midfielder, said, "Girls, when you see the outside back receiving the ball, you know that you are going to be one of her primary options, so you don't just have to be *ready* to receive the ball, you have to create separation so that you make an opportunity. That means a movement like this [he demonstrated checking away] to take your defender away—and then come back to the ball. As we work on these patterns, I want to see you making movements like that. Every time. Check away, then come back for the ball. Go!"

By the basic rules of feedback (see chapter 3), his feedback was strong. He explained one idea, demonstrated and described the solution clearly and quickly, then gave athletes a chance to try it right away. But he failed to do something so simple that most coaches don't even realize when they fail to do it. He failed to observe. He positioned himself well afterwards to watch for their follow-through, he looked at the girls cycling through the patterns, but after he said "go," eight out of the next ten girls receiving the ball failed to make a movement like the one he had described, and somehow he did not notice. Perhaps he simply assumed they were doing it and was only half-looking. Perhaps he was thinking about his next coaching point. But for whatever reason, he was looking but not seeing, poor execution went on without correction, and his next stoppage addressed a new detail.

He had taught it, but they had not learned it. Or even done it, really, and it's not hard to imagine a Saturday, not too far down the road, where at half time he would say with some urgency, and perhaps even frustration, edging into his voice, "Girls, we're static. We've talked about using our movements to create space to receive. We've got to be creating space." In that moment, he will be describing John Wooden's gap to them: *Girls I taught you how to create space, but you have not learned it.*

There are a wide range of reasons why athletes would not be able to execute something they did in practice in a game, and I try to discuss many of them elsewhere in this book. There could have been insufficient variation and spacing of retrieval practice so that athletes forgot what they did in training on game day. The training environment might have never progressed to a complex enough setting to prepare athletes to execute under performance conditions. Athletes might have failed to read perceptive cues telling them it was the right time to execute a skill they knew how to do. But in this example, I am describing something much simpler: the perils of observation. A coach asks players to do something, athletes fail to do it, right then and there, and the coach fails to see it.

To remediate the learning gap, the coach might have said something like "Girls, I didn't see the sorts of movement we discussed there. Let's try again." Perhaps he might have added, "I'll watch ten of you now and shout 'Yes' or 'No' to show whether I see a movement away and back." Perhaps he might have said, "Girls, we're struggling to make those movements and I suspect it's because we're trying to make them too late. Try to start them a little earlier and see if that helps." Perhaps something else. *But a coach can only respond to errors that he sees*. First you have to perceive the error, and surprisingly, that is the step where the process breaks down far more often than almost anyone would suspect.

In fact, if there is one thing I can offer in this chapter to help you teach better, it is to urge you to resist the temptation to judge this coach. Some version of this story has undoubtedly played out in one of your recent trainings, whether you coach seven-year-olds or professional athletes, whether you are a new coach or an established and respected veteran. There is a part of you that does not believe this, but *I am 100% certain it is true*. This is the remarkable part of the story. With some regularity, the athletes you train simply do not do what you have asked them to do, and you fail to see it. If someone showed you a video afterwards, they could easily point it out to you. *You asked for the combination to end with crosses on the ground. Count the number of crosses on the ground*. Or, *You asked them to practice using both feet. Count how many times they use their left foot*. What was hidden in the moment you were coaching would now be obvious. Players were not striking crosses on the ground. Almost nobody used their left foot. You fail to see what was right in front of you, therefore you fail to understand your athletes and their struggle to learn. We all do this. We are all, with some frequency, the coach I have just described. The only question is whether we will have the humility to accept this. Only then can we take steps to change it.

Science tells us that we see only a fraction of what's right before our eyes, and there are a variety of reasons for this. One is attention. We miss things because we're not concentrating on looking. We're looking passively. Observing carefully to see what 16 athletes are actually doing during a complex activity is hard work, and the brain is designed to only work hard when it must, when we force it to. What's more, "observing" doesn't feel like coaching, so we may be unlikely to focus on making the effort it requires if we don't see it as a critical task. Much of the time we should be observing intensely, we feel like we should be saying something or at least setting up some cones. Instead of really looking, we're thinking about what we're going to say or do next or who's going to start on Saturday. But looking well takes single-minded concentration. We have to see it as a task. We have to force our minds to do it actively.

2. Any cognitive scientist can prove its presence in seconds www.bit.ly/34vvA00

There are technical problems to overcome as well. Your optic nerve connects to the back of your eye in a spot about 15 degrees to the side of your center of vision, for example. There are no receptor cells there. Your cortex receives an incomplete picture of the world around you. To compensate, it fills in the gaps with what it thinks it's likely to have seen in the blind spot. It uses other sources of information—your other eye, what you saw when your eyes looked in the space you cannot see a few moments ago. The brain does this so seamlessly that most people never even know the blind spot is there,[2] but it is shockingly large. We often say that we see the world as we imagine it to be and mean that metaphorically, but it is often literally true as well.

Our perception is subjective and fallible. We just don't want to believe it's true. As Chabris and Simons put it, "We are aware of only a small portion of our visual world at any moment" but "the idea that we can look but not see is flatly incompatible with how we understand our own minds." We can fix the first part only if we fix the second. If we want to be better at developing athletes, we have to take the task of seeing them as they learn far more seriously.

Let's return for a moment to the session where the girls failed to make the checking movement their coach had asked them to make. The technical name for not seeing what is right before our eyes is "inattentional blindness," and one reason why I saw what the coach did not see is that I had been discussing the challenges of observation with a group of coaches just the day before. I walked in the door expecting it to happen. I saw it not because I am especially perceptive—I am as likely as anyone else to miss what is right before my eyes—but because I was prepared, and this, Chabris and Simons tell us, is the key to seeing better. "There is one proven way to eliminate inattentional blindness," they write. "Make the unexpected object or event less unexpected."

Seeing better in the classroom

Watch "Denarius Frazier teaching math" at www.coachguidetoteaching.com

When I work with coaches to help them develop their capacity to see better, I often start with a video of Denarius Frazier teaching math. In the video ▶, Denarius faces a problem similar to what almost every coach faces in training. He has 30 students in his classroom. They are each completing two math problems. There are multiple steps to each problem. It's extremely challenging to assess the progress of so many people at a complex task. But Denarius is a master, so it's worth watching how he approaches the task.

One key observation about how Denarius approaches the task of seeing is that he treats his observations as data and so tracks them in a disciplined way. He is carrying a clipboard and takes notes, for example. Most teachers do not do this. They take "mental notes." But it is unrealistic for a teacher to think he will observe 30 students doing two different problems with four or five steps each and remember everything of importance—or even most of it. What he remembers from a data set that complex will be an accident, and his efforts to remember important things he saw early on will disrupt his ability to watch later. Both observing and remembering require working memory where capacity is sorely limited. One of the tasks is going to lose unless he tracks his observations.

It's the same for a coach. It's beyond the capacity of anyone's working memory to remember general trends, individual strengths and weaknesses, and important details of what they observe over the course of several minutes of a complex activity. Whether you realize it or not, you will be forced to develop habits to compensate, and these will distort your understanding. You will lock in on the first thing you see or allow more recent observations to drive previous ones out of your memory; you will remember only hazy details of the positioning of the supporting players, or merely that they were incorrect, rather than the key crucial details. The human brain struggles to remember a seven-digit phone number. It cannot remember the details of how several players are not opening up quickly enough to create space, that your central midfielder's runs are too deep, that the other tends to play back into pressure and that four or five players (which ones?) need to clean up their first touch when preparing to shift the point of attack. It would be doubly implausible to try to keep that much data in your head and then analyze it to see an unexpected trend, to decide which was the most important topic to bring up now, or to reflect on how best to present and fix the problem. Believing that you can process that much information without tracking it in some organized way is incompatible with an understanding of how the brain works. If your primary approach to watching training is taking mental notes, you're not treating your observations as data and are missing a critical tool that can help your athletes get better faster.

One way to track observational data is to take simple notes—that is, to use a blank sheet and write down what you see. This would solve your working memory problem, so it's valuable. But Denarius does not appear to be writing out sentences and phrases, and this tells us that he is not taking simple notes. He has organized his thinking in advance to prepare himself to observe better. If you watch carefully, you will notice that the most common error among his students has to do with finding the remainder. He spots this right away and so his "stoppage"—the moment when he pauses the lesson and says *Here's something we need to change*—is built around fixing that issue. That seems simple, but it's a big deal. If his feedback consistently addresses the most common and/or most important error in the room— rather than something only that one or two people struggled with—the rate of progress will be multiplied. But look again—at 42 seconds when he spots a student whose remainder is incorrect, for example, he says, "Ooh, check that remainder," but merely makes a tick mark on his clipboard. This tells you that he has already anticipated that this might be a problem and has created a place to note errors with the remainder. In other words, he has thought through the problem in advance and made a list of the mistakes he thought students might make. He uses this list to organize his observation. It helps him remember what to look for and allows him to visualize the data quickly: six tick marks next to the word "remainder" and he knows where to focus his energy.

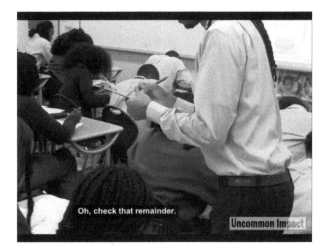

Oh, check that remainder.

Uncommon Impact

But careful observation reveals that there's something else written on Denarius's clipboard as well. Check what he does at 1:12. Explaining to a student why her work is incorrect, he quickly glances at his notes. He does this because he has written out the ideal answer, an exemplar, and it helps him to diagnose what she's done wrong much more quickly and accurately. "Your remainder is off because this value right here is incorrect," he says. He is able to spot the gap between what he sees and the ideal execution because he has a version of the ideal to constantly refer to. He doesn't have to strain to keep all of the information in his working memory. A glance down—it takes about a second—is enough to remind him. With this support, he is able to quickly assess each student in a few seconds, which means he can make it around the room before the time for the task runs out. If it took him ten seconds at every desk, he would never make it around the room. Efficiency is not a sexy word and TED Talkers and philosophers of educators rarely rhapsodize about it. But it's a big deal. Without it, only a few students would get individualized feedback, and Denarius would only gather data on a subset of the class. This is what happens to most teachers. They can't get to everyone. Not everyone feels seen. They are guessing at the experience of half their class. Efficiency matters and Denarius is efficient because he is always comparing the answer he sees to an exemplar. The differences pop quickly; a glance at the ideal response reminds him of what's missing.

ATUL GAWANDE

> Under conditions of complexity, not only are checklists a help, they are required for success.

It would be easy to overlook this step in preparation. Writing out your exemplar might seem like a waste of time, especially if you are an expert in your domain. You might argue that you have it "in your head": *I know what effective midfield play looks like. I don't need to write it out.* But I assure you Denarius knows what division of polynomials should look like. Looking at a list of what needs to happen for students to meet the standard helps him see all of the potential gaps and process information more quickly and accurately. The science writer Atul Gawande has written an entire book about a similar idea: checklists. "Under conditions of complexity," he writes in *The Checklist Manifesto*, "not only are checklists a help, they are required for success." He goes on to describe the fields in which trained professionals—surgeons and engineers, for example—use well-designed checklists to manage their decision-making with profound effect. He describes an effective checklist as being "precise ... efficient, to the point, and easy to use. They provide reminders of ... the most critical and important steps." A good checklist is a form of exemplar, in other words, though other versions of exemplars include more narrative than a mere list. Either way, the purpose is the same: to clearly describe the necessary characteristics of success and make observation for those things disciplined and efficient. Interestingly, Gawande argues that such tools are most valuable in two situations. First, when used during especially complex and sophisticated work. Surgeons and engineers who build massive skyscrapers use them, though they resisted them for years, because experts in particular know much more than they can keep in working memory while observing. The more you know, the more you need to organize what you're looking for. The second situation when checklists and other exemplars are especially valuable is when you want reliable results across a large organization with a lot of autonomy—a soccer club, say. If everyone agrees on what "right" looks like, it can reduce variability in execution while preserving autonomy.

PACE OF PASS
BALL STRUCK ON GROUND
RECEIVE ACROSS BODY
EYES UP

: Pace of pass
Ball struck
ground

COACH

1 Pace of pass.
2 Ball struck on ground
3 Receive across body
4 Eyes up

To put this in athletic terms, let's say you are working on building out of the back. Your session notes include details that you've thought through in a moment of reflection. You now know what to look for:

- Passes:
  - on the ground
  - struck at pace
  - to the front foot of the receiving player
- Open hips and eyes up to receive
- First seeking to break lines; failing that, seeking to change the angle of attack *quickly*—no lazy horizontal passes

You're more likely to attend to these details of execution because you have thought them through, and if you get distracted, there is a simple tool to return them to the top of your consciousness. Having written them down, you can now make notes or assemble data on them as you watch: a check next to *Passes on the ground*. "We're always doing that. Well, with the exception of Mathias." You write his name next to *Passes on the ground* so you or an assistant can work with him later, but there's no need to make a stoppage about one player's technical issue. You also notice that Kike is brilliant at scanning before he receives. If you ever need to have a player demonstrate this, he's your guy. You write "Kike++" next to *Open hips and eyes up to receive*. You decide to start observing methodically for the pace of passes and start making checks for good passes and Xs for poor ones next to Passes struck at pace. You see that you're about 60/40 and know you want to stop and address it. "Guys, I want you to be focused on speed of passes. They must be struck at pace. I am going to be scoring your passes. Every one of them. Go!" They might be skeptical that you're really watching them *that carefully*, but now they see you ticking off a small mark after every pass. They grow more focused. The numbers skyrocket. You can see their progress because the numbers are in front of you. "Pause," you say. "Boys, I didn't teach you anything new there. I just reminded you that the pace of your passes was critical. When I did that, we went from 40% of our passes being too slow to be effective to almost none. What does that tell us?" you ask, setting them up to realize for themselves that they have the ability if they maintain their focus.

In a moment, I want to share with you a really fascinating video of a coach using this idea on the field. And I want to return to the second half of Denarius's video where we see how he responds to the data he's gathered. But first, I want to pause to break out some of the things that have emerged in our study of Denarius's classroom that a coach can use to gather better data on performance during training.

The first key idea is that what you observe is a form of data, and mental notes are insufficient for data. You should watch with a tracker of some sort, a place to take live notes. In *Teach Like a Champion*, I call this "**Tracking, Not Watching**" to remind teachers (and now you, Coach) that observation is not a passive activity but an active one. You may be tempted to think that you are not coaching when you are "just watching," but in fact this is one of the most important—and overlooked—parts of the job. Merely taking notes on what you observe will make you more intentional about and aware of how you look. How carefully? At what? We are, science tells us, easily distracted. We are often blind to what happens right before our eyes. Our eyes follow what's bright and fast moving—for example, a soccer ball—almost by instinct, and it doesn't take much for our awareness to be drawn away from the quieter but more profound: the defensive side of the game; movements off the ball. Surely we watch different players more than others. Most coaches can and should decide more intentionally what they will pay attention to and the design of your tracker can help.

The second key idea is that you will be more efficient at seeing the learning gaps that separate your team and players from success if you "**Anticipate Errors**"—that is, if you take a few minutes when you are planning a training exercise and specifically ask yourself, "What are the things players are most likely to get wrong as they do this?" *And then write those things down.* Several positive things happen as soon as you do this. First, you make yourself more likely to see those mistakes when and if they happen. It's about making the unexpected less unexpected, Chabris and Simons tell us. Second, it is now easy to think through what you will do if the mistakes you have anticipated actually emerge. And of course you make it easier to design a tool to gather data efficiently as you observe.

Recently I watched footage of a coach who was being videoed as part of an advanced license course. He had a habit of talking to himself while being taped. This provided a window on his thinking. As his players executed a set of passing movements, he said to himself, "They're just not clean enough." Later, he repeated this to an assistant: "They're not clean enough. They're just not clean enough. I don't think we should do the next [progression]." Their technical skill, he was observing, was not proficient enough for them to do what he was asking them to do tactically. And yet, just a few seconds later, he blew the whistle and went on to the next progression anyway. He's not alone, I suspect. It's incredibly easy to see an issue and still not take action. You might call this burying the data. Often we acknowledge this to ourselves later: *I knew we didn't have it down…* Which raises a question: *If you knew, why didn't you do something about it?* That question is not rhetorical. The transition from seeing a learning gap to changing the session to reacting to it is far from automatic and the answer, I think, is often: *Because I didn't know what to do about it in the moment.* Or perhaps: *Because I didn't want to try to change the session live with my team and risk not knowing what I was doing.* Or maybe: *Because I'd planned the second half of the session really carefully and was excited to teach it.* There are of course times when you might intentionally choose not to address something right away because you may want players to struggle or you want to focus on teaching something else, but there are also times when you should act, when you know they need to go back and clean up their technique rather than go on the more advanced progression, and yet you fail to do so. One reason for that hesitation is that changes you make on the spur of the moment are uncertain and may involve downtime—moving markers or re-forming groups. They *may* help solve the problem you saw but they will *definitely* disrupt the practice as currently planned and that's not always a very compelling deal: trade your planning for uncertainty; trade what you want to do for what you grudgingly acknowledge you should. It's easier to try yelling, "Clean it up, boys. It's gotta be cleaner!" instead. Now you feel like you've done a little something and can get on with what you'd originally planned. But if you've anticipated errors, you can also anticipate responses to errors. So what you do after you decide to go back won't seem quite as spur-of-the-moment. If you know what you'll do about it, you're more likely to take action. And the action is more likely to work.

There are more intangible benefits to anticipating errors as well. One is that you practice anticipating what players will struggle with. Even if you're wrong about the mistakes you anticipate players making, you are getting better at it. And you are practicing seeing training through the eyes of players and are getting better and better at understanding the sorts of things that keep them from success. More subtly, if your planning process *presumes there will be errors and struggles*, you are far less likely to get mad at players when they emerge. You are far less likely to see struggles as signs of laziness or some flaw in the group—they're soft—than reminders that learning is hard. You're more likely to see a problem-solving challenge. It's no longer a question of assigning blame and you'll preserve their trust and faith in you when you don't falsely accuse them of not giving a damn when in fact, they do.

The third key idea is "**Exemplar Planning**," which is similar to "Anticipating Errors" but involves taking the time to describe what the ideal answer looks like. You will see the gaps between what you're getting and what you want much more clearly if you have a careful description of the ideal constantly at the top of your mind. The gaps in execution will suddenly be clear. To make an exemplar, you would ask: *For this exercise, what does a world-class team of U14s—or the best possible version of your team of U14s—look like executing this concept?* And then you would write it out. This would remind you of details you were semi-aware of. It would help you to think about the details. It will help you to see more clearly what athletes do well—and therefore what to reinforce and praise so you get more of it. And it will help you to be ready to describe what you liked in clear language so players know what it is they should replicate. It will help you to see what's missing too. And it's a great activity to do with colleagues. Take a topic like combination play in the attacking third with a diamond midfield or an exercise like a rondo and compare your exemplar with a colleague's version. I almost guarantee she will have elements in her exemplar you hadn't thought of and vice versa. It is a great tool to help you constantly grow your understanding of the game.

Watch "Kika Toulouse
data tracking" at
www.coachguidetoteaching.com

With that in mind, this video ▶ of New York Red Bulls youth coach Kika Toulouse is fun to watch because she takes several of the tools we see Denarius using but adapts them in useful ways.

Kika's topic is weak-side runs. She wants players to see opportunities to make such runs, and when they make them well, she wants their teammates to recognize the opportunities and get them the ball. So she sets up a tracker to help herself observe carefully. She treats her observations like data—tabulating for each team, times when runs were made and then in addition how successful they were at leading to scoring plays—in this case, playing to a blue neutral player just over the goal line and receiving the ball back. Then she does something fascinating. She shares the raw data with the players, notes that it is fascinating and then asks *them* to analyze it. Why, she asks, did the orange team create more chances through weakside runs but turn fewer of them into scoring opportunities? Message: analyzing what the data tells a team is not just the coaches' job. They wrestle with the idea, trying to connect the data points. The first player to talk is a central player who arguably spent the drill with his head down and failed to spot opportunities. His interpretation is that his teammates gave the final ball away. There's barely any response from his teammates. Or from Kika, who instead goes on to a second player who offers a more useful analysis. But the key takeaway is that data is powerful for players too.

Acting on the data

Let's return to the moment in Denarius's classroom when he has identified, through careful observation and tracking of observational data, a common critical error much of the class is making—in other words, the most important thing to talk about with them. Now his plan is to recreate that error—to make the problematic parts of a flawed solution as clearly visible as possible so the group can study it. If he can get his students to study their mistakes with openness, curiosity and interest, if they can reflect on their struggles and missteps without defensiveness or recrimination, and if he can make doing so a habit, then he will have created a learning culture that will be hard to surpass. And he will have made his coaching life easy. The response to every error won't be as simple as saying *Let's pause and take a look at what went wrong*—students who are new to a topic often struggle to diagnose errors, for example—but it will open to him the possibility of fixing a significant proportion of errors merely by pausing to examine them rather than designing a more complex intervention. In fact, ideally their comfort with and interest in error analysis will give rise to students inclined to constant reflection. But that will only work if the culture is right and participants embrace the idea that getting it wrong is often a critical step in the process of getting it right, where they study their own mistakes with openness and curiosity and without defensiveness or recrimination. When a team, a club, a classroom or a school has that kind of culture, I describe it as having a "culture of error," and for a coach it is profoundly important.

The gap between "I taught it" and "They learned it" is ten times easier to find and understand if athletes are not trying to hide their mistakes from you—even more so if they willingly share them. That sort of culture doesn't ordinarily develop naturally, nor is it built primarily through things like a team talk where a coach explains to players that they need to embrace mistakes if they want to be successful. In the places where it thrives most, it is "in the sauce," as they say: expressed subtly in a thousand tiny moments—in the language used to describe mistakes and the facial expression and body language that greet them. In Bob Zimmerli's math classroom, for example, there was the moment when, observing his students struggling to combine like terms, Bob paused them and said, "I'm glad I'm seeing the mistake I'm seeing. It's going to help me to help you." He's not afraid to call a mistake a mistake; he just makes talking about it a positive.

So it's worth watching the second half of Denarius's clip —starting at about 1:20— through that lens. First, let me explain what's happening. At 1:24 or so of the video, Denarius takes the paper of a student named Fagan. She's made an error in finding her remainder that is typical of what much of the class has done, so he is going to project her paper to the class to study it. Remember, it's critical to see the error if we want to understand it. But of course, this moment could go very wrong. Fagan could feel ashamed and singled out for having her mistake shown to the whole class. You can almost imagine the parent phone call Denarius could get that night. But right from the beginning, Denarius is keenly attentive to the culture he is creating.

His first move, as he prepares to study Fagan's mistake, is to signal to the class that what he is about to do is important and worthy of their highest level of attention and focus. "Pencils down and track me in 3, 2 and 1," he says. By "track me," he is referring to the classroom expectation that students will track the speaker during critical parts of the

Watch "Denarius Frazier teaching math" at www.coachguidetoteaching.com

lesson. This helps them to maintain their own attention and signals to others that they take this task seriously. Denarius then scans the room very carefully—invisibly—to make sure everyone is attentive. This is easy for him to do because tracking is an easily observable proxy for paying attention. And his scan is not just a formality. He spots one student not yet ready. "Waiting on one," he says, to remind students that he needs their attention but without saying the individual's name so as to not divert attention away from his task.

Once he's sure each member of the class is giving their full attention, he begins, "On a few of our papers, I'm noticing that we're getting an incorrect remainder." His language is critical here. First, it's all about the group: *we're* getting incorrect answers on *our* papers. He is deflecting any perception that this moment might be about Fagan. *This is a moment about all of us and that we are all responsible to study.* Notice also his tone as he prepares to study the mistake. He's calm and neutral and maintains what I call "**Emotional Constancy**." He doesn't get upset at the mistake but instead calmly focuses on the steps required to solve the problem. Many teachers might take one of two alternative approaches in terms of their tone. Some might let their impatience and possibly frustration show: *Guys, we've been doing these problems all week. We really need to start applying what we know about remainders.* Others might be singsong, as if to say, *Oh we made a mistake, but it's OK. Don't feel bad; don't worry too much.* The latter of these responses implies that students can't really talk about a mistake without someone pouring syrup on it and telling them that it's going to be OK in the end. Students do not need to be coddled and propped up so they can learn from mistakes. Why suggest to them that learning from one's mistakes is anything other than standard operating procedure? The former response betrays frustration with students. It's the first hint of blaming the learner. It may distract them from the study of their mistakes by introducing a whole series of extraneous questions in their minds. *Why is he angry at us? It's not my fault Fagan can't solve remainders.* But it will surely communicate to them that their mistakes are bad and when their teacher shows them, he is annoyed. Better to keep quiet. This language deserves further study and is something I will return to in a moment.

As he begins reviewing the problem, Denarius says, "Snaps first for Fagan for using long division." Denarius's goal is to build a culture where learning is a team endeavor and he uses snaps to make peer appreciation and support more visible. But his language and actions are critical in more subtle ways here too. First, he is reminding Fagan that her error is partial. Her first instinct may be to tell herself "I got the problem wrong" and perhaps throw up her hands—"I'm terrible at this"—but in fact she did not get the whole problem wrong. She got a key step wrong. That's why it's not just "Snaps for Fagan," it's "Snaps for Fagan for using long division." She got the big idea right. No need to panic; a bit of focus will fix things quickly. Further, helping her distinguish what she did correctly from the error she made is important because Denarius wants her to keep doing the correct things. Including a clear description of what went right will help her know to persist with them.

I want to take a minute to try to eliminate a common misunderstanding about what coaches and teachers do when they build a culture of error. To build a culture of error is to show that mistakes are normal and valuable to study so we can shift players away from doing things like deflecting blame onto others, rationalizing their mistakes, or seeking to hide them—from their coaches but also from themselves. The message is that mistakes are inevitable when we try to learn difficult things. So when we make mistakes, we want to acknowledge them and seize the opportunity they create to better understand the game. This is different from a culture where coaches are afraid to call a wrong answer or a poor decision a mistake—the opposite, in many ways. However, when I work with coaches, they sometimes struggle with this distinction. For example, I will share with them some examples of statements that build a culture of error when you witness a mistake:

- "I'm glad I saw that mistake. It teaches us something we have to fix before Saturday."

- "I like that your first instinct was to look for space and to go wide, but in this situation, we don't want space. We have the advantage and we want to go directly at goal."

- "What I am asking you to do is difficult. Even professional players struggle with it. But you can do it. So let's take a look at what went wrong…"

All three statements are different in some ways. The first flips player expectation; the coach is glad to have seen the mistake now and hopes it will prevent one in the match. The second gives credit to a player for sound understanding of the game—but makes it clear that she's come up with the right answer for a different setting. The third acknowledges that the task is not the sort of thing you just try once and get right. It normalizes struggle. But what all three have in common is that they are *explicit about the fact that a mistake has been made*. However, when I ask coaches to come up with examples, they sometimes come up with things that do the opposite—things like, "That's one way you can play the ball here, but something else you can try is…" This is a statement which avoids telling a player he made the wrong decision. It blurs the distinction between right and wrong (rather than clearly highlighting an error so we can learn from it) as if that was the most useful thing to do in the world—which sometimes it is. A response that says "that's one option; here's another" is fine if the two options really are equal. But blurring the line between right and wrong is different from teaching players to learn comfortably from mistakes. It turns out it's surprisingly hard to simply tell players they were wrong without making it a big deal and getting on with it. But that's what we seek—not a culture that is afraid to distinguish the right answer from lesser alternatives but one that makes it easy to talk about that distinction and why it exists.

There's a giant wall in front of progress

Jeff Albert is the hitting coach for the St Louis Cardinals. He's a voracious reader and a student of both cognitive and physiological science, so careful observation and establishing a culture that makes it safe to struggle are central to his work.

One of the most important things in coaching, to me, is actively observing. When I feel like I am really coaching, it's often when I'm in the cage studying what a player is doing or at home watching video, figuring him out and then setting up what I want to do the next day.

But to the players, all of that is invisible. They aren't used to it. Sometimes they ask: *Why aren't you saying anything?*

JEFF
ALBERT

I want to gather all the evidence before making a decision about what route we're gonna go. I don't want to be wrong. Especially when you're a new player. You're making this transition into pro ball, to a new city, to a new life. While that's happening, I'm getting to know you as a person. I'm observing what you do in practice and in the games. I have your history, your stats and scouting reports. I'm kind of putting together the puzzle pieces.

I overheard one of the players explaining it to one of the newly drafted guys: "Don't worry if Jeff isn't saying anything to you. It doesn't mean he's ignoring you. He probably knows everything about you, everything about your swing. He's just waiting."

In fact it's often really helpful to wait until the player has expressed a motivation and a desire. Maybe he starts asking questions or says: *I want to work on what that guy's doing.* He's seeking the information you've been getting ready.

Another thing that really helps is when you get small groups of players working on the same thing. They'd be watching one guy hit and a coach would say to another guy, *What did you see there*? He solves it. He tells the other guy: *Here's what it feels like I'm doing.* It's building knowledge together.

Baseball is a game of failure—that's what they say about it—so there's often not a lot of willingness to take on more failure, to get in the cage and risk looking bad in there. There's this giant wall in front of progress. But when the players acknowledge it and talk about developing, you're not hiding the struggle any more; you're actually working together to solve a problem, sometimes even consciously experimenting. That makes the cage a much safer place from a learning point of view.

The first place I saw that was in the Dominican Republic. The young guys down there do it all the time. In the cage, two or three or four of them, talking mechanics. It's a big part of the culture. But it also has the effect of building a culture of error.

In professional baseball, there are so many games and so few days off that you almost always prepare and develop on the same day. It helps to designate a specific time when you come to the cage and you're getting ready for the game versus a time when you're working on your development. Clearly define purposes. At 3 o'clock, we're working on this; at 4:30, it's a different task. Right before the game, it's getting ready to play. It allows the player to compartmentalize what they're doing and build attentional focus, but also to struggle safely and not worry that if they feel off it means they're not going to be able to hit that evening.

The next move for Denarius is to begin a round of questioning. "What's a way that we can quickly check to see if this remainder is correct?" he asks. The students are doing much of the work because he wants them to be able to practice analyzing their own mistakes. Spotting errors in thinking is as important as knowing how to fix them, of course. That said, the questioning works here because students know enough to troubleshoot. Without background knowledge and shared vocab, this is much harder (see chapter 1). If students had not been working on this topic for some time, Denarius would likely have to guide them more through the process or prompt them with key terms and ideas to apply.

Novices notice far less than experts when they observe and perceive, cognitive psychology tells us. They're just as likely to make incorrect observations or struggle to really see the problem, so part of your preparation should be to consider what you'll do if you "show the problem" to athletes and they fail to understand it fully. Most likely you'll have to teach them more directly.

The sequence ends with Denarius sending his students "back to practice"—that is, to more problems in which they will apply the concept he's just reviewed. If you've read the chapter on feedback, you'll notice, I hope, that his feedback here is fast and focused: it's about one single topic; students can see it and are then given the chance to use it right away.

I want to return for a moment to an observation I made about Denarius's **Emotional Constancy**, the benefits he derives from his measured tone in delivering feedback and the normalcy he communicates. He doesn't freak out about the mistake and he doesn't sprinkle his critique with sugar as if that's needed to make it go down. He is calm and steady and delivers his feedback with composed neutrality. If this topic is relevant for classroom teachers, it is doubly so for coaches, who are perhaps doubly likely to give feedback wrapped in strong emotion and just possibly to romanticize doing so—to believe that it makes them a better coach if their feedback frequently comes with a raised voice. That's how you show you're demanding and have high expectations, right?

There is very little research on this point that I am aware of, so I will make two arguments based on what I know about teaching and learning that I acknowledge are not based on science. The first is that highly emotional feedback is in some cases either less productive or possibly counterproductive. If feedback comes loaded with judgment, intense emotion or frustration, players may be more focused on these aspects than on the content of the feedback. If you say "Wider, Kevin" but your tone of voice says, "For God's sake, Kevin. Get wide!" or "Why do I have to keep telling you to get wide, Kevin?", then Kevin's attention is diverted from the fact that he needs to get wide and onto the fact that you are frustrated with him. A part of him will ask, *Is that fair? Does he get equally frustrated with Drew? Wow, his face gets really red when he yells*. For the most part, you want Kevin thinking about his positioning, so the distractions created by shouting at him in many cases keep him from focusing on the change he needs to make.

It is also true that coaching requires a bit of intensity—that in some cases, a lack of intensity among players is an issue. Or a failure to recognize the urgency of a situation. Or a failure to really attend. So my argument here is not that coaches should never raise their voices or be demanding in their tone as they give feedback. There will certainly be times when it's fitting. But many coaches overuse it, and this also results in a Boy Who Cried Wolf-like response that you might call urgency fatigue: if you are always yelling, if everything is a test of whether players "really want it," they will start to tune you out. Intensity works best when it is a variation from the norm. Generally speaking, if my feedback is technical or tactical—if it is focused on learning something—I would err on the side of emotional constancy. My colleague Chris Apple, who I will discuss more in chapter 5, offers this excellent piece of advice:

> When I plan a training exercise or game, I plan the activity, the coaching points, the likely mistakes *and* my demeanor. If it's a basic technical exercise, I am going to be incredibly exacting and firm. I'm not going to let them off the hook for the slightest

error in accuracy, concentration, etc. My voice and the stopwatch will generate the needed stress/pressure. If it's a complex activity or challenging technique (like crossing), I know the success rate will be low and they are going to get frustrated with themselves, so I need to inspire confidence and sticking with it. "It's OK, building out of the back against an organized defense is tough, keep going." I might even talk about the failure rate we expect in a given activity. If we are 90% successful, it just means the defense isn't making it tough enough. When we play attack vs defense tactical games, we intentionally set it up to have about a 50% success rate to be as gamelike as possible. It helps to know these things in the planning process so you can anticipate your own reactions and those of your players.

Your demeanor is a critical part of the learning environment, in other words. It should be intentional and mindful. Moving away from trying to accelerate learning by always opting for intensity and pressure may surprise you. And if you are trying to develop a coach who falls back on shouting to fill the gap when technical guidance is difficult, the first thing I might try is to challenge him or her to be emotionally constant, both in practice and, especially, in games. I'd want to know if my coach has more tricks in his or her bag than falling back on exhortations for "intensity," "desire" and "hustle" when the other team is dominating you in the midfield.

I know some coaches may have some reservations about this guidance. *Are you saying I should never raise my voice? If so, how do I demand more effort and intensity from players?* Let me say first that I think it is a gift when coaches demand intensity from athletes. It's also important to distinguish demanding intensity from shouting or the use of excess emotion. In some ways, even the demand for more intensity can be heard better when it is modulated to some degree. Sometimes at least. There will also be a moment when the stakes are high and the chips are down, and you will strategically be not-emotionally constant. Just make sure it's intentional and that you haven't romanticized the shouting and intense emotions as the same thing as high expectations. They are different. In training, shouting as the default mode of communication and as an indication of intensity is overused and overrated.

Questioning is also a means to CFU

So far, I've described checking for understanding primarily as an observational phenomenon—one that involves planning for what you should or might see, observing systematically and using the data to take effective action right away. These small adjustments in habit can have a profound effect. But there is another tool that coaches use to gauge their players' understanding: questioning. And it too deserves examination.

A brief return to Denarius's classroom: the video shows that once he presents the error, he begins questioning to assess what his students understand about it: "What's a way that we can quickly check whether this remainder is correct?" he asks. In a sport setting, this just as easily could have been Denarius asking how to solve the problem when a player is in possession in compressed space with numbers down. Quinietta describes the best means of checking a remainder in polynomial long division (taking the final term of the divisor and solving for it. In that case, the result will be equivalent to the remainder resulting from long division). This is good news. It reveals that students, or Quinietta at least, understand how to assess the accuracy of answers to all polynomial long division problems. Denarius's next question is to confirm that students know the name of the move Quinietta has used. Shared vocabulary, as I discuss in chapter 1, is immensely important to shared problem-solving; it allows groups of people to quickly discuss solutions and responses in a reliable and efficient way, and Isaiah is able to name the polynomial remainder theorem.

Now, Denarius asks students to play out the suggestion. *If we plug 3 (the term from the divisor) into the function, what do we get?* (The answer, 248, does not match the remainder on Fagan's paper.) They know what the solution is. Denarius's goal is now to assess whether his students know how to apply the solution in this specific context. Fortunately they do. Or at least, a few of them do. I'll discuss this issue in a moment, but first, because there's a bit of a gap between math and sports, let's imagine Denarius is a top soccer coach and his class is his team. We can then translate his questions in a context that's a bit more applicable to coaching. That might sound something like this:

Denarius: Pause. Hold the ball and make sure your eyes are on me. I'm waiting on one. [Pause] Good. One thing that I'm seeing as I observe us attacking is that we sometimes force a pass into densely packed pressure. We play ourselves into situations where we are numbers down as soon as we receive the ball and our odds of success are low. For example, Fagan's pass here into David pits him against three defenders right away. But if we make a pass like this and we realize we're in a bad position, we have tools we can use to play away quickly and turn it into an advantage. There are multiple strategies we can use. So first of all, snaps for Fagan for trying to play forward aggressively and unbalance the defense. But if we play forward aggressively and find ourselves boxed in, what's one way that we can break out of the situation and get the ball quickly to a preferential situation?

Quinietta: We could play a short backwards pass to a teammate who would then look to strike a longer first-time pass to the farthest accessible open player.

Denarius: Good, and what do we call that in our game model?

Isaiah: *Play back to play out.*

Denarius: Yes. And if we did that here—if Fagan played the ball back to Kevin, [imagine Denarius here now rolling the slow backward pass to Kevin] and Kevin tried to play out, what would he see?

Several players: Carla open in the right channel.

Denarius: Exactly. Ball back to Fagan. Play that from here. Go!

Whether in his actual classroom (in the video) or the imaginary training session above, Denarius has used questioning to reexamine the original problem and study it anew, allowing players not only to find a better solution but also to understand and recognize their own mistakes—a second and deeper level of awareness. He's responded to the data by taking fast action to close the gap between "I taught it" and "They learned it." That of course is the critical second part of checking for understanding: it's not just gathering data to understand the gap; it's taking quick action to close the gap. Speed is important and the phrase "snowballs are expensive" helps to explain why.

A "snowball" is an idea that grows in size and gathers weight the longer it persists. Like a snowball rolled along the ground, it can start small but soon become too heavy to lift. Misunderstandings are that way. They get worse overtime. By the time players have done something wrong multiple times, there's a habit to break—something to learn and something to unlearn. And one undeniable idiosyncrasy of the human mind is that it is prone to confirmation bias: we assemble evidence around the beliefs we hold to be true. The longer I hold a mistaken belief, the more evidence I assemble around it; the more I confirm it. You cannot (as I discussed in chapter 1) throw a switch one day and simply instruct a player who has been holding the ball all his life, regardless of positioning and setting, and expect him to suddenly start perceiving teammates in space. Years of seeing the game through the lens of me rather than we will have gathered way in his mind. It will be a snowball; better to catch it early. And snowballs—even ones that roll along only for a week or two—are expensive. By that I mean they cost time. If you spend three or four sessions on pressing and find yourself wanting to shout at half time on Saturday because your players are not doing it in a coordinated and consistent way, the best approach is of course to take notes and reteach the topic at a training next week. That's a far better response than shouting at your players to remind them that you taught them something they clearly didn't learn. But that's also an expensive solution. You've wasted several practices and you only get so many. A teacher who only finds out on the test that her students did not learn the key ideas is a teacher who will not cover the necessary material for that year. In other words, checking for understanding is most powerful to the degree that it allows you to make real-time adjustments in your training sessions while you are still running them. Lost sessions are expensive from a player- and team-development point of view. If you only find out afterwards, you will never get ahead.

Snowballs are expensive. Prompt action is so important. But he's also used his questioning to gather data: do they know how to solve the problem? Do they know the principle they are applying? Can they spot a quality second pass? His questions reveal a stream of data about students understanding and when coaches can start to think about and use real time data about learning they're more likely to be successful.

Affirmative checking

I want to share one last video with you to show some ways that coaches can be more intentional about observing for mastery, in this case with very young players. In this clip , Steve Covino is working with a group of U8s, teaching them how to do a scissors move. They dribble slowly around the field and when Steve blows the whistle, they are supposed to accelerate and attempt a scissors in which they must change direction. Steve's done a really nice job designing this skill development exercise with such young players. Everyone is moving the whole time, getting time on the ball even when they're not working on the scissors. But he's also made it so the move he's looking for—the scissors—happens at a specific and reliable time. He knows when to focus and observe most carefully. And players do the move lots of times, but because he paces them with his whistle, they do it with slightly higher focus and execution. He's also connected the move from the very beginning to its context—the reason why you'd use it is to change direction deceptively, and as you can see, that influences how Steve teaches it. You can also see evidence of his exemplar planning: to be effective, players must accelerate out of the

Watch "Steve Covino
affirmative checking" at
www.coachguidetoteaching.com

move, they must change direction sharply, and as important as the dummy leg that waves over the ball is the surface of the foot that strikes the ball on the training leg: it must be the outside of the foot. Steve's done his homework even on this apparently simple move of thinking through what excellence looks like and now knows what to look for.

Watching carefully, he notices that several players are not changing direction sufficiently, so he pauses them to demonstrate. Like Denarius, he's careful to ensure that he gets full attention from his students as a matter of habit: players are expected to put their foot on the ball to keep it from becoming a distraction and have learned to put their eyes on Steve to ensure their focus. His stoppage is fast and focused. He quickly models two side-by-side-versions—the incorrect version and the correct version—so players can see the difference. Then they're off to try it.

After that, many of his young athletes are doing great, but Steve wants to know if everybody is getting it. He's specifically looking for the strugglers. If they don't get the basics now, they'll continue to practice it wrong and will perhaps never learn; and it's easy to watch the group and get the overall sense that "they get it." Steve wants to know that everyone gets it, so he tries something even more methodical. He observes the players working on half the field. As he sees each player execute correctly, he sends them to the other end of the field to happily practice more, allowing him to focus his attention on a smaller data set. He watches each player carefully to make sure they have it. As he winnows the group, he corrects individuals. He's far less likely to miss someone now. There's visual affirmation that each player is ready

THE POWER AND CHALLENGES OF MODELS

One of the key tools coaches use to reteach after spotting an error is a demonstration or a model, so I want to take a few minutes to talk about them here, in part because they are so challenging to do well. That might seem like an unexpected statement. What could be simpler than just showing athletes how it should be done and sending them back to practice? But with a bit of planning and intentionality, I truly believe coaches can get a lot more out of their models, and this is especially important for coaches who bring deep technical mastery and skill to the job. They are able to show athletes how to do what words can never fully describe...if they can get those athletes to truly lock in on what they do.

There are two parts to every successful model: you doing it and them seeing what you do, and the first does not imply the second. A common problem with models is that observers often aren't looking in the right place or focusing on the right things. "Here's how to do it," you say, demonstrating proper footwork, but half your team isn't watching your feet. Or they are, perhaps, but the real key is how you put your weight on the front of the plant foot, and their eyes are drawn to the foot on the ball instead, where they assume the critical action occurs. You've demonstrated perfectly, but they haven't really seen the solution clearly enough to understand and use it. Often after a model we'll ask, "Did you see that?" and everyone will of course say "Yes!", but unless we've defined carefully what "that" was before the model, it's very unlikely that there's much truth to the affirmation. Or perhaps you'll ask, "What did you notice about what I did?" but this is a classic case where the responses deceive us. You hear various mumbled answers and wild guesses until you pick out one voice saying, "Your plant foot!"

"Yes," you say. "Good. What did you notice about my plant foot?" but most of your listeners have just told you they were not looking at your plant foot, so the true answer to *What did you notice about it?* is "almost nothing." And of course, realizing now that the crucial piece was the plant foot doesn't help them. Hearing you or other observers describe what they might have seen won't help. They can't go back and see it.

So one of the simplest ways to improve models is to provide a focal point in advance. I sometimes call this "calling your shot." You say, "I'm going to model the scissors here. Watch my left foot." Now you've directed everyone's eyes, and players who would have been watching the ball or your right leg or something else at random will now be looking at the thing you want them to see. If you want to ask them to analyze our model—"What did I do there?"—this is a doubly important preliminary.

It's easy to overlook the importance of this step because experts perceive more than novices.[3] Expertise, after all, is knowing where to look, and Kirschner and Hendrick reminded us earlier that novices see superficial details while experts see underlying principles. If you are an expert, you are unlikely to realize how much less novices notice during a demonstration. You show your players a short clip of combination play from La Liga and see sublime artistry in the dance of movements off the ball; they see a series of passes leading to a shot from the top of the penalty area.[4] They walk away thinking that the goal is shots from the top of the area, not the subtle spacing and positioning in the build-up play that you were watching. Observers are also less likely to see what you want when there's more to watch for. Even elite players watching 12 seconds of footage from La Liga involving 12 players' interactions at midfield might be watching any number of things. With novices or complex demonstrations—or with video—provide more contextual guidance than you think is necessary. As in, "Watch my left foot. I want you to tell me which surface I use to carry the ball forward" or "Don't watch the ball; watch what the left back does after he plays the ball."

Steve Covino's model in the video provides a useful case study. Interestingly, Steve uses a bit of a variation on what I'm describing. First, he lets his players identify the "focal points" by asking them what he should be focusing on: "Where am I supposed to take my touch? With which part of the foot?" It's a handy bit of retrieval practice (chapter 2) that will help encode the key elements of the move in long-term memory. Perhaps it engages them in the model a bit more too. Of course, there's the risk that their answers will reveal that they don't know what to look for, so if you ask a question like this, listen carefully and address misconceptions. "I heard some people say X. What I'm going to show you is more important right now. Watch for whether I change direction and what part of my foot I use..." But here, Steve's players get it right: they should be looking for whether he changes direction to play into space, and they should be looking to see if he uses the outside of his foot to get there.

A second variation is that Steve is deliberately modeling a mistake. He's been watching carefully before the stoppage and has noticed what some of his young athletes are doing incorrectly. He wants to give them the opportunity to identify and correct it. This is a powerful move. It's critical for players to be able to perceive mistaken execution on their own. Knowing whether to correct something is as important as knowing how to correct it. But there are risks here as well. There's the risk that players may remember his faulty

3. It's the same with video models or having another coach model, incidentally.

4. Or uniform colors, or that the play is "really fast," or...

Watch "Steve Covino affirmative checking" at www.coachguidetoteaching.com

execution—"Ha, ha so funny! Coach Steve made a mistake"—better than the correct one—"Wow, look how Coach Steve shifts his weight." Or, they may feel so successful by virtue of having spotted his mistakes that they fail to attend to the solution.

This is a risk John Wooden wrestled with constantly as a coach and in the end, he came to believe that order of events in a corrective model was the most important thing. When you spot an error, he advised, stop the player and model how to perform the move correctly (M+), then show them how *they* did it (M–), and then model the move correctly once more (M+). The "recency effect" in psychology is the tendency of listeners to remember the most recently presented information best and it suggests that Wooden's model is a strong one and that, at minimum, coaches modeling mistakes should end with a correct model.

Comparative modeling—whether via Wooden's formula, Steve's approach, or some other—can also be adapted for more advanced learners. Recent research in the field of "comparative judgment" suggests that people are able to discern subtle distinctions that differentiate excellence when presented with two similar but slightly different models. That is, rather than presenting one model that is obviously wrong and one that is clearly correct, athletes may learn more if coaches present one that is almost right, or right in many ways but missing a key detail, and one that is better, or perhaps even one that's good and one that's great, and then letting players observe the subtle difference. This approach—analysis of subtle rather than obvious differences in models—is powerful for expert learners in particular. "The newer the content," Marc Mannella advised one team, "the more contrast there needs to be in the comparisons. Once learners have more experience with the content, you can ratchet up the similarity and home in on finer points."

There are lots of plausible variations, but a good rule of thumb is that if you model different versions during a demonstration, *the last thing players see should be the exemplar.* You can see this in Steve's model. After the incorrect version, he quickly follows up with a correct version that will remain in players' working memories as they practice.

Complex models and the power of planning

Some demonstrations require multiple modelers. Someone has to pass you the ball and make a certain movement so you can demonstrate the direction of the first touch or the subsequent pass. Perhaps there are multiple secondary roles required. Perhaps players from your team whom you draft on the spur of the moment play this role. Perhaps you have an assistant you can call into service. But one of the things that most commonly undercuts a model is that these participants don't know the model is coming, may not fully understand what it's intended to show, and/or don't fully understand the role you want them to play. Realizing that you need a supporting cast to demonstrate *pass and move*, you say "Pass me the ball, Coach" or "Stand over there, Jose." But where exactly and how should Jose stand? And then do what? And how should Coach pass you the ball? You've given them no time to prepare and no guidance on their role, so there's a decent chance that the model will break down. There's too much that has to go right for it to be an improv performance. Without a bit of planning and preparation, some demonstrations won't give observers high-quality information, so when in doubt, plan your models. Ideally, sketch them out before training and put them in your session plan. Who will demonstrate what? What will they say and do? Perhaps you even want to map it out. If not, at least talk it through with your assistant or your fellow modelers beforehand: "Here's what I want you to do." With an assistant, you can even run it through quickly while players are still practicing in a sort of mini-rehearsal. Even if all you do is eliminate the obvious mistakes and ambiguities—pass it a little harder; pass it on the ground; pass it to my other foot—it will increase the quality and efficiency of what goes on stage for your players dramatically. I offer this advice based on experience. I lead frequent practice-intensive workshops for teachers and have come to recognize, by virtue mostly of the wisdom of my co-presenters, that planning and rehearsing our models makes practice ten times better, especially if the models are complex and we want to include specific points of execution or show common mistakes so we can fix them.

In fact, here's a page from the "modeling document" that my colleague Darryl Williams and I used at a recent workshop. In column 1, we've named our practice. In column 2, we define our roles. Here, Darryl is going to explain what I am going to try to do and I am going to play the role of the teacher. He can comment on and guide people's attention to things I'm doing. The last column has a rough script of what I'm going to say and do. We do this for every activity we model. Of course, these models are initial models to start an activity, as opposed to feedback models in response to errors in training, but we often also list out how we'd model a response to a common error. It's how we respond to the errors we anticipate—something I'll discuss in the last section of this chapter.

MODELLING DOCUMENT

| SHOW CALL TAKE & REVEAL PRACTICE GROUP SIZE: 2 TIME: 2 MIN/ROUND | DW: FACILITATOR DL: TEACHER | NO FEEDBACK | ENGAGEMENT IMPORTANT IN OUR CLASSROOMS? AFTERWARDS WE'LL DISCUSS, GO AHEAD

DL
• **TAKE** (Circulating around the room)
"Darryl, I love your explanation here. Can I share the hard work you've done to learn from it and make it even better?"

• **REVEAL** (Places work under the document camera)
"Snaps for Darryl for sharing his work. As always, let's think of one thing that he did well and one thing he could improve. Start your feedaback by taking directly to Darryl by saying 'Darryl it was effective that...'"

ROUND 2
• Let's focus our feedback specifically on where Darryl could improve his use of vocabulary.
• What's one place where he used strong technical |

Marc Mannella described something similar that one team he worked with does to prepare. After the coaching staff conceive of a new drill, often in the conference room, they go out onto the floor and walk through it in detail with each other and with all the personnel who weren't involved with the planning but will need to be involved with the execution. They decide who will play which role in the drill or the modeling of it, etc. This makes demonstrations and explanations more efficient—when the players go out there, the coaches and staff know exactly where to go and what to do to model the activity.

Before I wrap up this chapter with a handy activity you can use to prepare for sessions that are more likely to be responsive to errors, let me discuss one other place where checking for understanding is useful.

Reject self-report

Here are a few examples of some of the most commonly asked questions in training—for any sport. See if they look familiar and then consider what the likely response is:

- "So the wing backs have to make sure that they seize those opportunities to push up the field. Is that clear?"
- "So, with my first touch, I want to play away from pressure and cause my defender to be uncertain about my direction of play. Everybody get it?"
- "If Shannon goes forward, Kelsey or Carly have to drop in. Understand?"
- "So we're in groups of eight. One player in each section of the grid, two floaters and two defenders. Are we good?"

Let's start with the answers. The answer to questions that end in phrases like

- "Is that clear?"
- "Everybody get it?"
- "Understand?"
- "Are we good?"

is almost always a few nods, maybe an "Uh-huh," but mostly silent and inaccurate assent. There's a decent chance that it is not clear or that everyone does not get it, and if that's the case, it's highly unlikely that they will respond by telling you. Which means that in the case of "So, with my first touch, I want to play away from pressure and cause my defender to be uncertain about my direction of play. Everybody get it?", they are likely to go off and practice poor first touches; and in the case of "So we're in groups of eight. One player in each section of the grid, two floaters and two defenders. Are we good?", they are likely to spend six of the ten minutes figuring out the activity. For their part, Kelsey and Carly are likely to fail to drop in when Shannon goes forward or perhaps spend the whole match dropped in in fear that they'll miss the cue when it happens.

The questions I am describing here are self-report questions, and it is inevitable that every coach will ask them from time to time. It would be strange not to. They are a verbal habit for most people. But it's important to recognize that we often ask them because we have realized we are at an ideal moment to check for understanding: we have just explained a concept and are getting ready to practice it, or we have just explained a new exercise and want players to break off into groups and do it. So we ask, "Got it?", which a little reflection reveals is an unreliable instrument. The annals of psychology are full of studies on the unreliability of self-report data. If you ask people even something very simple like how much time they spent on their smartphone in the last 24 hours, the data will almost assuredly be inaccurate. Respondents won't be aware of how much time they actually spent (looking at you, every teenager on earth), or if they are, they will know better than to tell you (still looking). And if you ask people a less cut-and-dried question like whether they understand something, the answers will be predictably inaccurate:

people are very unlikely to understand whether they understand something—the less they understand about it, the less they understand the gaps in their knowledge, in fact. So when you hear yourself asking, "Everybody get it?", remember that in many cases it suggests you have realized it would be a smart time to check for understanding and you are now failing to do so. If that's the case and you really do want to know if everybody gets it, consider some alternatives.

The first option would be not to ask at all and just vow to watch very carefully as they practice. You could verbalize that differently to help players focus on it, too. "Now let's try it so we can see if everybody gets it." Or you could ask a question that is more likely to get a response: "What questions do you have?", for example. This is far better than "Do you have any questions?" because everyone over the age of ten knows that the answer to the latter question is "No, Coach," whereas the first question assumes there will be questions and so is more likely to encourage confused people to speak up.

Or you might ask a series of fast, targeted questions to assess understanding. That might sound like this:

> *Great. So how many players are there per group, Kevin? And how many per grid, Antonio? And who starts with the ball, Demarcus? Good. Off you go.*

Or

> *What surface will we use, Marcos? Good. And after my move, what do I want to do, Rodrigo?*

Or

> *Great. So when Shannon goes forward, what tells me I have to drop in, Kelsey? Same rules for you or different, Carly? Good. Let's try it.*

As you did this, it would be important to cold call. This would help you move faster and ensure that you didn't just hear just from the people who were inclined to volunteer to speak (and who are more likely to answer correctly than the rest of the group).

Another possible response is to use a show me—which involves asking listeners to demonstrate a simplified version of the thing you want them to do during training from where they are currently standing before they practice it fully.

A show me isn't always possible but when it is, it's nice because it can be quick and replace

- *If Shannon goes forward, Kelsey or Carly have to drop in. Understand?*

with

- *Great. So, Kelsey and Carly, show me where you'll go if Shannon moves to here.*

or

- *OK, Carly and Kelsey, point to where you'll go if Shannon goes forward. Good. Let's play.*

Or you could replace

- *Everybody clear on what body posture looks like when we're defending?*

with

- *Great. Very quickly, show me your basic defensive body posture now.*

Then you might scan quickly to confirm and remind:

- *Very good, Carly. Nice, Sara. Lower, Jessica. That's it, Kelly. Foot forward, Karin.*

before putting it to practice.

Or you could replace

- *Does everybody know what group they're in and where to go?*

with

- *Right. Before we split up, please point to where you're going. Good. Let's go!*

Preparing to win

"The key is not the will to win. Everybody has that," the iconic basketball coach Bobby Knight is reputed to have said. "It is the will to prepare to win that is important." What happens on the court in a game, Knight argued, was determined by a thousand more mundane decisions in practice in the previous days and weeks. That's a compelling argument to coaches, and having read the above quotation, perhaps you'll want to quote it to your players. Do your homework, it reminds us, and the results will come. Don't expect greatness to emerge when the chips are down just because you want it to.

As with so much of the advice we give players, there's benefit to reflecting on the wisdom of this guidance for coaches as well. Want to run a great session that grows and develops your players? Want to run a hundred great sessions that transform your team? The answer is in your preparation, and on the topic of checking for understanding, I have a particularly useful tool to help coaches prepare to win in training (and therefore ultimately games).

It's a four-step process and is great for individual coaches and even better for clubs or groups of coaches as professional development. Here's how it works:

Step 1: Write out your training objective for the session. The key here, as I discuss in chapter 3, is specificity. Precise goals mean rapid progress, Anders Ericsson reminds us. Vague goals mean slower progress because we're less focused. "Building out of the back," for example, is a general topic and describes generally what we're working on. What do we want to accomplish today in terms of our ability to build out of the back? A session goal should therefore be specific and manageable—defined as something you could actually accomplish in the time period allotted. *The goal is to improve the speed of our play when building out of the back.*

Step 2: Write out your exemplar. What does excellence in speed of play when building out of the back look like? What are the details that separate good from great? Or that separate our approach to it from some other? As we've discussed in this chapter, writing it out will help you see more clearly whether it happens or not, and it will guide and focus your feedback.

Step 3: Anticipate at least two errors. What are your players likely to get wrong? To misunderstand or struggle to execute? This too you will see more easily if you've anticipated it, Chabris and Simons's research tells us. Right or wrong in your predictions at first, you will get better at them over time. And whether your guesses are right or wrong, they will prepare you psychologically to respond to error with equanimity.

Step 4: Plan your response. What will you do if the errors you anticipate occur? Will you model what you want players to do? Perhaps a comparative model that shows the subtle difference between what they did and what they could do? If so, planning out the demonstration in advance—who will help you, where they will be placed, etc.— may help. But then again, perhaps you'll need to briefly simplify the task or slow it down or increase the space if players struggle. All of those decisions will not only be better if you think them through in advance but they will also make you more likely to take action when you see gaps between your teaching and your athletes' learning.

There's one last element of planning that you might consider here: planning your affect. Being strategic about the emotions and values you reinforce is a critical part of building culture, which is the topic of our next chapter.

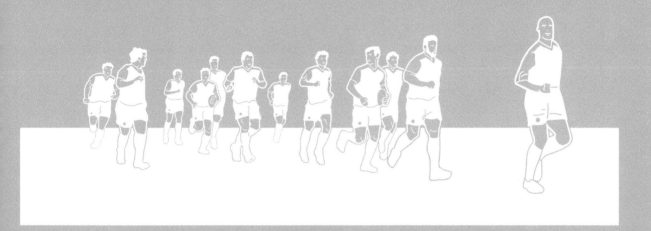

> I want you in there as players... jog a slow lap together... thinking *'This is the team'*... We're building towards next year.

CHAPTER 5

BUILDING CULTURE

Several years ago, I observed Chris Apple training a group of boys at Empire United's Development Academy in Rochester, NY. Chris is also men's soccer coach at the University of Rochester, and I have learned a lot from him in a variety of settings over the years, but that particular session was especially memorable. He saw and taught the hidden sides of the game more than almost any coach I'd observed. His guidance and his stoppages were almost always about what was happening away from the ball, for example. And when I asked him why he'd chosen to work on pressing during so much of the session, he replied with a phrase I've thought about frequently since: "The great majority of coaches spend the great majority of their time on the offensive side of the ball." His coaching focused on what players did in the moments away from the spotlight. Compared to that, what they did with the ball was easy.

Fittingly, then, what turned out to be perhaps the most significant takeaway from the session was also away from the spotlight. At the time, I simply jotted it in my notebook as an afterthought.

And then, a few years later, I was asked an unexpected question during a workshop for the US Soccer Academy Directors' Course. A coach wanted to know how he could help players to forget more effectively—to put mistakes behind them and focus on the next moment. The question caused me to remember that moment from Chris's training, and a few days later I asked him about it. His answer revealed a great deal about culture—arguably the single most important aspect in determining a club's outcomes on the field and in players' lives.

Here's the interaction I'd seen at that practice. After technical work and a series of exercises on pressing, Chris's session ends with a chance for the boys to play, full field and relatively uninterrupted. The quality of play reflects the culture of Chris's team more broadly: intense and competitive. In the waning minutes of practice, the game is deadlocked, and you can feel the tension.

And then suddenly there's a clear chance for one of the strikers. He finds himself in the center of the box, with a bit of space and the ball arriving at his feet. No one but the keeper to beat; it's a sitter. His first touch is perfect; two defenders lunge desperately to close but it's hopeless. He leans into the shot and...fires four feet over the bar. A bad, bad miss, and infuriating to most coaches.

But Chris, on the sideline, shouts nothing, says nothing. The sound of the ball slamming against the wall echoes inside the training facility. The player jogs slowly back, head down, and a teammate jogs nearer. "Next play, kid. Get it back," he says.

In retrospect, I'm not sure why I bothered to describe that in my notes. I suspect I was stuck by the contrast between Chris's response and the counterproductive things I had heard so many coaches yell in similar situations:

- "Caleb, you gotta make that!" [Pretty sure Caleb knows that, Coach.]
- "Aw, get over the ball, Caleb!" [True, though it doesn't help much now, unfortunately.]
- Turning to the players on the bench in exasperation: "What is he *doing*?"

Coaches make statements like that in response to player errors in part to protect their own ego, suggests Stu Singer, a consultant who works with coaches to develop their mindfulness and self-discipline, told me. "The statement lets everybody know: *I taught him better*. It's about protecting the self instead of responding to the athlete."

Chris didn't remember this specific play when I described it to him but there had been a hundred like it since. So many that Chris had a working theory on what to communicate in such moments.

"He knows he missed, and me pointing it out adds insult to injury," he said. "It's the last play of a scrimmage he really wanted to win; he's upset, angry, maybe feeling he let his team down, maybe trying to break into the starting 11, and he feels he just blew it. He'll be thinking about that play the entire car ride home. If anything, I could have told him to shake it off or remind him of the three he scored that day."

As I understand it, the term "mindfulness" refers to teaching oneself to make intentional decisions about what to pay attention to, particularly in moments of intensity and importance, and Chris's response strikes me as being especially mindful. He was able to see past his own emotional response and focus on the player, the long-term goal and (most of all) the culture of the team. What does he need now? What will make *him* better? What do I want the rest of the team to think about his mistake and what it will mean to make a similar one? "You have to *respond* versus *react*," Singer advises. "Emotion is OK. But the question for a coach is always the same: did you choose it, or did it choose you?"

Culture is built in a thousand smaller moments when we're not fully aware that we're building it. The aggregate message of those moments is at least as influential as the moments when we are aware that we are building culture—talks before or after games or before the season when we discuss how we want to interact as a team and what our mindset should be. Those aren't irrelevant. But culture really is the thousand unacknowledged half-second interactions in which our response communicates mindset and relationship. For Chris it was *When you make a mistake, I will stand by you; so play fearlessly rather than When you make a mistake, I will seek to establish blame; therefore, play self-consciously and be ready to point the finger at others.*

The difference between responding and reacting is worth some consideration. Much of athletic performance, as I discussed in chapter 1, is about honing the "fast" systems in an athlete's mind so they can react in the fractions of a second before they can engage conscious thought. Coaching, by contrast, is often about slowing down, about giving ourselves more time, often just a moment, in which to respond intentionally. Reaction is instantaneous. Response is slower—often only by a fraction of a second, though sometimes by an hour or a day—and lets the brain's more advanced centers of planning and logic (the prefrontal cortex) take precedence over its instinctual ones (the amygdala). Even a second's delay can allow a coach to think about the larger context in which athletes play—culture, in other words.

Chris's response was memorable because he had chosen not to say anything. Over time, Chris had found himself thinking about the importance of the things he should not say. This also communicated culture. Saying less gave players more space and autonomy and ownership. If he commented on everything his players did, they would never learn to judge for themselves. In fact, they would hear him more when it mattered if he chose more carefully when to speak. He would earn their trust and appreciation if he did not seek to judge every action.

It had not always been that way. "Early in my career, I was abysmal at this," Chris noted. "I'm not sure I was even conscious of it. I coached everything. Imagine your boss was looking over your shoulder and correcting every error. Not fun, not sure how much I'd learn, pretty sure I'd become resentful." For Chris, learning to coach had been learning to be intentional about when to remain silent, to let the story play out, to focus, in the heat of the moment, on long-term relationships. Over the years, Chris had given a name to this idea: coaching by not coaching.

* * *

Culture, the topic of this chapter, has been written about extensively in a thousand settings. In part, because culture is so powerful. "Culture eats strategy for breakfast," the management guru Peter Drucker said. Want to run a successful organization? Take everything you do, says Harvard Business School professor Frances Frei, and "multiply by culture."

"Group culture is one of the most powerful forces on the planet," writes Daniel Coyle in *The Culture Code*. The introduction to his book is called "When two plus two equals ten," an allusion to the idea that a team that inspires people to give their all, causes them to work together, and brings out their best will win out over one that lacks cohesion and unity, often even if the latter has a better game plan or superior talent. You can get a lot wrong if you get culture right.

It's interesting to note how strongly we are drawn to the idea that culture is the ultimate source of strength, and that cohesion and unity will beat talent. We desire in a deep and instinctive way for that to be true. How many movies can you think of that tell the story of underdogs who manage to come together and triumph through camaraderie, collaboration, and self-sacrifice? In those tales, the opposition are never another, similar group who have also managed to cobble together some success through shared culture. They are always more favored by life: they are twice as big, have nicer uniforms and snobby attitudes. Count, by contrast, the number of movies about the under-matched group who win because they prepare better, study hard, and learn to understand the subtleties of the game. The trailer to that movie would start with a quote from Bill Belichick—"You can play hard. You can play aggressive. You can give 120%. But if one guy is out of position, then someone is running through the line of scrimmage and he is going to gain a bunch of yards"—but it doesn't matter what's in the trailer. No one is going to go see a movie about how we win through knowledge, preparation and understanding. The story we want to be told again and again is the story of culture triumphant.

It's almost as if some deep truth has been demonstrated in the triumph of the group over superior talent based on "chemistry" and principles of shared culture. And no wonder. Humankind's triumph as a species is, as Hollywood might describe it, the story of a bunch of underdogs who must learn to work together despite their differences. In learning to value the group as much as themselves, they win out over fangs and claws and other superior evolutionary talent. The opposition in the story of evolution is often groups and species with superior physical attributes whom we outcompeted by understanding the nuances of working together. The triumph of culture is the story of our species, but it's not a simple one.

It's worth hearing how an evolutionary scientist describes it. The sociobiologist Edward Wilson describes the success of humans as being the result of two parallel forms of natural selection, one that rewarded strength and intelligence among individuals and another that rewarded coordination and cooperation among groups. "The strategies of the game were written as a complicated mix of closely calibrated altruism, cooperation, competition, domination, reciprocity, defection, and deceit ... Thus was born the human condition, selfish at one time, selfless at another, the two impulses often conflicted." A weaker individual in a stronger group might be more likely to survive through the eons of prehistory than would a stronger individual in a weak group, in other words; but the best case of all was to be the strongest individual within a strong group, though of course the conflicts that arose from seeking that position could destroy a group. The evolutionary pressures that shaped us as individuals sometimes jibe with and sometimes conflict with the equally strong (if not stronger) pressures that shaped us as groups and group members. We are all of us jockeying for position within the group, often through alliances, even as we seek to ensure that the group succeeds. It is true that individuals come together to form groups that are greater than the sum of their parts, that they are evolved to do this, but not easily. The natural state, Wilson is telling us, is one of tension created by deep-seated and conflicted instincts. Building culture is the story of how we reconcile that tension as we seek to achieve things.

"We all want strong culture," writes Daniel Coyle. "We all know that it works. We just don't know quite *how* it works." Many people look to build it mostly through dramatic public moments: a meeting to talk about cohesiveness or how to respond to adversity, say. One of the themes of this chapter is that such public moments may end up being less influential than daily actions—rising above adversity, and seeing one's teammates and self do so, over and over, even if you don't realize it. Culture is, first and foremost, a set of habits. It is what you do, not what you say. You can exhort players to fight hard at half time, but unless they have competed at their limit as a habit in training, the results will be mixed. You can tell them to be humble or unselfish teammates, but it won't help much unless they have lived in a culture that has steadily and consistently reinforced those things.

Culture is built, sustained and transmitted across an organization indirectly: communicated in a series of small moments, many of which occur when you're most distracted by other things. Building culture is in large part about our ability to sustain focus on what's important when something else feels more urgent.

There's a simple but telling scene in *The Test*, the documentary series directed by Adrian Brown tracing the efforts of Australia's world-renowned cricket team after a cheating scandal. The scene occurs just after newly appointed manager Justin Langer has taken over. On tour and preparing for a crucial test match in England, the players amble onto the field at Lord's Cricket Ground for one of their first trainings with Langer. But his mind is on the long term rather than the coming match. Culture comes first and it needs rebuilding. "Right boys," he says, "before you start, I want you in there as players, a real tight-knit group, just jog a slow lap together. Start thinking, 'This is the team. We're building towards 14 July next year.' Real close. Nice slow jog together." Culture is built in how groups of people do the familiar, the mundane, the everyday, Langer knows. It starts with doing the simplest tasks, as a team, in a way that is mindful of and intentional about who we are and who we want to be.

There is a paradox implicit in this kind of culture-building. How we play and how we interact has to be shaped and honed by a coach who has a clear vision for those things. "As managers, we have no choice but to impose what we think," Marcelo Bielsa observes in the documentary *Take Us Home: Leeds* United. "We can't convince [players to do] something that we don't believe in." But in the strongest cultures, the vision almost always feels (and is) shared. It has to feel to members of the team like something that belongs to them as well—an "ours" rather than a "yours." Thus much of a team's culture-building must be fostered and inculcated in the reactions between and among players.

This duality—the design by the coach and the ownership among the players—can be glimpsed in one crucial detail from the session when Chris's player missed his sitter. The scene ended, you'll recall, with a teammate jogging over to show his support. "Next play, kid." Small but profound. A show of camaraderie in the moment of distress. That kind of signal earns faith and loyalty and builds a sense of belonging. The response was the player's choice, but the words he used were guided by the culture. Chris and his staff used the term "next play" constantly and deliberately to describe where players' minds should be. "We have two sayings that we use so much, the players now use them," he told me. "'Next play' and 'aggressive mistakes.' The first we use after an action where we see a player or team hanging their heads over a mistake or upset about something that just happened. You can't change it; move on and focus on the next one. The second is something we use going into an exercise, small game or match to remind the player to go for it, take risks, make impact plays. If you aren't making mistakes, you are playing it safe and not making impactful plays, and consequently not stretching yourself to be better." Once culture is encoded in the words we use, it spreads easily. The teammate used Chris's phrase but his words were a mash-up. He'd added his own phrase, "kid," the term and his tone reflecting his knowledge of the exact right way for one teenager to express casual support to another in a moment of duress. Building a teammate up rather than tearing him down felt like the right thing to do because in Chris's club, that was what you did. The teammate had recognized the moment and enacted it perfectly.

The interaction reveals another fact about culture: most of the interactions that shape a player's experience in a club will take place outside the coach's knowledge and they will be at least as influential in building culture as the things a coach and his or her staff do and see, so it's critical that they are positive and ideally align to the larger vision. Strong peer-to-peer culture is no accident.

Merriam-Webster defines culture as "the set of shared attitudes, values, goals, and practices that characterizes an institution or organization," and that definition helps a lot. It reminds us that culture is shared among everyone, a mindset (attitudes), and a set of regular habits and rituals (practices). But there's one thing anthropologists often remark on that's critical to culture and is missing from that definition: language. Cultures are demarcated by their language—if they don't share an official language, cultures have their own argot or vernacular. Often, we know who belongs because of how they talk. You know you're getting old when you no longer understand how the younger group talk, for example. We build belonging by shaping the words group members use. Crucially, the words the teammate used to build Caleb up expressed the culture perfectly because Chris had put them there.

There are several important ideas about culture that I've been describing in this chapter so far, and I want to pause to give names to them and define them a little more. I'm going to share two lists:

1. The first list is a set of principles for building culture. They describe how a vibrant culture is built and maintained. Chris Apple used habits, reinforced through language and enough buy-in that they showed up in peer-to-peer interactions. Those sorts of moves are on the principles list.

2. The second list is a set of characteristics. They describe the types of values and beliefs that are communicated by the most productive cultures. In his silence in the moment of his striker's error, Chris's was trying to express psychological safety. *When you make a mistake, I will stand by you; therefore, play fearlessly and embrace accountability.* The messages a culture might communicate once it works are discussed there.

PRINCIPLES: HOW CULTURE IS BUILT AND MAINTAINED

- **Culture is designed...**
- **...and it must be shared.**
- **It must be distinct.**
- **It is expressed in habits...**
- **...and language is the most important habit.**

The first two principles go together. They are yin and yang. Both true; each dependent on the other: a paradox. The first part is that culture is designed, which is to say intentionally planned and built by the coach around his or her vision for the team. That is what it means to lead—to bring a vision to reality. But it also must be shared, which is the second principle. Even a very clear and detailed vision requires buy-in from and agency for participants. And it evolves. Imagine you wanted to create the perfect garden. You would decide what you wanted where and plan the rows. The seeds would have to be meticulously planted, the more carefully and thoughtfully the better. But if the "right" culture—the one in which athletes are most likely to thrive and grow—is to emerge, it must take on a life of its own. It might unexpectedly require enriched soil. Or staking or pruning. You'd have to observe and react.

The third principle is that culture not only must be unique to each particular group but also needs a bit of a wall around it. Not so much to keep others out but to signal to those within the culture that they are part of something special and distinct.

The fourth principle is the idea that culture lives in what you do every day. You can tell your children to value generosity, but unless they see it from you every day, unless they practice it every day, they will not likely grow to live it. In many ways, ironically, the less aware you are of a habit, the more it influences you. Imagine you play cricket for Australia under Justin Langer. Imagine that players running a lap "as a team" starts to happen every day. Over time, players do it in that manner—whatever the details are—automatically. It becomes the norm. To them, this is how you run a lap. The expectations are more influential because you no longer think about them. They are part of you, as are the beliefs they express.

The fifth principle is a reminder that of all the habits, the most powerful, the one that shapes beliefs most, is language—our choice of words. Most of the concepts we know and can think about because we have a word for them. A word for a concept—"gratitude," say—solidifies it and notes that it is worthy of mention. It now exists in my mind. I can talk about it and direct my own or perhaps my children's attention to it when it occurs. I not only put a value on it; I become more aware of it because I can name it. In fact, as Shawn Achor points out in *The Happiness Advantage*, the more I use the word to point out things to be grateful for, the more I perceive the world to have things worthy of gratitude in it. Having the word doesn't just allow me to see it in the world but changes my conception of the world. The Inuit, the legend goes, have fifty words for snow. I do not, and therefore do not see the distinctions they see between one type—light and fluffy, perhaps,—and another—windblown and granular. "Snow" is mostly one thing to me. The Inuit see and value distinctions and gradations that I miss because they have words to differentiate them. "Language," W.H. Auden wrote, "is the mother, not the handmaiden, of thought." We name things into being and cause others to see them more readily or conceive of them by putting a word or a phrase on them.

Now think for a moment about Chris Apple's team and the phrases, "Next play" and "aggressive mistakes." Chris invented phrases for his players to use and in so doing caused them to perceive, focus on and value them. Like different types of snow to the Inuit, these are things that other cultures do not see and value as clearly. The "aggressive mistake" will exist in the mind of his players; they will believe in it as a necessary step in learning, if he can coin that word and have them make a habit of using it.

What does it mean to do it "together"?

Imagine you are Justin Langer and your team has just come out to train, early in your tenure, and you have said to them, "I want you in there as players, a real tight-knit group, just jog a slow lap together. Start thinking, 'This is the team. We're building towards next year.'" Let's say they did it, perfectly. What would happen? What would it mean to "jog slow a lap together as a team"? Would it be tightly organized—in step and chanting like marines—or loose and casual? A bit of banter and some joking? Would it be quiet or loud? Would everyone chat equally or might there be reminders from the captains about goals and how we practice? Surely it would be different for you and for me. It's important to be intentional, to recognize that culture is being communicated and also that the habit can communicate a variety of different things.

The next step might be to frame the expectations in words. Perhaps you and your captains get together to do this. When we say we want to run "together," what do we mean? Then perhaps you express that by defining the term with the team:

> When we say we run our laps "together," what we mean is, we're building each other up, reminding each other of our vision, showing appreciation as teammates. The lap starts casually. A bit of easy banter; anyone can talk. We're reminding ourselves of why we like to compete together and calling out things teammates have done so we can show appreciation. Keep it light. If you're

smiling, you're doing it right. Then, when we make the turn at the far side of the field, the captains take the lead. They remind us of what we need to focus on as a group, get our minds ready to train.

Suddenly you've defined your culture by defining a few words: "together" has a specific meaning on this team. It means camaraderie and then focus. "Making the turn" means shifting that focus from mutual appreciation to the task at hand. It reinforces the role of the captains.

Culture, Daniel Coyle points out, is "dialing in to small, subtle moments and delivering targeted signals at key points." The language helps keep those targeted signals coming.

Let me try to show you these principles in action through a few stories.

"When I came to New York," former New York Red Bulls and now FC Red Bull Salzburg manager Jesse Marsch told me, "I realized that positive energy was really important to me. The feeling of wanting to work. All of us. Of loving effort. I wanted to be about that every day. It was important to create the environment physically and to embody it. When people saw me, I wanted them to see that I loved being there, loved working hard. I wanted them to see me smiling, happy to see them. I wanted them to hear me thank them for the work they do."

Hearing this was a bit redundant. I'd visited Marsch at the Red Bulls' training facility, and I'd felt it already. I arrived early one morning with few people around. I poked my head into the first office by the door, expecting to find a reception desk and saw, instead, Marsch himself, smiling and in the midst of greeting a player. He immediately waved me and a colleague I was visiting with inside. Suddenly we were bantering like family. Then another player arrived and joined in. It felt suddenly like a family wedding. The energy and the inclusion were palpable, and this was the first thing I experienced because Marsch had planned it that way. He had moved his office to where he could greet everyone when they arrived, where there would be foot traffic and group interactions, and where he could shape the culture he wanted from the first moment every day. His office door wasn't just "always open"; his office was always abuzz with players and staff coming and going. He knew everyone's name. Asked about their families. No one had to be told, "You matter to this club. We are a family." They felt it.

But Marsch had gone even further in building culture. "Ali Curtis was sporting director at the time. He was big on measurables. When I started putting together a description of how we wanted to play, he kept asking me about KPIs [key performance indicators]. 'How will we know if we are successful at playing the way we want to play?' he'd ask me. So I came up with words to describe what I wanted that we would try to measure. I wanted guys to be all in every day. I wanted everyone to empty the tank and leave nothing on the field, so those ideas became part of our terminology: 'empty the tank.'"

You can hear the level of intentionality in Marsch's story. He reflected deeply on who he wanted the team to be, on the field and off. He planned how his culture would be expressed, how he'd measure it. But he wasn't done.

"I asked the players to define it. I said, 'What does "empty the tank" mean to YOU guys?' They got together and defined it as 'giving everything you have every day to the group, especially when it's difficult for you.' And so that's what we used as our definition. Because it can't just be about me; it has to be a reflection of everybody involved." The yin is an intentional vision for culture, but the yang—sharing the process of envisioning it with players—was also starting to emerge. His concept; their definition. Shared culture.

"We developed other phrases. Like '*Roger Bannister*,'" Marsch continued. This was intended to evoke the story of the famed distance runner, who set out to break the four-minute mile when people said it could not be done. "When, after years, he finally broke it, something like 23 other guys broke it in the next ten years. It tells you that fatigue is mental. Break that barrier! That's what the word means. I had them read the article and then we talked about it. Then we started using the word 'Roger Bannister' to capture the idea in the story."

"Muhammad Ali was another one," Marsch said, referring to the phrases they used to mark the touchpoints of their evolving culture. "In NY, they had never won [the MLS cup]. They wanted to be the first to win so badly. It resulted in a lot of fear, actually, at playoff time. They were waiting to fail. That's where Muhammad Ali came from. I read this article where he said, 'All that talk? I was trying to convince myself that I was a champion, could be a champion, before I actually was a champion.' I told them that story and we used the phrase. '*We're going to Muhammad Ali the hell out of this*,' I told them." The phrase meant something like "Walk right up to opportunity bravely and with a bit of swagger; talk like you belong, and you will start to believe you do." There were more phrases. Dozens of them. They became the language of the team. They expressed its ideals and culture.

You've probably spotted many of the principles for building culture in the story. Language is the most important habit, for example. Marsch was literally inventing a new language for players and coaches to use to express their values and culture: *Muhammad Ali, Roger Bannister, Empty the Tank*. He had the phrases painted in the lockers and on the walls. Not just in the locker room, but in each and every locker. Visual signals were critical to Marsch. "When I went there, the facility had just gray walls. No phrasing, no logos, no *feel*. It was cold. It needed to feel like a home. When they came in, I wanted them to feel energy. He had inspirational photographs and slogans posted, but vocabulary was just as important.

"Environmental design" is the idea of engineering the environment to shape culture, to "alter the spaces where you live and work to increase your exposure to positive cues," as James Clear puts it. Its effects can be profound. "In the long run, we become a product of the environment we live in. To put it bluntly, I have never seen someone stick to positive habits in a negative environment." But Clear adds that "environmental design is powerful not only because it influences how we engage the world but also because we rarely do it." It was the first thing Jesse Marsch did.

Before I discuss language a bit more, it's worth thinking about what designing a culture might look like if you don't have a large facility and a budget to emblazon it with images and phrases that embody your vision. The first step would be to examine the environmental cues that do exist. The first is the field. What does it look like when players arrive? A field with grids and markers already set up carefully and pinnies laid out in anticipation sends a clear message, for example. *What we're doing today is important enough to be thought through and prepared for. I am ready.* The field also shapes players' behaviors when they arrive. Part of playing for Matt Lawrey at Atlanta United is the habit of showing up early to training, getting your boots on and joining in with high-energy joyful rondos, not because Matt tells you to, but because the culture does. But Matt subtly facilitates this by ensuring that the grids are set up before players arrive. The cue is in the environment. See the rondo grids? They are ready for you! Again, the elements of careful design and shared culture are both present. The minute training starts, Matt strides onto the field and gives a direction to begin shaping the rondo. Something like "Two touches. Burpees if you give up 20 passes. Go!" But before that, the rondos belong to players. They form up groups as soon as six new players have arrived. They race to get their boots on. They chatter away happily and play in a full-of-tricks risk-free way that they wouldn't with Matt supervising. And Matt, if he is there, is careful only to walk around chatting and joking and connecting with players. *When he blows the whistle, it becomes his exercise. Before that, it's theirs.* It's a shared culture, though of course only because Matt has designed it that way.

Another thing I noticed on visits to Atlanta United's Academy was the environmental design around player interactions. New player today? Perhaps they're a guest, perhaps trialing. Either way, the players initiate a warm greeting. Welcome. Shake hands. Names. It's the same for adults, by the way. The graciousness of saying "Welcome to our club" instills values and character but it also establishes ownership. I can only welcome you to something I have agency over.

Maybe you don't have guest players at your club, though. What about the ways older players and younger players interact as one training ends, another begins, and you switch fields? Do the older players make the younger ones feel like an important part of the club? Do they greet them, high five them as they walk by? Interact like older sisters and brothers? Or do they walk mutely past with their headphones on? Speaking of ending practice, do players pick up their trash and stray tape and take pride in the field? This too is part of culture.

Of course the environment today for young people is as virtual as it is physical. Environmental design could show preparation and excitement for practice before players arrive. "Girls, we'll be working on pressing today. Here's 30 seconds of Bayern Munich pressing. This is gonna be how you play soon. Get ready!" Or just "Great training in store for you all this afternoon. Bring your best and make sure to hydrate." Or "Thought this video of great tackles from the Premier League would get you fired up."

Many of the things I have been describing are "different." Most clubs don't have older players greet younger players like family. But if you did things like that, not only would it set you apart to others—I'm trying to imagine the parents that would not appreciate kind and gracious older players making their athlete feel a part of something larger—it would set the club apart to its members. Everything that is distinctive about a culture that the group knows sets it apart from others has this effect. It says, *That's how we do things. Or We do things differently.* Notice the pronoun in those statements: "We." Creating clear distinctions in your culture—things that outsiders might find unusual or not understand—clarifies to insiders that they are a part of something unique. That's the third principle: distinctness. The language on the walls at the Red Bulls' training facility had the effect of reinforcing distinctiveness. Not only were the words unique to the team, but the language was like a code word. You could say "Muhammad Ali," but only some people would know what you were talking about. To speak the language was to be in an inner circle.

Here's perhaps a clearer example of the idea of the inner circle. I once observed a coach of a professional team enter a room for a meeting with his players. Late by a few seconds, as it happened, and the room exploded in an excitement that I could not make sense of.

"201. 201!" some players were shouting.

"Get the wheel!" shouted another. It had been quiet before, but it was uproarious now. Players laughing; coach laughing.

"Boys, you know I'll spin," the coach said.

"You better spin," a player shouted.

"Got a cookie?" shouted another.

The coach gestured like Tom Brady under center, quieting the crowd. He was suddenly pretending to be very serious. Or maybe he was serious. It was hard to say at first.

"Do you think I fear the cookie?" he asked, pausing and scanning the room, grave and somber. "I am the manager of the [team name here]," he said slowly, like Winston Churchill addressing Parliament. "I do not fear the cookie. If it is the cookie, then let it be the cookie!" His voice edged higher.

Wild cheers.

Now here's the back story. The coach had a "fine wheel." Various small infractions of team culture required a spin of the wheel, which then assigned a fine or consequence, some of which were more straightforward and some of which were hilarious and embarrassing. The whole team had suggested fines to put on it. (Principles 1 and 2 there. Designed by the coach; shaped by the players.) I am authorized to divulge the secrets of the cookie only in my final hours in this world, so I cannot say more, but suffice it to say that "cookie" was a tiny sliver on the wheel. The worst place one's spin could land.

So, the players chanting "201" were chanting the time: it was 2:01. The coach was late. He would have to spin the fine wheel. They wanted the cookie. (Alas, they were disappointed.)

Observing as an outsider, I understood very little of that until the coach explained it to me, and that in some ways is the point. Elements of a culture that are incomprehensible to "outsiders" remind "insiders" of their belonging. Inside jokes and nicknames work this way. One of my favorite clips from the first version of *Teach Like a Champion* is of a history teacher named David McBride greeting his students at the door before class: "Mornin', DJ. Mornin', Red," he says as his students arrive for class. "Prime Time is here!" Every single kid has a nickname, which is to say a special name given to you by the people who are closest to you. The message David is sending at his classroom door is: You are family; we are a team. This is not to say that I think it's worth your time to give every player nickname or that youth teams should have a fine wheel. Instead, I am arguing that successful cultures are subtly marked off from the outside world. Belonging, Daniel Coyle argues in The Culture Code, is the most important emotion in strong cultures, and it is paradoxical. "Belonging feels like it happens from the inside out, but in fact it happens from the outside in. Our social brains light up when they receive a steady accumulation of almost invisible cues: we are close; we are safe; we share a future." Strong cultures constantly find ways to remind players that they belong.

In *The Only Rule Is It Has to Work*, their book describing their efforts to manage a minor league baseball team according to principles of data—and as it happens, social science—Ben Lindbergh and Sam Miller seek the advice of clinical psychologist Russell Carleton. How can they create a sense of chemistry and belonging? They ask.

"Have an absolute non-sequitur item that is given out," Carleton advises. He suggests letting the team vote to award it, but you could also have the coaches nominate a player for unseen culturally valuable things (e.g. tireless defending; building up teammates). "You might try a crazy toilet plunger (spray paint works wonders). The guy who gets it gets to keep it in his locker ... but with the caveat that if the toilet gets clogged up, he's got to go in there and plunge it out." The award, depending on your culture, could be a simple straightforward honor or communicate a bit of silliness and humility—both an honor and a leveler. The advantage of the latter approach being that the more fun it is, the more players will want to participate in the giving and the more a ritual will develop (see further, "fine wheel"). But of course, this award is powerful precisely because it would be so incomprehensible to anyone not part of the culture. It establishes belonging.

The fine wheel did this too and at the same time was both carefully designed and shared. It reinforced the coach's expectations of key tenets of team culture, including timeliness, but ensured players' buy-in. It was his idea, but they helped build it and chose the consequences to reinforce the standards he had set to help them succeed. "[Culture] cannot be merely top down," Jesse Marsch told me. "If the players hold each other accountable, it always has more weight.

"When I got to [Red Bull] Leipzig"—a sort of apprenticeship where he had coached briefly as a transition to the European game in between his jobs at New York and Red Bull Salzburg—"my office couldn't be out front, so I had to adapt. I had to constantly spend my time out walking around. Now this team [Salzburg], they win all the time. In NY, we had to teach them how to win. This team, I have to teach how to lose. That it's normal to lose. It's natural to fail. It's the only way to get better." I'm sure there's a word for that on the wall in Salzburg, though I didn't ask what it is. The principle at work here is the second one. Same coach; same plan. But a different team, so the culture has to adapt and evolve.

In discussing Marsch's efforts to build culture, though, I have not gotten to what may be the most important part yet: the key to culture is building habits. Here you need what Coyle calls "steady signals" to communicate what the culture is about. It's what you do every day, often when you don't realize you're doing it, that expresses what you believe. All the talk and the painting of the walls would be meaningless if Marsch couldn't shape his players' physical and mental habits.

His next step was to think as deeply and intentionally about tactical culture on the field as he had about culture more broadly. Taking Curtis's idea of KPIs, he wrote a list of the things that made a player a Red Bulls kind of guy—a fit for the team. He started with the defensive side of the ball. "What we did against the ball was always very important to me," he recalled, so his list included statistics most players would be familiar with—steals and intercepted passes—but also ones he had invented. Marsch again defined new words to describe the details of tactics and in-game culture he wanted on the field, especially when Red Bulls did not have possession. They were things like *forechecking, hunt the ball, ball thief.* There was a chart where players earned points individually and in groups—"attitude points." The video guy would go back after the game and score all the interceptions. "After the game, if a player won the overall attitude points, we would have him pick his song for the highlight video and in it we'd show the moments of his attitude points to the whole team."

LESLE
GALLIMORE

We get to carry each other

Previous to being appointed commissioner of the new Girls Academy League this year, Lesle Gallimore was head coach at the University of Washington—the winningest coach in program history, with a career victories total that puts her among the top 25 all-time in Division I women's soccer. Despite leading the Huskies to the NCAA tournament 15 times, her priority was often culture: "Every single player who has memories, it's of the culture. The connections. It's everything else other than the wins in their college career that made them who they are." Here she describes some of her methods for building it.

People would often ask me *What's your culture going to be like this year?* And I'd say *They're not even here yet.* You can't just stamp a mantra or a culture on a team. In college athletics, it's a new team every year. There were a lot of things that we did that were threads that connected us over time; but every single fall, it was a new group and a new dimension and a new feel because of the people in the culture. And that was the art of trying to manage them—to figure out how to weave that thread in a way that wasn't always top down. And you hopefully had enough leadership returning on your team that they could teach it to each other.

We tried to do a lot of relationship building in advance. Almost every year, we'd read a book in the summer. Something that we felt would provide a theme or leadership and team-building lessons. *Unbroken. Legacy. Boys in the Boat.* Real-life stories; often about sport, but not always; often tied to Washington. If you can get young women to understand what people have been through to make it happen, it's pretty cool.

One year, our mantra came from a song. 'One' by U2 with Mary J. Blige. One of the lyrics is, "We get to carry each other." I turned the lights off and said *listen to the lyrics.* They pulled that out: we don't *have* to carry each other; we *get* to carry each other. They latched on to it.

We had a great season, but at the end of the year, a couple of players were struggling— on the field and off. But we still made an Elite Eight run. When they needed to, they carried each other. Everyone had that love for one another. It was very real. It's what you dream about as a coach.

In the early days, we were always trying to do as much layering of smaller group time as we could—time together where they were constantly with different people on the team. By positions, by age, by where they were from. Really trying to get them all to be in the presence of different people all the time. The key was for everyone to get to know one another.

We would do things on the field that would mirror that too. The first day we had the "Dawg Bowl," our annual 4 v 4 tournament. Winning it was a big deal. The returning players definitely communicated that. But the teams would always be mixed. So let's say there were two freshmen on each of the five or six teams in this tournament, they'd have the opportunity right away to compete with different people. They would right off the bat understand the importance of how we played from a competitive standpoint. That tradition would breed the right culture and make everyone bond and feel included right away.

But it wasn't just games. If you want to build culture on the field, the same rules for building culture apply: habits are everything. Referring to the scoring of the hidden aspects of on-field culture, he said, "We did it in practice as well. We'd have individuals and teams that would win." Players hunted the ball when defending in games *because they hunted the ball when defending in training*. It was their habit. And they hunted the ball in training because Marsch and co. built it into the culture. It was everywhere.

Many of Marsch's measurables were tiny things, by the way. *Ball-oriented* meant staying compact when pressing and controlling space in front of the ball; *fore-checking* meant preventing an opponent from turning with the ball and facing forward. Some coaches might call an idea like "hustle" measurable, but that would be far too vague for Marsch. Culture was about the tiny details that would make us who we wanted to be, captured in precise vocabulary. Only then could it be turned into habit. "Changes that seem small at first will compound into remarkable results if you're willing to stick with them," writes James Clear. "In the long run, the quality of our lives"—and you might add our sporting endeavors—"depends on the quality of our habits."

The chart is a funny idea. It seems a bit juvenile as far as management tools for professional athletes go, but clinical psychologist Russell Carleton mentions something similar when he gives Ben Lindbergh and Sam Miller advice in *The Only Rule Is It Has to Work*: "Start a sticker chart," he tells them. "Ten stars and you get a burrito ... Stars can be used for anything you want to reinforce. The first rule of child psychology is that it applies throughout all of life. They will scoff at it and three days later be checking out how many stars they have." I read that passage to Marsch and he laughed. "I used to think 'Oh they're professionals,'" he said. "I thought 'it will be too cheesy.' But I'm never afraid to try things. So I tried it and it worked. Now when someone has an idea, I think: let's try it. If Luis Robles wanted to have Olympics in preseasons, I'd say, 'Yeah, let's try it.'"

Again, I am not necessarily arguing for a chart here. The point is the importance of measuring and recognizing what you value so it turns beliefs into habits. "What gets measured gets done," the management adage goes. The outcome was Marsch's Red Bulls teams playing relentless team-oriented pressing defense without the ball and doing it joyfully as if they were wired to. It seemed like part of the team's DNA. Could you accomplish that via other tools? Of course. If you were a small club with limited resources, could you steal Ruth Brennan Morrey's idea from chapter 1 and have players observe for and chart their teammates' subtle actions during games to shine a light on them? Sure? Could you end practice by observing and praising one tiny easily overlooked moment that expressed "who we are as a team"? Could you let players do this? Yes, yes and yes. The point is that public recognition is a powerful tool in building shared habits.

The other way to get strong habits is to teach them. This is one of the biggest lessons from successful classrooms. They are full of "discipline" but not necessarily in the manner most people use the word. Discipline is better defined[1] as "teaching people the right way to do things." This means for anything you do frequently, teach people the proper way to do it—or *how we do it*—and reinforce it or have them practice it until it becomes habit. Then you have discipline.

In *Teach Like a Champion*, I shared a video of a teacher named Doug McCurry teaching his students to pass out papers, which might seem like an odd thing to focus on, but McCurry knows his students will do this hundreds and hundreds of times during the course of the year and the more frequently you do something, the more important it is to think about how it should be done and the more you should consider installing that "how" as a routine. You can see that in the video. McCurry explains passing papers carefully and in detail to the class: "Denzel will take one and he'll pass the stack to James. James will put one down then he'll quietly go to Bruce." Then the class practices it. McCurry times them, "Twelve seconds, back in ten…. Eleven seconds, back out in ten." Why is he doing this? Why not just start teaching on the first day? The most important reason for it is that in a typical classroom, it might take a minute or two to pass out or collect papers. If McCurry can do that in ten seconds—and thus save perhaps a minute on each of the hundreds or even thousands of times his students do this task—he will manufacture hours and hours of time with which to learn more about the Civil War or adding fractions with unlike denominators. But he will also allow himself to make his classes more engaging and energetic. As students wait for the papers to get passed out in a typical classroom, ideas begin to fade and energy ebbs. Surely you have felt this in training. A slow transition from A to B. Players who don't come together quickly when you want to tell them something. A water break that is three minutes instead of 45 seconds. These things not only waste time but also affect culture more broadly. Players lose their concentration and come out of "the zone" when they stand around waiting. They want to play but instead find themselves waiting for the transitions to end.

Once, at a workshop, I asked teachers how long it typically took students to pass in or out a set of papers in a typical classroom. I was asking because I wanted to make the point that if you could save a minute ten times a day for 180 school days, you'd gain 30 hours of instructional time over the course of the year, but the teacher who answered gave me an unexpected answer. "How long does it take?" I asked. "Zero seconds," she said, "because it wastes so much time that teachers in my building have stopped giving out materials as often as they should." There's an analogue to that in coaching sports. Why do so many people advise coaches to not talk during training and to never make stoppages? Because they have seen stoppages that are painfully long and ruin the energy and flow of practice and leave players yearning to play. But saying we shouldn't use stoppages removes a critical teaching tool. A better solution is to *streamline* stoppages. Short, focused stoppages of 30 seconds or less and where the coach quickly shares one idea and players try it right away (as discussed in chapter 3) help. These stoppages are much better and more viable

1. I'm pretty sure Ronald Morrish was the first person I heard use the word this way intentionally. His book *With All Due Respect* is excellent

Watch "Doug McCurry paper passing" at www.coachguidetoteaching.com

as teaching tools. But doing this only works if the procedures are sharp and routinized. If you are fast with your feedback but it takes 30 seconds for everyone to listen, you've lost. If everyone isn't locked in and clearly listening, you'll be more likely to say things two or three times to attempt to ensure that everyone hears you. Or you'll have to stop and remind players to listen. Much better is to do what Doug's done and teach them to listen. To make a habit of the everyday things you do. It might sound like this:

> Right. Sometimes during training I'm going to stop our games to explain things to you or ask you questions. My goal will be to talk very quickly and get you back to playing. Because I know you want to play. So when you hear me say "pause," stop right where you are and give me your eyes. If you pause very quickly, I can recreate the scene quickly and we'll be back to playing. If your eyes are on me, you'll listen better, and I'll know you're listening. Let's try that now. Start with the ball, Kevin, but listen for me saying "pause."

After a minute, you say "pause," and perhaps you take a play from Doug McCurry's playbook and say, "That was pretty good, but I think we can be a little better. Make sure to stop right away and give me your eyes so we can learn and get back to playing. Let's try it again." Then they're back to playing and you say "pause." Let's say their response is better. Now you want to build the routine of hear-and-try. So perhaps you give some real feedback: "Good. Thanks for your eyes. When we're receiving the ball, we want to make sure we snap our hips open like this. See if you can do that every time you receive the ball. Go!" In this case, you might deliberately give very short and very actionable feedback because what you are really trying to do is to have players feel the difference. To understand what it's like when they pause very briefly, perhaps for 10 or 15 seconds, get some useful advice and then try it right away. Next of course you'd want to build the habit of using feedback so you might narrate back to athletes that you see them using it. "Yes, Jason. That's the way. Good, I saw how you received that ball, Miguel. Big time!" You'd want to build a habit of using the feedback after they hear it and perhaps curate it and make it feel positive. You'd be doing essentially what Jesse March did with his charts but in a simpler way.

Take another look at this video from chapter 3 of James Beeston building habits with his players. You'll notice that he's explaining procedures for how he'll call on them and how they should react. Cold calls, turn and talks, raising hands. Now they know how to do these things. But notice that the video starts with him explaining how to listen. Come over here so you can see me. He brings them in close. Most coaches overlook this. But your physical behavior while you are listening affects how well you listen and how well those around you listen. If you are fussing with the ball or staring off into the distance, you will gradually give more of your attention to those things—and encourage those around you to as well. And players will gather round and listen to your feedback hundreds, perhaps thousands of times. Why not teach the right way to do that? "When I'm explaining an activity to you, like I'm doing now, make sure you come in close so you can hear. Leave the soccer balls where they are. Just you. Make sure your eyes are on mine. If you do that, I can tell you what you need to know quickly, and we can get back to playing faster." Notice that a good "roll-out" always explains the why.

Watch "Steve Covino
start and stop" at
www.coachguidetoteaching.com

This is especially important with younger players, as significant portions of training can be lost to distractions. Watch this video ▶ of Steve Covino playfully but consistently reinforcing his procedures for start and stop—and incidentally socializing attentiveness, which, as we will discuss, is a critical characteristic of a successful culture.

When designing and implementing procedures in your training sessions, be sure not to overlook the importance of language. The words you use are part of the procedure, and using the same word each time will make the actions more of a habit. Consider the video of James Beeston we watched in chapter 3. Every time he stops players, he says "freeze" to stop them and "play" to send them off. It's the same terminology each time. He wants a fast and consistent response. If everyone is attentive two seconds after he says "freeze," then he can get his work done quickly and keep the energy flowing. If the practice snaps to life when he says "play," the intensity will be higher. Choice of words is important too. James's choice of "freeze" reminds players of one of the critical things they need to do to maximize outcomes from stoppages: stop where they are so he can recreate the scene. Smart. I myself often prefer the word "pause" as it implies brevity: players will be moving again soon.

A final connection between Steve's session and Doug McCurry's class: the kids are all really happy. This is counterintuitive to many people—even many teachers—who assume that structure and clarity mean joylessness and soul-crushing rigidity. But in fact, students in both cases seem to appreciate the implicit faith in them expressed by a coach who wants them to do little things better. It looks different with older players and perhaps adults, but ultimately they appreciate the respect for their time and development implicit in a more focused learning environment with less downtime. You can see this in James Beeston's U19 session and also in Denarius Frazier's classroom: when he quickly calls them together, they are instantly and willingly attentive, with eyes on him in exactly the way he's taught them, and then are back into their math.

CHARACTERISTICS OF SPORTING CULTURES

So what kind of culture does a successful team have? ("successful" here is defined as that which maximizes people's growth and development and fosters behaviors among participants that support that goal for themselves and others. As I will discuss in chapter 6, this definition of success is different from one that defines success as winning the most games. That said, in the long run, such a culture is often a (game-) winning culture as well.)

There's no one right answer, of course. Every culture is different—that's one of the principles of developing cultures—but I'll offer here some thoughts on five characteristics I've seen in both strong classroom cultures and top sporting environments. I think these characteristics are worth developing in their own right, but not surprisingly they also align with and foster the teaching concepts described in this book. In other words, these are characteristics that help cultures get the best out of people. Still, everyone's vision of culture is different. Assuredly I'm less aware of some things that are critical to you and obsessed with something that will be less urgent to you. Adapt or discount as you see fit.

To me, **positive learning cultures are characterized by:**

1. A culture of error, or 'psychological safety'
2. Inclusion and belonging
3. Attentiveness

4. Excellence

5. Character and candor

Psychological safety

In chapter 4, I discussed the phrase "culture of error," which describes a classroom—or a training environment—in which learners willingly reveal their mistakes to their teachers and peers. They do this because they believe doing so will help them to learn. When this occurs, it is far easier to find and remediate the gap between "I taught it" and "They learned it." In chapter 6, I'll share some scenes from Iain Munro's training where he encourages players not to hide behind what they can do well but to push themselves to try—and therefore fail, at first—at what they cannot do. This is critical to their learning. Psychological safety is the term psychologists use when referring to a state where moderate risk-taking is tolerated, people can speak with honesty and candor, and where creativity flourishes. When Jesse Marsch sought to get New York Red Bulls over their fear of failure, he painted the phrase "**fear to fail = failure**" on the wall. He delivered a similar message to his Salzburg team, despite their differences. They had to get comfortable with the idea that they were going to lose. They had to understand that this helped them learn and grow. They had to approach losses as learning opportunities. This is to say that mistakes should be studied rather than punished. When teachers gradually socialize students to acknowledge and examine their errors without defensiveness and anxiety, they learn faster. It's the key to trust in learning and performing organizations, argues a recent article in the *Harvard Business Review* that begins with a quotation from the head of industry at Google: "There's no team without trust."

2. www.bit.ly/2HcsBlo

LAURA
DELIZONNA

> When the workplace feels challenging but not threatening... Oxytocin levels in our brains rise, eliciting trust and trust-making behavior. This is a huge factor in team success.

"When the workplace feels challenging but not threatening ... oxytocin levels in our brains rise, eliciting trust and trust-making behavior. This is a huge factor in team success,"[2] writes Laura Delizonna. We've seen examples of this throughout the book: Chris Apple not screaming at Caleb for his obvious miss at the beginning of this chapter; the math teacher in chapter 4 telling his class "I'm so glad I saw that mistake. It's going to help me help you"; Denarius Frazier's emotional constancy in the face of his students' mistakes. These are not cultures where people tiptoe around mistakes to avoid hurt feelings. They're cultures where people are not afraid to discuss a mistake and say it was wrong. Why would they be afraid when it's not a big deal.

How does one accomplish this? First, remind players that struggle is normal. James Beeston, training his players to break down a low block, sees them struggle and says: "This is extremely difficult. I wouldn't expect you to get this the first time. Let's try this...." When appropriate, praise smart risk-taking. I'll discuss this more in the next chapter under the heading "Coaching decisions, not outcomes," but saying, "Good. I'm glad you tried it" or "That was a good time to take a chance. Too bad it didn't work out," are examples of this. In chapter 6, you can also read about Steve Kerr helping Steph Curry focus on the signal—the right long-term decision—not the noise—the fact that in a given moment the right actions are not getting results. Kerr wants his star player to worry less about a few missed shots and to play boldly—or at least to know when and how to play boldly.

Apparently, this is one of the talismans of Jurgen Klopp's culture. "He would say: 'I don't watch you shooting all week [in training] to try to be [Andres] Iniesta and thread a pass,'" Alex Oxlade-Chamberlain told an interviewer.[3] "He would scream at me 'SHOOOOOT!' It goes in or it misses but, in his head, it is, 'So what? Mo [Salah] and Sadio [Mane] are running in.'"

3. www.bit.ly/35jacLU

It's worth noting that a culture of error where people willingly expose their struggles and mistakes because doing so will make them better is not relevant merely for athletes. It is critical for adults too. A club must foster it among the adults, so they do not hide the difficulty of the work from one another. If you ask a coach, "Can I come watch you train tomorrow?" and he or she says, "Don't come. I'm doing something new," they are telling you they are afraid to be seen struggling. A good response might be to model what you want yourself: "OK, fine. Then come see me. I'm doing something really challenging tomorrow and I'm not sure it's going to go well. I'd love your feedback."

Inclusion and belonging

Psychological safety alone does not make for an inclusive culture. Being included has to make players feel important, happy and supported, and, in a strong culture, it must protect against cliques, which are essentially subcultures that come to be more important than the larger culture. Among the most useful concepts for defending against the sort of social fractures and divisiveness that can tear apart the cohesion of a group is the idea of "fault lines," which comes from management professor Katerina Bezrukova's research and which Ben Lindbergh and Sam Mitchell discuss in *The Only Rule Is It Has To Work*.

Describing how Bezrukova's research might play out in a school, they write, "If five friends all love cheerleading and five other friends all love marching band, then those ten people are divided into two groups that don't interact. But if girls from each group are also into, say, running the school's canned-food drive, there is now a third, overlapping group. And if there's a conflict between a cheerleader and a flutist, there are networks for resolving it."

"When I first went to Leipzig," Marsch told me, "there were a series of individual rectangular tables where everyone ate. They were all separate. It would always be the African players at one table. The French players at another. The German players at another. Staff over here. The first thing I said was that we have to totally change the meal dynamic, so the tables are continuous and there's no separation. We have to sit together. And then we have to tell them why. I tried to bring subtle pressure to sit down where the next seat was. Not to sit where it was safe. And then, in time, you'd start to see on the road that the guys were mixing more there as well. The routine became that we would change where we sat."

Russell Carleton also stressed the importance of mixing across "fault lines" at mealtimes to Lindbergh and Miller. The first few days of their team's season featured a "Don't eat with the same person twice" rule.

Of course meal times are only one example of the many settings in which players can mix and cross fault lines. Matt Lawrey's rondos before training are a great example. They were social as much as anything else, but "The rule was you made a group with the first six guys who were ready. If you're there and not playing, it was 'Hey, why are you waiting around? Get going. Get in there.' It was so important for the guys to get to play with different kids, and the system was designed to randomize." But it often wasn't that easy.

"There were guys who would come in the same carpool," Lawrey told me. "They'd arrive together so they tended to always play together. And over time, they'd subtly start to engineer it so they could play with the guys they knew. Sometimes it was by positions, but at one point they suddenly were forming groups literally by race: the black guys, the white guys, the Hispanic guys. We had to figure that out fast. So I started using an intro task: 'Guys, it's 100 juggles with your left foot when you arrive. When you've got that done, start your rondos.' We had to always be ready to find new ways to shuffle the groups."

The way you teach and the habits implicit therein, of course, are among the biggest drivers of culture. In *The Culture Code*, Daniel Coyle notes that when people feel like they belong, their behavior changes. They become not only more productive but also more creative, more risk tolerant and more selfless. But belonging, Coyle writes, "is a flame that needs to be continually fed by signals of safe connection."

"Our social brains light up when they receive a steady accumulation of almost invisible cues: we are close, we are safe, we share a future." You can hear some small echoes of the habits and routines we saw teachers like Denarius and coaches like James Beeston reinforcing above. Eye contact and body language, for example; it's important that people track, that they look at the person who is talking. This behavior says, "What you are saying matters to me." When Denarius speaks, he asks students to track him, but he also expects—and has explained to them that he expects—them to track each other. Compare that to so many American classrooms where students are asked to share their thoughts and opinions with a room full of people with their backs turned and their eyes averted as if to say "I'm not even listening." Who would possibly share an important thought in such a place? Players in James Beeston's training are similar: the body language and eye contact are peer-to-peer signals (that James has intentionally made part of the culture) that you belong and that your ideas matter.

Coyle cites studies by social scientist Alex Pentland, who researched the behavioral drivers of team performance. Compare the first three items on Pentland's list to the behavior of players in the group James runs:

- Everyone talks and listens in relatively equal measure, keeping contributions short.
- Members maintain high levels of eye contact. Conversations and gestures are energetic.
- Members communicate directly with one another, not just the group leader.

Attentiveness

Interestingly, the discussion of the nonverbal habits that drive team culture has already begun a segue to what is, for me, the third characteristic of learning cultures: attentiveness. Attentiveness to others—eye contact, focus, constant cues that say that I am listening, that what you do and say matters—is the driver of their belonging and engagement. And as a double bonus, it helps people pay better attention. And this is both fundamental and fundamentally overlooked. Let me put it in the words of a teaching colleague: "The depth of our attention creates our capacity for learning." And attention, Cal Newport points out in his profound book *Deep Work* (which I discussed in chapter 3), is a habit, a capacity, grown and developed by practice and eroded by constant distraction.

Success in spaces of intense competition require you to "hone your ability to master hard things." You must be able to sustain focus and concentration when others waver and you must be able to master new and difficult content again and again. The key is the ability to sustain states of unbroken attention and deep concentration. Those who can focus best for the longest separate themselves from the crowd.

So we want players as locked-in mentally during training as they are physically, but this is not easy to accomplish. Attention tools like tracking help. So do means of participation tools like cold call that constantly engage players and signal that they cannot tune out. So do training sessions that aren't interrupted by off-task behaviors or slow, shambling transitions. Crisp transitions from idea to idea harvest and husband states of attention. This is a big deal.

One topic—a hidden one, perhaps—that deserves attention is what to do when athletes are not attentive. When you circle players up to listen—at a stoppage, at half time—and eyes are wandering, or you hear an undercurrent of whispers or giggles. Or that one kid who is kicking the ball against the back of a teammate's legs. Being able to fix small disruptions like this without creating a larger disruption, not responding to off-task-ness by interrupting the task for everyone, is one of the hardest skills for a teacher. You can read more about it in *Teach like a Champion*, but here's a short recipe of steps.

First, a caveat. The best solution is to have taught people the right way to do things. Want players locked in and attentive at half time and not on their phone? Explain the procedure you want them to follow carefully. ("I'm going to give you three minutes to get water and talk to your teammates. Then I'm going to ask you to bring it in. When I do, come near so you can hear. Give me your eyes and be where I can see you. No soccer balls. Know that I may ask you to respond to questions and thoughts and to problem-solve with me.") Include the "why." ("This will let us study the game whichever way it's going quickly but with focus. It'll help us succeed and the routine will make half time feel calm and focused for you.")

"If students aren't doing what you want," Doug McCurry told me, "the most likely reason is you haven't taught them." So start by teaching them.

The clip of James Beeston's session from earlier in this chapter isn't of half time, but it's a great example of how to teach expectations, explain a process and share the why. I especially love "Sometimes I may call on you even though your hand isn't raised, because the game requires you to be switched on at all times." He's so clear about how to participate and what "focus" looks like.

If you have taught your half time expectations and you're not getting the behavior you want, the first thing to do is to "be seen looking,"—that is, to show athletes or students that you notice and care who's paying attention. Look at this very short video of an elementary school teacher named Katie Kroell. Notice in the foreground there's a student who's distracted. Maybe there's something he wants from his backpack. Could be something perfectly appropriate; could be something distracting. It doesn't really matter

Watch "Katie Kroell sacrifice" at
www.coachguidetoteaching.com

which. What matters is that when he sees Katie looking at him, he decides to change his own behavior. Knowing his teacher sees him changes his decisions. When a teacher shows students that she sees what they do and cares, much of the behavior will desist. On the other hand, if students think their teachers won't notice or care what they do, they are more likely to engage in off-task behaviors. Oftentimes, teachers use a bit of subtle pantomime to show students they're looking, to make it a bit more obvious. Perhaps it's a slight tilt of a head like you're looking around something. You can see Denarius do a bit of this at 1:33 of the video from his class. He steps out slightly from his cart, raises his chin slightly and gets on his tiptoes just the slightest amount. Message: See me looking at you? I notice and I care whether you follow through. Here's a still shot of the moment:

The next move might be a quick low-key reminder to the group describing the expected behavior very simply, ideally in a way that assumes the best (see chapter 3) such as "Make sure you're tracking Donnell while he's talking, boys."

The next move is a nonverbal correction. A small gesture that says, "Please turn around" or "Track me" or "Ball behind you, please." There are two benefits to a nonverbal correction as compared to stating the above correction to a player—or not saying anything and allowing the behavior to persist. The first advantage is that, done subtly, your nonverbal is private. It allows you to reinforce expectations quietly while preserving relationships. You can do it with a neutral face or even an understanding half smile so that players feel understood. But culture is also preserved. The other benefit of the nonverbal is that it allows you (or a player who's speaking to the team) to continue talking. You keep the task going and preserve attention and focus.

If these things don't work, a private individual correction afterwards is a sensible move. It allows you at least to make sure the behavior doesn't happen again. It might sound something like this: "David, before you go warm up, give me a moment, please." [David walks over.] "David, when Donnell was talking, it looked to me like you were possibly making a remark to Kevin. You definitely weren't tracking him. It's important as part of the team to be locked into our conversations about how to improve and to show that you're locked in. I'll expect to see that next time. Thank you. Go warm up."

You'll notice that there are no questions here—"Were you? Why were you?"—just a careful statement of the expectations and the reason for them and a reminder that you will expect better, ideally done in a calm voice, perhaps even with a gentle hand on the shoulder to show you are not angry.

I've modeled this sequence with half time talks, but of course it's a plausible recipe for reinforcing expectations around listening and attention in any setting.

Excellence

The pursuit of excellence—learning to seek the best versions of ourselves as individuals and members of a group—is one of the primary purposes of athletic endeavor. Perhaps it's *the* primary purpose. Some might argue that enjoyment is the primary purpose of athletic endeavor. Probably so. For many athletes, that's as far as it goes. But for many others, especially those who pursue a sport beyond a basic level, enjoyment and excellence are intertwined. The enjoyment comes in part from the growth; it is more fun when you understand it better, see yourself improving, accomplish things.

In building a culture of excellence at a club, a few key ideas are critical. First is the idea that excellence is in large part about a dialogue with oneself, the process of mastering a series of concepts and challenges through diligence and teamwork. Second, excellence is not zero sum—"More for you means less for me"—but is achieved communally. When your teammates get better and improve faster, it's likely to cause the same for you. We push each other by giving our best. Finally, excellence is about taking the risk of giving one's best and finding out what one is truly capable of. That means the willingness to compete fully, to compete every day. And doing that includes psychological challenges coaches should be prepared for.

I once asked a coach at FC Dallas, perhaps the most successful academy in the US, what was the single most important thing they did to develop players. "We compete," he said. "We try to make everything competitive. Our players are always competing, so they are not intimidated by challenge. We tell them: *iron sharpens iron.*

The phrase "Iron sharpens iron" expresses the idea that we give our best every time, both for ourselves and for our teammates, and that when they fight hard against us in training, they are making us better and preparing us for competition. At the same time, we're not looking for the Hunger Games. Our work is youth development and education. We want healthy competition when we step on the field but balanced by support and a culture where athletes feel a sense of belonging. Competing can go wrong if it's not also humane and athlete-focused and if the challenges are not framed properly for athletes. Providing language to help players manage the intense emotions engendered by a competitive culture is critical, for example. Again, the phrase "iron sharpens iron" is a good example of this. It explains to players how to frame the intense emotions of the field or court. You can easily imagine Jesse Marsch telling an "iron sharpens iron" story and building the phrase into his club's vocabulary. But language is not enough. The next step would be to build habits to express the ideas you describe. Perhaps after practice we thank each other for pushing us by playing hard; maybe we hug or shake hands. Maybe we do this first with any teammates we feel anger or tension with about what happened on the field. We know we have to resolve it productively to be teammates. The ritual of saying thank-you to those who test us reinforces the phrase "iron sharpens iron," encapsulating a competitive mentality but also helping athletes make sense of the sometimes difficult emotions competition will give rise to.

Of course you don't have to use this language or this ritual. This is an example of how beliefs need habits to turn them into culture, and that some of them should address the complex psychology of being an athlete—of putting it all on the line at the time in your life when you are just beginning to figure out the relationships around you.

Character and candor

In the end, what matters most about the work that coaches do? We set out to help people achieve their athletic dreams, to maximize their potential and find out what it means to pursue excellence, and to learn to work together as a group. For most, the journey itself will turn out to have been the gift. Playing will end. They may not even know it when it comes. There will be an interruption for work or school; an injury or a spot on a team they do not make. Suddenly it will be over. Or they'll hold out believing there will be another chance, but it will never come.

No matter. They will go on to other (hopefully greater) things, our athletes. They will be husbands and wives and partners, mothers and fathers. Presidents—of nations and sports franchises and banks and nonprofits. Mayors and doctors and nurses and teachers and coaches and everything else. If we have done our work well, our coaching will have helped them to thrive in those endeavors as much as, or perhaps even more than, the goal they and we primarily thought they were pursing in all those years of training.

Would we coach differently if we knew that was the true outcome?

In the end, our work should first and foremost help our athletes thrive by helping them to become the best people they can be. Would we knowingly train a locker room full of World Cup champions if we knew as a result that they would also become selfish spouses and distant parents? Self-absorbed members of communities? Takers instead of givers?

We would not. Or at least, I would not. I assume you as well.

Character must always be at the soul of the cultures we build. There are in fact various types of virtues that participation in athletics can reinforce: moral virtues (compassion, courage, honesty, humility, gratitude), performance virtues (determination, perseverance, resilience, teamwork) and civic virtues (community, civility, citizenship).[4] They must always be foremost in our minds because they are the true purpose of what we do.

4. I've taken this from the Jubilee Centre's framework for character education, which I highly recommend. www.bit.ly/37I0MSp

CHAPTER 6

ISSUES IN GROWTH & DEVELOPMENT

The previous chapters in this book were about the details of a coach's day-to-day interactions with athletes—giving feedback or designing a session, for example. The sum of those interactions becomes, in effect, a methodology—a conscious or unconscious philosophy about how athletes learn. Hopefully, those chapters will help you to develop your methodology even more intentionally.

But technical questions only cover part of the teaching life of a coach. There are broader issues that intersect with methodology, and at almost any workshop or club visit I've done, one coach, or several, will end up asking questions about them.

At a workshop on feedback, a coach asked how he could get parents to stop shouting counterproductive things from the sidelines, both psychological ("If he pushes you, push him back, Kevin!") and tactical ("Get it up field, boys!").

On my visit to a professional academy, a coach asked about a player we had just watched train—a model kid in every way, except that he wasn't quite good enough. How to tell him? *What* to tell him?

At another academy, the question was about a coach. He was constantly shouting and didn't take feedback but his team was a steady winner. How could the club get him to change his mentality? How long should they keep trying?

The coach of a national team wrote to ask for reflections on what to do (and not do) during half time talks.

And every coach seems to have questions about the effects of technology on players' motivation and focus.

Often those questions would stay with me and I would wrestle with them for days. What were the answers? Were there answers? This chapter is an effort to reflect on some of those questions and the broader issues they raise.

The first section considers topics in long-run player development and growth: whether everyone on a typical team gets coached equally, for example, and how more equity of teaching might be achieved. Or how likely we are to be right when we say, "That kid—that's the one who's going to be special."

The second section is also about long-term development and trajectory, but in this case focusing on coaches. How does the desire to be recognized for our achievements—as every professional wants to be—affect our decisions? How does one manage one's own emotions?

Finally, there's a section on related club- and organization-level issues. How can we help parents to be intentional about their sideline behaviors and how can we help to align long-term incentives with them?

TOPICS IN PLAYER DEVELOPMENT

Coaching everybody

In the introduction, I described one professional coach's realization (after watching Denarius Frazier teach math) that many times, much of his team went uncoached during training—which is to say, undeveloped. This suggests a major difference between coaching and teaching.

In school, it is more or less understood that the goal is to reach everybody: the greatest amount of learning for the greatest number of people. A teacher like Denarius will tell you it's his job to make sure everyone learns, even those who are reluctant or poor at math. There had been a time when a teacher could legitimately react to students who struggled or signaled that they did not care and more or less write them off. Not my problem. *If you want to fail, that's your choice. Some people just aren't good at math.* But not anymore. Teaching has changed; a teacher's ability to reach everyone is a key aspect of his or her skill set.

Coaching is more likely than teaching to accept differences in who gets a coach's attention and the benefit of resources. Sometimes this is by design. It's just part of how things work. At the professional level, a coach only keeps his job if the team wins. In that system, some athletes' performance and progress is more important than others'. Pro teams invest millions in first-round draft picks and "projects"—each with immense upside but raw skills. Of course they invest more resources in their development. Similarly, the goal of an academy is to develop elite players; the coach's job is to invest in the top of the class—the handful of players on each team who have a shot at making it as pros. When allocating resources, the rational decision is to allocate them to the most promising athlete.

But the tendency to prioritize some athletes over others prevails even at levels far below the top tiers of sports. Powerful, often deeply ingrained tendencies and incentives determine who receives attention and opportunity—and who does not. The tendencies show up at every level of the game. The result is something coaches often think too little about: that the teaching (and therefore the learning) on any team is almost always asymmetrical, allocated more to some than to others, sometimes because of decisions a coach isn't even aware he has made.

Consider the story of Xavier from chapter 1. Kids who shine early because they are fast or flashy are often showered with attention at the expense of slower, smaller peers, or perhaps the kid who's cautious because he is thinking deeply—an ugly duckling who might emerge later as a swan. Which means there are a lot of swans that never develop. But also consider the potential for positional disparities in coaching. Chris Apple's observation in chapter 5 was that *the great majority of coaches spend the great majority of their time on the offensive side of the ball.* Training exercises at the youth level are often designed to teach the attacking side of the game, and most of the time the defense is there essentially to provide opposition while the players on the offensive side are learning. The back four are often mostly a foil to the "real drama" unfolding up front. Perhaps there might be a little positional work and a few reminders for the center backs to get stuck in, but rarely was there a focus on technical aspects of play for defenders: body position, footwork, what cues to look at to make decisions. You could be on a great team with a great coach and still not get much coaching as a center back.

And even in open scrimmages when feedback is at least theoretically given to everyone, the guys who are on the ball are more likely to get the pointers from most coaches. A decent corollary to Chris's observation might be *The great majority of youth coaches spend the great majority of their time coaching the players on and nearest to the ball.* Draw a circle of ten or twelve yards around the ball and you also often have a circle of where the teaching goes. There are a lot of players outside that circle. On how many teams does the kid waiting for the pass from the point guard get as much feedback and as many pointers? Doubly so if the point guard reliably holds the ball herself. On how many teams does the shortstop get twice as much guidance as second base? On how many teams is the coach not aware of the balance, the equity, of who gets taught? Athletes are often fighting for the attention of their coaches. The kid who's a bit of a thinker and who at age ten still lingers at the margins can receive in return a lack of guidance that can ensure that he or she stays marginalized.

Or consider the influence of the relative age effect, which Malcolm Gladwell's book Outliers brought to broader awareness in 2008. Typically, Gladwell writes, 40% of elite Canadian junior hockey players will have been born in January, February, or March. It seems like a statistical anomaly until you factor in the influence of an annual age cut-off. If the cut-off month is January, players who are born in the first two or three months of the year will be significantly more physically developed than athletes born in the last months of the year. This is a huge advantage when they are young. "Coaches start streaming the best hockey players into elite programs, where they practice more and play more games and get better coaching, as early as 8 or 9," Gladwell told ESPN in a 2008 interview.[1] If you're looking for "potential"—kids to tap for the first team or an elite program—you're more likely to choose kids who are 107 months of age versus 96 months of age. And kids moved to a more advanced environment tend to get more coaching, more challenge, higher expectations. To be slightly older is to gain more access to opportunity and thus to be more likely to succeed: a self-fulfilling prophecy'

1. www.es.pn/3dLT8C3

Even if a coach isn't actively sorting players into programs and onto teams, his tendency will likely be to give more teaching attention and more opportunities on the field to kids who look like they're more committed and have more potential. It's a lot more gratifying to give feedback to a kid who can apply it successfully than a kid who struggles. The weaker player stumbles and does it clumsily or does it right but loses the ball anyway a second later. The stronger kid makes you feel successful. Look how good he is! He's got it already. He scored twice. He's going to be special and you'll have been a part of that triumphant journey. It's like catnip. It's almost impossible that any coach is not at least a little bit biased in who they observe and give feedback to—for reasons that are mostly about being human and fallible. But the athletic and the precocious are magnets; they draw attention. Which means that some individualized version of the relative age effect—the relative talent effect; the early developer effect—is happening within each team.

Hidden things draw our attention to some athletes more than others. In their book *Soccernomics*, Simon Kuper and Stefan Szymanski describe how this is a factor in scouting, for example. "At least one big English club noticed that its scouts kept recommending blonde players," they write. "The likely reason: when you are scanning a field of 22 similar-looking players, the blondes tend to stand out (except, presumably, in Scandinavia). The colour catches the eye. So the scout notices the blonde player without understanding why. The club in question began to take this distortion into account when judging scouting reports." But of course there's a coaching version of this too. We are always "scouting" in a sense, subconsciously scanning the field to decide which athlete we'll focus our teaching on. And it's rarely equal.

Like relative age, issues of symmetry are not *only* about fairness. On the Czech national soccer team, when Gladwell examined the data, no players had been born in the last three months of the year. The team had reduced its potential talent pool by 25% or more. Twenty-five percent of an 18-player squad is 4.5 players. Imagine the effect of replacing your weakest four players with four players who are distributed normally across the team in terms of skill. It would be a massive improvement. But we also narrow the pool of potential late-developing performers when we, unintentionally or not, focus on only some of our athletes' development.

A few years ago, visiting a major league baseball franchise, I spent an hour or so chatting with the club's GM, a highly successful devotee of analytics. What was new that the data were telling them? I asked. "Well, one thing we're discovering is that the guys we think will never make it make it a lot more often than we thought," he said.

"The minor league system was built for the purposes of entertainment but is now used for the purposes of education, and the two rarely connect," the executive of another MLB team told me, so a minor league club is often a deliberate exercise in asymmetry. A roster at the Class A level might have six or eight or ten guys who the club is committed to growing and developing, but you need a lot more guys than that to play a season of baseball. You want to grow a shortstop? You'll need a decent second baseman. So teams fill out the roster with a lot of "second basemen": decent players they're not really looking to invest in. The time, the energy, the effort, the doting—those things are going to the left side of the infield. What those "other" guys get is a chance to play. In their hearts, though, the club knows they aren't likely to get above Double-A.

"At least that's what we thought," the GM told me. "What we've learned is that those guys make it to the majors much more than we thought." Now they were thinking more about how to invest in them—in spreading the developmental tools the club had across a wider array of players. Analytics and player tracking had revealed that more efficient and more symmetrical teaching was a performance issue.

Symmetrical coaching is also about team chemistry. I was struck by this recently while observing Marc Mannella, who helps teams develop their teaching capacity, as he worked with members of an NBA coaching staff. He showed them a video from the HBO series *Hard Knocks*, which profiles NFL teams via behind the scenes footage, in this case the Houston Texans. In the clip Marc showed, a coach is reviewing film from a pre-season scrimmage with players on the defensive line—specifically, a great play made by J.J. Watt, the team's star.

"This," the coach says, "is excellent," as he rolls through footage of Watt pushing a tackle upfield and bursting inside. "That angle, and running like that, is excellent," he says, freezing the video to show Watt racing laterally along the line of scrimmage. "That's excellent. *That's excellent*," he says twice more as the video shows Watt bringing down a running back from behind on the far side of the field. "That shit will win us a game," the coach says as the scene fades out.

Marc, I know, had chosen the video because he wanted the basketball coaches to observe how the football coach could strive to be more specific, his analysis more technical. Calling it "excellent" without defining specifically what "it" is doesn't help other players in the room understand how Watt accomplishes "it" or how they can replicate "it." The coach will need to roll back the tape and ask the players to analyze carefully how Watt generates leverage, times his move, places his hands. He'll want to explain what "running like that" means and how it's different from how they currently run. Only replicable praise gets replicated. At least that's what Marc wanted to talk about.

But that's not what the basketball coaches saw, and the conversation quickly went in another direction.

"The question that came to mind for me is, 'Was he the only one that did something right on that play?'" the first coach to weigh in asked. "I'm not a football guy, but there must have been at least three or four other people that did their job, that allowed him to get that lane or that forced the running back to where J.J. could do his job," he says.

"I just think in general, it's easy to coach the best player," another pointed out. "He gets paid the most. He's supposed to do that. Is there a way to include other people?"

The coaches bristled at the idea of lavishing praise on the team's star without acknowledging the rest of the team or taking steps to develop them too.

"If I'm a roster bubble kind of guy, I look at that play and I think, 'Yeah, that's the best defensive lineman in the league,'" Marc said. "The question is, what can somebody else learn from it? And the thing you can learn can't be 'Be six foot five, 290 pounds and able to bench press 740.' That can't be the lesson.

"I think people might be surprised to learn how this dynamic exists at the very highest levels—I've seen it in the MLB, NBA, and NFL. I was shocked when I heard of it in my first experience with professional athletes. I was working for an NFL franchise. I'd felt it myself as a high school athlete, but surely these grown men are past that? Nope," Mannella recalled. It's the hidden story of teams. At every level, players are constantly asking: *Am I important here? Do I matter? Is this coach vested in me? Does he see what I do? Does he care if I succeed?* It's lurking constantly just beneath the surface and it only takes a few seconds of video to release it.

Which perhaps explains why the soccer coaches had such a strong reaction to the very simple observation that Denarius was coaching everyone, seeing everyone, and most of all communicating to everyone that their progress mattered. If you were Denarius's student and did poorly on a test, you still knew that Denarius wanted you to succeed. He had proven it, day in and day out, by coaching you, investing in you, letting you know he saw you. Similarly, a coach should be able to say, "You're not starting this weekend" or "I want you to play with the farm team for a few weeks" and have the player feel that it was coming from someone who believed in him and who was vested in guiding him forward, even if the decision was a disappointment. That's very different from thinking "He doesn't give a damn about me. I'm not on his list. I'm not one of his favorites." Coaching everybody is one of the primary ways we build inclusive culture and relationships; ignoring players is often where resentment starts.

So if coaching everybody matters, the next question is *What can you do about it?*

A simple starting point is to vary your coaching position more intentionally. At Chris Apple's session, we were standing pleasantly on one sideline when Chris suddenly excused himself and walked to the other side of the field. Was it something I said? "I always try to split my time between various coaching positions," Chris told me later. "When you stand on the near side, you see the near side players more clearly. You coach them more. Not on purpose; it's just one of those ways that, over the course of a season, you can get really unbalanced about if you're not careful." Sometimes the simplest observations are the most powerful: the average coach typically notices and teaches the players who are closer to him most often, and if you always stand in the same place, there will be a long-term asymmetry. So you might use a timer to remind you to switch which side of the field you're coaching from every ten minutes, say, in a typical training activity, so offense and defense—or first team and second team etc.—get equal attention.

A periodic retrospective review of your week's coaching activities might also be a useful habit to get into. Do you run six activities on creating overloads in the attacking third but only one on defensive topics?

Finally, this is a great area for teamwork. Ask a colleague to observe you—it doesn't even have to be another coach—and make observations merely about who you interact with. We often do this with classroom teachers. We call it a "heat map"—a concept that should be familiar to coaches. It involves simply having a colleague track who gets questions, feedback and comments directed their way. Are you primarily talking to three players? Are you ignoring the backs or the quiet kids? This is a good way to find out.

Talent identification

With athletes, we are always sorting—always guessing who has potential and trying to create new opportunities for them. We do this for valid reasons. Players deserve opportunity; they deserve challenge; one of the major reasons to play a sport is to commit yourself to the pursuit of excellence in order to see how far your potential can go. The problem is not that we sort. The problem is that when we sort, there is a near inevitability that we will be wrong in who we choose, and we are far less aware of this fact than we should be.

In advance of a 2016 FA Cup tie between Manchester United and Shrewsbury Town, *Guardian* journalist Stuart James profiled Shrewsbury defender Mat Sadler, who had played alongside then Man United star Wayne Rooney on a highly successful England U17 team that had done brilliantly in a tournament of European nations 14 years prior. An injury to Rooney prevented the 2016 reunion, but the point of James's article was to highlight the different paths the two men's careers had taken. Rooney had gone on to become one of the most highly regarded players in England, if not the world; but Sadler's career, James observed, had not quite panned out. He had been tapped for the England squad early. He appeared twice in the Premier League for Birmingham City that year as a 17-year-old. His success seemed assured. But his time at the top was brief, in the end—15 total matches spread over three seasons—after which he began a "disappointing" career as a player in the lower leagues: six transfers and five loans to Stockport, Rotherham,

Shrewsbury, and Crawley Town, among others. He would never again be on the same field—or in the same league—as Rooney.

But in fact, the implication that Sadler was an underachiever and that his journeyman career was a mark of unrealized promise isn't quite accurate. The data suggest that playing in the third tier made Sadler a *success* among the alumni of the youth national team on which he and Rooney played. "Only five of the 18 members of the [U17] England squad," the article noted, "are still playing professional football."

"We all thought we were going to be big hitters then, I tell you. We really did," Sadler is quoted as saying. English football did too. To the keenest football minds in the country, Sadler and his teammates were the best of the best, and that assessment was made just a few months or years shy of their professional debuts, which is to say after the real uncertainty was passed: they'd done their growing and maturing physiologically. They were on the brink of adulthood. And yet ten or so years later, the pick of the litter were as likely to work for the gas company as to play for a Premier League side.

That players overestimated their own talents is fairly understandable. In fact, it's fairly understandable that professional coaches and scouts and evaluators *also* wrongly assessed their potential. In the US, we react with shock every time there's a Ryan Leaf or a Darko Milicic, but we somehow ignore the fact that about half of first round draft picks don't pan out despite millions of dollars spent on assessment and development. Professional evaluators routinely get it wrong, not because they are bad at the job but because the job is so hard. That is really where the story lies.

Consider an article in the *Telegraph* in 2007[2] which describes how in 2003, David Platt and other senior members of the FA's technical department organized a "player audit" in which they evaluated promising youth players on their likelihood of playing one day for the senior England men's team. They were categorized as "certainties" for full England honors, "on course" or "having no chance." "The audit," the article notes, "severely over-estimated the quality of the player within the system."

2. www.bit.ly/34hVCF9

"Out of 25 players graded as becoming certain senior internationals, four have achieved this status to date," Platt reported years later. If there's a 16% success rate for the "certain" players, then in fact there are no "certainties." Learning curves, physiological growth curves, attitudes, health, commitment, and psychology are all too unpredictable. *The mistake isn't in guessing wrong; it's in betting too heavily on the guess*—even at the elite levels. We think we see the future, but we don't.

For the FA, the data means one thing, but what does it mean for youth coaches and clubs that are interested in long-term development? First, let me reiterate that leveling is often a good thing. It's not without its difficulties, but it creates opportunities for players to grow, challenge themselves and compete. It is one of the reasons why sports are valuable and is a form of fairness. Players who love the game and want to play it at a high level have a right to be with others who approach it similarly.

Interestingly, schools I've helped run have often chosen to group students by achievement levels as well, even though some in the education world object to this. That might seem like a contradiction in schools that explicitly seek to ensure every child's success, but ironically it has helped us to see how to do grouping and leveling in a way that jibes with the idea of teaching everybody equitably and with what we know about the challenges of selection. In the classroom, for example, grouping by achievement level only works if it is fluid—constantly changing and responding to progress of students—rather than fixed: *Here is the top group; here is the bottom group.* So, sure, there should be an A team and a B team in your club, but how you structure that dynamic is critical. You must select wisely, you must coach everybody, and you must believe in their potential no matter where they are in the hierarchy.

The first rule of sorting is to hedge your bets. If the only thing you know for certain is that you are wrong, that you have chosen some Ryan Leafs and overlooked some Tom Bradys, do not bet too heavily on your selection. Do it in stages, with lots of re-sorting and alternative ways for players to earn opportunities.

The second rule is to group for performance, not for potential. Once you have made selections, remember that you have evaluated where you think players are *right now*. One of our first changes when we sorted students into groups for math in a school I led was to change the way teachers talked about it. It wasn't "ability" grouping. It was "achievement" grouping. We were vigilant about correcting the verbiage. Our words had to remind us that the sorting was temporary—not a measure of what students could do but of what they were doing at that moment. Getting people to change the way they talked about it helped to remind them of this.

If it's true that achievement level is temporary, the next step is to coach everyone as if they will be the best player on your team in three years. The problem is not A teams and B teams, it's B teams that are an afterthought where players aren't taken seriously and where there is no clear pathway up. Players should choose different levels of commitment. Those who choose to make a strong commitment should be allocated by their clubs to the most appropriate level competition. But once there they should all benefit from instructional excellence and a belief that all doors remain open to them.

"Fail fast" is common advice for projects in technology and entrepreneurial sectors of the economy. If you know you don't know the right answer when you start, design your organization not to avoid mistakes but to learn from them quickly. This means that the frequency with which sorting decisions are made is a critical factor in any leveled environment. In the case of our school, the second change we made was to fix the idea of putting kids into math groups annually. A year is a long time in terms of learning and a longer time in terms of a young person's mindset.[3] If we're really grouping for achievement, we should re-group as frequently as possible, which for us was three times a year. And we constantly referred to when we re-evaluate so it was a foregone conclusion to teachers.

3. For the most part, students did not know we were grouping them. We did not say we were, though I am sure many of them figured it out.

I encourage you to ask: how frequently can you look again at your player pool and consider which players are advancing rapidly and need new challenges, and which need more confidence and might benefit from time on the ball at a lower level? There should always be players moving up to the first team from the second team. The message it sends to players to see other players come up and teach everyone a lesson or two—in hunger, in skill, etc.—is a gift to second team players who are reminded, even if it wasn't them who were chosen for the chance, that the door is always open. But it's just as much of a gift to the first team to see hard-working players competing in a system of meritocracy and to know that their current status is not a permanent and God-given thing. In the *Guardian article*, Mat Sadler suggests that being anointed is what did several of the players on that U17 team in. Want players who compete on your club? Give them a real chance to compete for what they value over and over. Show them the door is always open and you will get competition.

In reality, having players "come up" to the A team once each year is far too infrequent. Why not give a few players the opportunity to play up at every tournament? Why not invite them up for a practice? For a week of practices? A year in the mind of a kid is a very long time; and besides, if you presume you were inevitably wrong on your selections, you'd want to constantly see how the ones you didn't pick stacked up (or how the ones who were struggling did at a lower level). One reason talent is hard to spot is that context changes performance and it changes it differently for different players. Mix a young Andres Iniesta in with lesser players and you might misunderstand his potential. He'd be waiting for the pass that didn't come. Put him in with Xavi and suddenly you see what he can do. What athletes do depends on the setting; you will never know who can do what until you give players new challenges. Somewhere in your club there is a player waiting to show you his inner Iniesta when placed in a different (and more challenging) setting.

Going down a level temporarily can also be beneficial: sometimes the best developmental opportunity for a player is to take on a different role—maybe one where he has to learn to take more decisive action in shaping the flow of play. A colleague described this happening to two players who were sent down from an NBA franchise to their developmental league team. For one player, it was a success. Dominating stints in the developmental league boosted his confidence and he came back up to the team firing on all cylinders. For another, it wasn't. The coaching staff speculated that the first player created for himself and the latter relied on others and therefore regressed more to the level of play around him. But maybe, in the long run, he was the player who most needed to learn to step up.

But consider the cultural context as well. If you make a point of sending some of your best players from the first team to play with the second team early in the season, you make it normal and natural for everybody else. You could tell them, "Everybody's going to go up and down this year. I want you to show them how it's done from a leadership and attitude perspective." You could set your club up to do this by not maxing out the A team roster and taking 16 instead of 18 or 10 instead of 12 on the assumption that there would always be two players rotating up. Or on the assumption that you'd promote two more players mid-season. Now you have a system built to reward players who show they are ready for more challenge.

Whatever you decide about sorting, the messaging to players is as important as the decision. Do you say, "You're on the A team," or do you say, "You're in the club and you'll be on the team that best suits you within it at any given time. Either way, work hard and learn as much as you can"? Do you prepare athletes for the psychology of moving up and moving down? Both for the naturalness and the inevitability of it? The only thing worse than telling a kid "You are a B team player" is telling them "You are an A team player." You are a player. Give your best; love the game and learn it. We will endeavor to teach you as much as we can no matter which.

One of the things that must happen in a club if you are serious about fluidity of selection is not just universally high quality of training but universally high quality of curriculum. If you really believe in the potential of all players to succeed, shouldn't they be learning the same ideas and the same language to talk about them? This not only signals your expectations for the potential of all players but also allows for fluid movement up and down as merit and development change the equation. If 14-year-olds are learning different things on different teams within the club—e.g. if one team has a coach who builds out of the back and possesses the ball and another has a team where the goalie is perpetually punting and players are encouraged to shoot yards from the end line and near the edge of the penalty area, time after time—there is little chance that players will be able to move from one team to another. The message is: If you are on the A team, please learn the game model. If you are on the B team, please ensure that payment is submitted on time. In fact, moving players frequently is a great way to hold coaches accountable for being consistent in what they teach at each level. If players can't move fluidly because they aren't learning the same things, you have an organizational problem.

Playing to win

Does winning matter? Is it a beneficial part of participation in sports, especially youth sports? The answer to these questions is yes. Athletes take pleasure in competition and in measuring themselves against others. It is hard to achieve your best, or even understand what your best is, without being pushed there by a desire to compete and win. To compete, and in so doing learn about ourselves and see what we are capable of, is, in the end, the purpose of the endeavor. And while striving to win drives all athletes, it plays a double role in team sports, where participants make a tacit agreement to make their individual desires, decisions and behaviors secondary to the shared goal of coming out ahead as a group. In that way, team sports mimic not just society but the pathway of human evolutionary success. Yes, having an opposable thumb is a big win from an evolutionary point of view, but perhaps less so than is having a willingness to coordinate and sacrifice. Animals that are willing to do this are known as eusocial. Humans are perhaps the only truly eusocial mammal and the traits this engenders (duty, sacrifice, selflessness)—which sport often reflects and reinforces—explain more than anything else why we sit atop the food chain. Perhaps that's why we love team sports so much and why cooperation and selflessness are the lessons we value most from participating in them. Whether or not we actually win, seeking to win teaches us how to achieve more and learn more about ourselves long after the games have stopped. So I am not out to tell you that winning and seeking to win are bad.

At the same time, a misunderstanding of why and how winning matters can be counterproductive and hinder the accomplishment of other goals, some more important. And ironically, focusing on winning too much in the short run can cause athletes to win far less in the long run. So, yes, winning matters, but not when we lose sight of its place. And because winning is powerful and feels good, it is especially easy to misunderstand.

The most obvious way a misunderstanding of winning disrupts the achievement of more important goals has to do with behavior. Who hasn't stood on the sidelines and listened to parents (or a coach) whining about the referee's craven efforts to fix yet another local U14 match? Truly, it is hard to live in a world where a referee, perfectly positioned and 25 yards from the play, can call offside against Kevin when his less-biased parents can see perfectly well (from 80 yards away, and despite a hazy knowledge of the actual rule) that he was on. Somewhere, a dark cabal of referees is meeting, even now, to conspire to deny little Kevin and his teammates their just deserts.

And who has not heard the same parents (or coach) rant about the opposition, who are not merely playing just as fiercely as their own children but who are in fact *playing dirty* and have been *coached to play that way*, as their whole club is taught to do, which pretty much everybody knows? How do the people in charge not see the cynical machinations—*Look how they're wasting time on the throw-in!*—and dirty play of every single team we have ever played against (except the one we beat 5-0)? And speaking of the people in charge, where is our trophy for selflessly holding the moral high ground when everyone else is using their elbows?

Apologies for the sarcasm. I'm still processing years of sideline idiocy: by our team, the other team, and every team. A game where someone hasn't completely lost the plot when it comes to winning sometimes seems like an impossibility to this sports parent. Is it getting worse? I suspect so, but who's to say? That it's bad is bad enough.

Winning is a worthy goal *because it causes us to give our best and compete with honor.* It is a gift of mindfulness to remember that, much though you want to shout in the moment, the referee is far more likely to be correct than you are. It is a gift to recall that competition benefits us to exactly the degree that the opposition challenge us. If they play hard, all the better. As Steve Freeman, director of Black Watch Premier, reminds his club's parents, you don't want to win every game anyway: "If we won every game, it would only tell you we weren't playing good enough competition." When, in seeking to win, we lose the plot, the winning is no longer beneficial.

Perhaps most relevant in a book about teaching, though, is the fact that by seeking to win in the short run, we often undercut our athletes' development and their ability to win in the long run. This is a counterintuitive idea. It would seem logical that the more you win, the more you are likely reinforcing the things that will continue to cause you to win; but this is not true, so it's worth taking a deeper look where conflicts emerge and why.

First, let me acknowledge that some coaches must play to win more than others—coaches of professional teams are the obvious example. Others—college coaches, for example—must take into account winning in the interest of the institution they serve, though hopefully they are clear that as part of a larger institution, they should be supporting educational goals like instilling character first and foremost. But for the great majority of coaches in the great majority of interactions, the goal is to develop players: to teach them the game and teach it right, to help them be the best players—and just possibly people—they can be somewhere down the road—when they are 17 or 19, say, perhaps even as a group six months from now. "Some youth academies worry about winning; we worry about education,"[4] says Xavi Hernandez about Barcelona's world-renowned academy. And in a recent interview,[5] Red Bull Salzburg head coach Jesse Marsch—among the two or three most highly regarded American coaches in the game—suggests that even professional coaches take a nuanced view of the tradeoff between winning and learning. Marsch described the primary challenge of coaching a professional team as being "how to create a learning environment." At the outset, you want to emphasize learning, even above avoiding mistakes. Players need to learn your system and how you want them to play. As the season progresses, Marsch observed, a shift occurs and things begin to tilt more

4. www.bit.ly/31y1dVY

5. on Gary Curneen's *Modern Soccer Coach* podcast: www.bit.ly/31yWFP3

towards outcomes. Results become relatively more important. The narrative that learning even at the expense of results is a worthwhile trade becomes less prominent, but the theme is that a performance culture has to be a learning culture. "Your ability to create a [learning-focused] process is vital to your success," Marsch says. "It ultimately leads to being result based." You win at the end of the season because you learn more at the beginning. Even in the pros.

Sometimes, you can coach for long-term development and make decisions that maximize your chances of winning each game in the short run, but not always. Sometimes, to do right for your athletes, you have to do things that will make it less likely that you will win now. That's a big ask. It requires a quiet ego. A coach has to be willing to appear less successful in order to help his athletes be more successful later on.

Where are the potential conflicts between winning in the short term and long-term development of players? Let's start with style of play. Is there a right way to play to develop players? I would argue yes. Or at least there is a range of right ways, and if embracing playing the right way means you lose the odd game as a result, so be it. You should still do it.

JEFF
ALBERT

You're not just blindly following a process

Prior to his job as hitting coach for the St. Louis Cardinals, Jeff Albert was minor league hitting coordinator for the Houston Astros, which meant he had to align hitting instruction across affiliates and focus coaching on long-term player development.

Alignment of the coaches is the first step to players' long-term development. Players want to impress everybody. Especially when they're new. And you're saying to them, *Hey, we want you to perform in the game, but we also want your long-term development. We want you to do well in the Major Leagues, not in A-Ball.* For the hitting coordinator, it only works if the manager and the coaches are also encouraging you: *Hey, your development is the most important thing. You're playing tomorrow whether you get a hit tonight or not.* It's important for the coaches at the affiliate to deal with that fear.

The games matter, but so do the other things we measure. The first step was that everybody had to know what we were talking about. When we talked about loading the hips, when we talked about swing plane, guys knew what that was. What we saw was that it was critical for everyone to have access to the same information.

But you can't struggle forever. The process has to eventually produce a great outcome, so you have to be able to show signs of progress along the way in whatever objective way you can—video or the data we can measure on a swing. Or data on not swinging at pitches out of the zone.

If I can measurably show you your swing plane is getting better, your lower half is getting better, we can start to be confident that the outcome is going to be good. You're not just blindly following a process. If we can find consistent objective ways

6
CHAPTER

to measure those landmarks, measure your progress, and if we can make coaches accountable for them too, then we can all be working on long-term development.

If you're the player, I want to supply you with the right problem to solve and the right pieces and let you solve it. Then I want to let you know if you're passing the landmarks, and I want to make sure you have enough encouragement. My role really is to provide those things.

Style of play

In group invasion games, the average player spends a fraction of his or her time on the field or court with the ball. In soccer, a typical player spends about a minute or two on the ball in a 90-minute game. The numbers are different for hockey, basketball, rugby and the like, but the principle is the same. What you do when you don't have the ball is the majority of your work. How you position yourself and move in support; how you align your body; where you set up to defend: this is the work of the team athlete. The priority for a coach should be to maximize opportunities for players to react to and learn from the movements and decisions of teammates.

In soccer, there are a variety of styles of the game that one might call *possession-rich*.[6] I don't intend to be overly dogmatic about what that means—you can play possession-rich soccer from a variety of formations; you can emphasize different aspects of possession; you can shift in and out of it occasionally, and learn to counter-attack, say—but if you want to develop players for the long run, the default should be a system that values and teaches it. This means 1) rapid ball movement and a priority on keeping the ball so there are lots of decisions and interactions; 2) a focus on movement and possession *everywhere on the field* so decisions and interactions are distributed to all players; and therefore 3) guiding principles that shape actions during open play so that players learn off the ball as much as possible.

Let me start with an extreme example. I know a coach who advocates for players to dribble whenever they can, even into a 1 v 2 or 1 v 3 situation. "Just dribble. You'll get more touches," he tells them. You're accelerating your own development, the argument goes; but the math is wrong. When a player loses the ball, she effectively distributes touches from her team to the other team. Our young dribbler gets five touches, but the rest of the team loses the 10 or 20 they might have had if she hadn't given the ball away. And when they know she's not passing, they lose opportunities to learn to support and play off a dribbler productively.

Further, all touches are not of equal value. On every possession, a player will make a first touch. She must receive and control that first touch—the ball having arrived in any of a thousand ways in a thousand contexts—and, in so doing, protect that ball, possibly deceive the opponent, and set up further actions. The first touch is inherently the most challenging and the most important developmentally. The second touch also has heightened value developmentally. It requires a player to prepare for further options. The technical and mental demands are highest on those two touches and their quality will determine if a player gets more. Once the ball is solidly in a player's possession, all

6. For coaches of other sports, there are analogies, I am sure. There's a way to play basketball or rugby or hockey that emphasizes ball movement, full team involvement, decision-making off the ball. I'm going to go a bit deeper here into the details of soccer in hopes that you'll see the connected tactical decisions in your own game.

touches are about equal in value. Earlier touches have higher value in success and in development. So it's not just that our dribbler is losing touches for her team overall; it's that she's turning more useful touches—a series of first and second touches spread across multiple players—into less developmentally beneficial ones—a fifth, sixth and seventh touch, all for her.

This doesn't mean there aren't times to dribble—of course there are. We want players who are not afraid to take risks, to spot and exploit and even create opportunity. But strategic ones, ideally, and coaches should explain the full story developmentally: to give the ball to a teammate is to preserve the opportunity to get it back, is to *learn how* to get it back. To give the ball away is to give away opportunity for everyone. There's a big difference in how much you learn when you have the ball for 60% of a game versus 30% of it, just as there's a big difference in basketball in how much the team learns if the player bringing the ball up court launches a shot before anyone else has touched the ball.

Even if it helps you to win now, it will result in fewer wins later.

But possession-rich environments—environments that emphasize the "group" in group invasion games—are most valuable because they create "mental touches," decisions made off the ball to create space and opportunity. This is where the great majority of decisions are made. When it is said of great players that they make others around them better, it is because they have mastered these arts, and the higher you go in the game, the more true it is. To learn to understand the game, players have to participate in a version of it that values positioning and movement off the ball, that is characterized by consistent logical player interaction, and that rewards smart decisions reliably. If a player can reasonably expect to get the ball a certain percentage of the time by making a sharp movement into a good position, she will persist in making such movements. She will watch carefully for more such opportunities and learn to read the game. Learning to read the game is a useful expression because much of it happens the way that learning to read language happens. The brain learns to read by the compounded experience of a thousand tiny perceptive experiences in which it decodes successfully or not. It's AI: a process of constant trial-and-error simulations. If players on the ball look for teammates only in certain places, or if they look too late after they have taken three touches when one would do, and if the odds of a player receiving the ball when she makes smart movements therefore become poor, learning will suffer. Our athlete will become a poor reader. She will learn to make random movements since logical ones are rarely rewarded. If the chances of getting the ball drop to near zero when she is positioned behind the ball, say, or is lateral and far away, *she will stop moving off the ball when in those situations*. In short order, the number of players actively involved in reading the game will be reduced. Brains will switch off. More and more athletes will play as if watching a faraway event in which they have no immediate involvement. It's a cognitive death spiral. It only takes a few players always forcing the ball forward or failing to see teammates open in a range of positions—or relentlessly keeping the ball for themselves—before the long-run effectiveness of the learning environment is destroyed.

Teams where coordination is not prioritized, where players do not learn to read a logical version of the game, are everywhere, and they are sometimes quite successful. There are plenty of opportunities to win basketball games by having your best player bring the ball up, work the ball with one other teammate and take a shot himself. His actions reduce the risk of a mistake and increase the likelihood of points scored. You've seen coaches rack up wins that way, or when precious few players know how to play in combination, handle pressure or more importantly support a teammate under pressure. Playing with poor ball movement in basketball or rugby or soccer, or poor puck movement in hockey, reduces both physical opportunities (on the ball) and mental opportunities (away from it) and means that the lessons learned from playing will be random rather than logical, progressive and productive. Sometimes a less team-oriented approach that rides the coattails of a few individuals can work against superior competition, but mostly it's a way of winning "against the run of play" and borrowing against the future. It's actually the run of play that matters most in the long run.

For soccer coaches: Building out of the back

As a default, developmentally oriented soccer teams should build out of the back. If they do not, the most useful and transferable learning opportunities will be allocated only to some players, which means you are guaranteed to coach asymmetrically. A decent rule of thumb is that half of goal kicks and goalie possessions should involve throws (in the case of goalie possession) or short distribution. More, ideally. Even if you won every punt or long kick, the result would be asymmetrical development. Backs never touching the ball except to win it and get rid of it. It would all but guarantee asymmetrical coaching. But you wouldn't win every punt or long kick. Fifty percent would be a miracle because really the numbers are about 1/3 won for the kicking team, 1/3 won for the opposition and 1/3 never really won by anyone, with the ball bouncing out of bounds or into space to no one's real benefit. So the odds are a bad bet over the long run. Building out of the back, on the other hand, means everyone must play under pressure, must learn to use skill, must decide. Over and over. This means your team will lose the ball, especially if you try to build from the back in challenging circumstances. You will give up a bad goal. Parents will moan. At some point, it will cost you a game. But that's a short-run consideration. In the long run, you will build skill, poise and comfort with the ball among all of your players in a wider variety of high pressure settings. You will teach them to link play. This will allow them to play anywhere on the field and enjoy the game for the rest of their lives. Which of those, a coach has to ask, is more valuable: the 2-1 win in a boot-fest against FC Crosstown or a 2-2 tie in which the half the players on the team who would otherwise rarely get on the ball learn to play as a team and with poise while under pressure?

De-emphasizing athletic-based success

You probably have a player who is really fast. You can put him on outside and he will race by defenders. He can reliably get in on goal even with sloppy technique. He can skate past the opposition no matter how questionable his puck handling or his decision-making. He can be out of position and still recover. You have a player who is big enough to rebound without having to learn to rebound. You have a player who can succeed because of athletic gifts. You owe it to him (and his teammates) to ignore the easy trick that leads to instant gratification, even if it means you'll miss out on winning some games. Over time, teams will figure out how to defend pure speed. Or the difference between his speed and others' will erode. Or we will be in a league where everyone is fast. Or big. Or stronger than the average kid. A coach who is committed to teaching for the long term must teach that player not to rely on physical prowess in unsustainable ways now, even when it causes the team to win; even when it makes the coach himself look good. If he does not, the result is an athlete who cannot play a more sophisticated game later, whom the game passes by. This situation is endemic. Some of the kids we coach the very worst are the kids who dominate when they are young. We let them become limited and one-dimensional players to keep the wins coming.

"We had one coach who would constantly have his teams play super direct because they had a really quick forward who would constantly break through and score two or three goals a game," an MLS academy coach told me. "But when that player moved [up], he wasn't as dominant. He was being tested against kids with similar physical qualities and it went badly." He needed a different skill set but had wasted a year playing in the past. This situation is all too familiar, though the response by the academy was less so. The coach was released.

Most parents are blind to this issue, however. They see the hat-trick and begin to dream of the future. It's a coach's responsibility to understand what the dreams awakened by early success will require to reach fulfillment and to recognize that their own self-discipline is one of those things. This is a difficult thing to do. Many parents are not aware that the coach who makes their child a star at 14 is not necessarily the coach that is preparing her to succeed at 16 or 18. A good club should see that issue coming and be prepared. Asking parents of successful older players who've been through the process to weigh in and share their perspective is one way to do so. Asking players themselves is another.

Coaching decisions, not outcomes

Here's a story an MLS Academy coach told me. His team one year was made up of a significant number of boys who were playing up in age by one and sometimes two years. Things were rough at first and they lost a lot of games. "The other team would celebrate like they'd won the World Cup," he told me, but the coach persisted. "We didn't alter or change anything. We continued to try our best to build out of the back play through midfield, switch the point of attack and dominate possession through all those matches and yes, sometimes that resulted in a pass picked off by a bigger or stronger player who then went in and scored. The communication from us on the sidelines was, "That's OK! Same again!" We let those young guys know that it was perfectly fine to make mistakes because we knew this would help them when they are 16, 17 or 18 years old and hopefully in contention to sign a homegrown contract."

How a coach reacts to the outcome when a sound decision results in a poor outcome is one of the most important factors in players' development. In the great majority of cases, when the decision is right but the execution goes wrong, it is a good thing. The execution, after all, won't always be insufficient. It's the easier part to learn, and as a result coaches should want players to make decisions *slightly ahead of where their skills are*. A good decision with an imperfect skill is not only preferable to proficient skill with a bad decision, it's likely to result soon enough in both good decision and good execution.

But the short-term cost can put long-term development—and long-run success—at odds with winning. There will be a game a good coach loses because a player had the guts to try the right play—to use his left foot; to take the high-percentage shot; to switch the point of attack—but failed. A coach should see both parts of the process and respond to both—whenever possible giving implicit priority to the former. This doesn't mean a free pass for execution or that the coach must say "Great play, Carlos!" when, in the waning moments of the finals, Carlos drops the ball. In the end, learning what you can execute reliably is part of the decision. And focusing so that you do what you are capable of is a skill. What it does mean is that the coach should differentiate two parts to most plays: a mental part and a physical part. While the physical part may be more dominant in determining whether you win now, the mental part is more dominant in determining whether you win later. That's the part that players can choose to replicate or avoid. A first step then would be to split your feedback. Saying "Great decision; better execution" to Carlos helps him understand both parts—to see the difference himself. He has to understand the difference between what he tried to do and how it worked out. This is something players are often not aware of—even elite players, as you can see in one of my favorite videos of Steve Kerr and Steph Curry.

Watch "Signal and noise: Kerr and Curry" at www.coachguidetoteaching.com

"That's your shooting totals," Kerr says to Curry, seated near him on the bench during what appears to be a timeout and pointing to stats showing plenty of missed shots. "That's your plus/minus," he continues, pointing to the data showing the larger and decidedly positive influence of Curry's decision-making, even though the outcome does not appear readily positive to Curry. After all, it's easy for a competitive athlete to over-focus on the immediate outcome. The coach's job is to help identify the signal amidst the noise.

"It's not always tied together. You're doing great stuff out there. The tempo is great ... It shows up here [in plus/minus]; it doesn't always show up there [in shooting percentage]," Kerr says. He is helping Curry to see that his decisions are right even if the execution was imperfect and he's missed more than his share. The right shot, in basketball, is usually a higher percentage shot and the task is to make decisions that will create more of them. But the phrase "higher percentage" implies misses too. It's a weighted coin toss, but still a coin toss. The outcome will never align perfectly with the right decision. Which is why Kerr, speaking to arguably the best basketball player on the planet, stresses decision, not outcome. "Carry on, my son," he says, as Curry heads back onto the floor.

Growth mindset: fear is the enemy of success

To be successful in the long run, players must embrace risk. They cannot grow if they live in fear of being wrong. You might think this is an issue most critical for weaker players and early learners who need lots of encouragement, but a visit to Philadelphia Union's academy a few years ago convinced me otherwise and reminded me that growth mindset is important for all athletes and especially important for elite players.

I was observing Iain Munro who, before arriving to coach in Philadelphia, had managed three teams in the Scottish Premier Division, played for Rangers, Stoke and Sunderland, and earned seven caps for Scotland. A theme in Munro's practices was that fear was the enemy of success, specifically the fear of making mistakes. As became clear, his interest in helping players overcome fear of mistakes should not be conflated with lack of high standards or precision. The words "Do it *properly*" echoed throughout practice and technical detail was at a premium. "Safe side in, safe side back," he called to his boys, demanding a pass to the foot away from a pressuring defender.

But consider this interaction during technical training in which he was teaching players to play the ball with their left foot, under pressure, and direct a first-time ball to a player on their right. Their first instinct was a crisp first-time touch with the inside of their left foot, something they could do with ease. But Munro pushed them to take the risks required to learn something more sophisticated.

"Don't side-foot it! I want you to play it with the laces!" he called. "Hook it with the top of your foot so you can disguise the pass." He demonstrated a back-spinning chop he wanted the boys to strike. For elite players, though, talent can serve as a barrier to learning. Many of the boys wanted so badly to strike each ball perfectly that they reverted to what they could do well (using the side of the foot) to avoid what they couldn't (using the top of the foot). In essence, they were trying to prevent themselves from learning something new so they could keep doing what they were good at.

Munro, however, was onto them. "I know you can hit it with the side of your foot," he called, as one boy struck a perfect side-footed pass. "Don't be scared! Play it with the laces! *Don't be afraid*."

"That's it," he called to another, whose first clumsy effort at the disguised chop lacked spin. "Keep at it. It'll come."

"They're so pressured to be successful, sometimes they are afraid to fail," noted Union co-owner Richie Graham, observing from the sidelines. That fear, Carol Dweck has shown, can stand in the way of long-term growth. Dweck studied the mindset of children and its connection to learning in school. Some students—often very capable ones—had what Dweck calls a fixed mindset. They believed talent to be something you *were*—often because they were praised for being "smart," she posited. Students with a fixed mindset developed a belief that if they failed, they would no longer be smart. Result: they avoided risks to avoid failure. Over time, though, they fell behind students who had a "growth mindset," who believed smart wasn't something you were, it was something you developed through struggle. Those students *liked* rather than *feared* challenge because they understood it made them grow. Students with a growth mindset didn't say, "This would be more fun if it wasn't so hard," or even, "This is going to be hard but it'll probably still be fun." They said, "This is going to be challenging; how fun!" It was they who tended to be the ones to emerge from childhood full of flexible adaptable talent backed by resilience and tenacity. It was they who succeeded in the end, even if they started behind. Dweck's groundbreaking research suggested that teachers—and parents and coaches—could shape the mindsets of the young people they worked with to make them more growth-oriented and that, over time, this just might be the most important determinant of success.

It doesn't take much to see the connection to coaching in Dweck's work. Elite players are often told they are good or talented—the soccer equivalent of "smart." If they come to see their ability as something given rather than earned through struggle, they can become risk averse, afraid that playing poorly or making a mistake will undercut people's belief that they are "good." A great coach then must actively encourage players to risk error and normalize the getting it wrong that leads to getting it right. When that happens, you have something I called a "culture of error" in chapter 4: a culture where it's safe—encouraged even—to make mistakes so that learners come to love the challenge of learning, and this, even more than his vast technical knowledge, is what set Iain Munro apart. You can't get to great, he reminded the boys over and over, unless you are willing to fail.

LESLE
GALLIMORE

I listened carefully when they talked about school

Former University of Washington Head Coach Lesle Gallimore, one of the top 25 winningest coaches in Division 1 women's soccer history, describes how important mentality was and how she looked for players who would be receptive to an approach that stressed teamwork and growth mindset.

We were competing in the Pac-12—the "Conference of Champions"—with the likes of Stanford and UCLA, just to name a couple. These are schools that win a lot. I always knew we might not be the deepest team; we might not always get ready-made players, but I felt we could win by developing players. That was a big part of what I was looking for and a big part of what I sold them on: "You'll be better than when you got here. And we're going to be a team." It was all about trying to find players that understood that. The phrase I used a lot was "You have to trust that I know that you are better than you think you are." That's my expertise. To be able to get players with a growth mindset who were taking feedback right up front was really important.

They're tough to find sometimes. It was often a case of talking to their coaches and watching their body language at training and in tournaments. And listening carefully to how they talked. How they answered when you ask why they play, for example. Are they intrinsically or extrinsically motivated? Sometimes they want to get something: they want to be all-conference or a starter. But if they never talk about being a teammate or how hard they want to work, or what kind of help they need, you worry a bit. You want someone who talks about how they want to improve. A player comes in and she says, "I'm strong finishing anything from my waist down; but above my waist, heading—I have to get better." That tells you something.

And a lot of times, honestly, you can learn a lot about them as an athlete by hearing them talk about their academics—if they want to know about the size of classes and whether they can ask questions of professors and how office hours work. To me, that's the same person that's going to ask me to watch film and be proactive in their own development. Not all the time, but fairly regularly, the student-athletes who want to understand the pathway academically are also the ones who wanted to find it athletically. So I listened very carefully when they talked about school.

TOPICS IN PROFESSIONAL DEVELOPMENT

A discussion of Carol Dweck's book *Mindset* provides a useful point to shift from the topic of players' long-term development to the equally important issue of coaches' development. It is often immediately apparent to coaches that athletes should seek to embody a growth mindset. They should embrace challenge and seek not so much to be proven smart or skilled but to simply improve and to end each day a little better than they were the previous one. Do that, and the outcome will take care of itself. Process is the driver of long-term success.

It is sometimes less obvious to coaches that growth mindset is equally beneficial to—and critical for—themselves. To succeed, they too must embrace challenge and seek not to be proven smart but strive instead to improve a bit more each day. For them, too, seeking that will likely cause the outcome to take care of itself.

"Coaching is about developing people to become better, to reach their potential and—for team sports—to become better than the sum of your parts," Scotland Rugby head coach Gregor Townsend told me. "It's about problem-solving and constantly working out how we can do things better ... how the next day, next session and next selection can be done differently to improve the team."

"There are ... so many things that I do where I try, and sometimes I fail. Or maybe I see that if I did it again and I did it a little bit differently and found a way to iron it out this way, [it would work]," Jesse Marsch told Gary Curneen.[7] "It's almost like it's trying to find a way to get to the core of what I want to be, who I want to be and what I want our teams to be that's the thing that's ultimately going to be the measure of how well I do as a coach."

7. www.bit.ly/31yWFP3

For elite coaches, process is the driver of long-term success—and also probably happiness. Plenty of winning coaches are burned out by the job because the job itself—the daily tasks and challenges—does not fascinate and engage them, and crafting solutions does not bring them joy. If winning is the only prize, it's probably not enough to sustain you for the long haul.

Rewind to the conference room in Chicago I described at the beginning of this book where I had the chance to interact with some of the top professional coaches in the US as they stepped back to focus on their own learning by watching video of teachers and coaches far less accomplished than themselves with humility and purpose.

Watching video is often an interesting litmus test—especially watching video of other coaches, doubly so when one is watching coaches of "lesser status." When the video ends, coaches have two choices: they can criticize the video and talk about what's wrong with what the coach on the screen did, or they can talk about what's useful in the video. Almost any video you can show will portray moments that allow for either of these two responses, but if there are five things a coach can already do better than the coach portrayed in the video and one thing that the coach in the video can teach them, despite his or her humble status, *it is the thing the video can teach them that's worth talking about*. Who cares what the coach got wrong? The purpose is not to judge him. The purpose is to get better. Seeking to extract whatever is useful from an unheralded source is growth mindset at work. Seeking to establish that some coach you've never met is not very good or that his players are unskilled is a sign of fixed mindset. The radical humility of that room in Chicago was a profound lesson. Did every coach love watching a fifth-grade teacher from New Jersey or a U14 coach from California? Probably not. But how amazing that several asked afterwards, *Can I get a copy of that video?* I want to watch it again. I want to study it. That, more than anything, explains why they had reached the top of their field.

Hunger and humility, relishing the journey of maximizing other people's skill by relentlessly seeking to maximize your own, focusing always on the things that can make you better—these are, I believe, the hallmarks of successful coaches. Give me a room of coaches who live in the crucible of *must get better every day* and I will show you a room full of coaches who have the focus and humility to learn from a coach like Steve Covino, masterfully running a session for U8s at an unheralded club. In fact, Steve joined me at a session with directors of MLS and Development Academies. I showed a video of him coaching U8s (it was from the same session I shared a clip from in chapter 4); he was practically besieged at the coffee break. The coach across town might be looking to prove he's smarter than Steve; but at the top, their first thought was *Tell me everything about what you did and why.*

It wasn't much different in New Zealand, where I held a session with coaches from New Zealand Rugby and showed them video of a ballet teacher giving feedback to her protege. These coaches—half of them 6'4", 240 pounds, it seemed, and most having played for the All Blacks—watched, studied and asked questions until, with apologies, I had to cut things off. We just had to move on. That mindset is the marker of cultures whose trajectories lead to the top. Is there more to success than that? Of course. There's knowledge and competitiveness and an ability to forge relationships. But if, as they do, you want your national rugby team to be the best in the world when you are a nation of just five million people, a culture of constant learning is a great starting point.

It is the same for individuals. Once, on a visit to a minor league baseball club—a Class A park in a tiny city most people would struggle to find on a map—a question reminded me of Nobel Prize-winning psychologist and economist Daniel Kahneman's book *Thinking Fast and Slow*, which I discussed in chapter 1. As I struggled for the exact term Kahneman used, a coach pulled his well-thumbed copy of the book out of his backpack and found the reference. I don't know where he is today but I am betting on him—and the players he coaches.

Coaching and ego

Managing one's own ego is one of the most challenging tensions in a coach's development. Not surprisingly, it has come up indirectly several times in this book. In this chapter, for example, there was the issue of a coach's willingness to take actions that develop players for the long run even if it means fewer wins for his team now—a move that requires suppressing one's ego in the service of larger goals. In chapter 4, there was the moment when Chris Apple chose to not call a player out after a terrible mistake. One reason many coaches would have yelled there is to exonerate their coaching: "It's not my fault. I taught him to score from there." In these cases and a hundred others, the battle to keep ego in check is waged.

It's natural to want to be recognized for one's performance and achievements, to take pride in one's work, to want to be the best. After all, coaching is a competitive profession;

everyone pursues recognition to some degree. But to develop players correctly, to coach effectively, is to be willing to forgo credit, to be invisible, or give the credit to someone else. Part of us has to be driven to win and perhaps even dream about the moments when we will stand on the podium, and part of us has to put that all aside.

Atlanta United Academy coach Matt Lawrey shared a major takeaway from the French Football Federation's coaching course: French trainer Jean-Claude Giuntini advised that "a youth coach should always be in the shadows. Never the spotlight."

"I refer back to it as often as possible," Matt said, "sometimes quoting it to myself on the bench when I want to stand up and berate a referee. I try to constantly ask myself why I do the things I do. 'Why did you make that coaching statement? Why did you make that substitution? Why did you change shape?' And if the answers to these questions are anything other than 'It will help the kids develop and grow,' then I know it is the wrong decision."

Perhaps seeking the shadow is not just for youth coaches, though. "I would argue that to develop players and teams correctly, you have to be willing to forgo credit most (if not all) of the time," Scotland Rugby head coach Gregor Townsend told me. "There are some coaches that will promote their own importance to a team's success, but I don't believe that is sustainable or compatible with long-term team success."

"I remember when I started coaching the professional team I had just retired from," Ulster Rugby head coach Dan McFarland told me. "it was very important to me that my knowledge (and by extension me) had credibility. This manifested itself in 'Do it my way and I will prove to you my way works.'" In retrospect, this was "unsustainable," McFarland said. As a coach who values and seeks to develop athletes' capacity to think for themselves, he found it exhausting and himself more controlling than he wished to be. In the end, he was able to step back decisively and into a role more suited to his own style and to learning—but he also offered a fascinating observation: his shift might not have been possible had he not started as he did. "I also believe that without demonstrating clearly at that stage, through results, that my knowledge and detail was good, I would not have had a foundation of credibility on which to develop."

Good coaches solicit input, adapt the plan, and delegate leadership. But they don't get far if they don't have a vision, a game model, a process of their own that they expect others to embrace. "We have no choice but to impose what we think," Marcelo Bielsa says. Selflessness is required, and so is decisiveness and self-assurance. A coach has power and must know when to carry it lightly, delegate it or forbear using it. Gregor Townsend put it like this: "A good coach seeks to make the players feel that it is they who are responsible for their actions, decisions and game plan." A good team often includes elements of democracy. But it is never truly a democracy. A coach delegates decisions to players, invests them in the strategy, gives them discretion to adapt and decide, but only with the understanding that he also sets the terms of the delegation—how much; when—selects the participants, and has the right to take it back. A coach who does not believe his process has some answers and who cannot set and enforce ground rules of membership and culture cannot survive.

Ego is a constant companion—necessary at times, disruptive at others; beneficial to some degree, problematic if unchecked.

With that in mind, it's worth considering ways that ego can subtly influence our decisions as coaches. Consider the following two options for the outcome of a game in which you are the head coach:

Option A: Your team is tied in a big game and has been struggling. With 30 minutes to go, you shift to a new formation and make a series of unconventional substitutions. On the sidelines, your voice is a constant, your exhortations heard above the fray. Gesticulating, you move players into decisive positions. It's clear to all that your interventions are making a difference and though it's far from the best game your team has played, your actions shift the tide. There's a late goal and you win. As you walk to your car, you overhear a parent say, "Coach really pulled one out for us today."

Option B: You prepare your team carefully all season, instilling strong knowledge of your game model and understanding of tactical adaptations your team can make. A week before a big match, you recognize a key tendency in your opposition and prepare your team to recognize and exploit the opposition's weaknesses so that each player understands their role. The game goes according to plan. You sit on the bench and occasionally make tactical adjustments by speaking quietly to players, reminding them of what they learned in practice, but these interventions mostly pass like ripples on a pond. The team plays with understanding and skill. They win 3-0. As you walk to your car, you overhear a parent say, "The guys did everything right today. Coach barely had to say a word."

In the first case, you get all the credit. In the second, you've done your job better. Now ask yourself this: how many coaches would choose the second option? How many would choose it throughout their career, reliably, across the years, and while some rival danced in the spotlight of theatrics and won visibility and acclaim?

If the hunger to learn is one of the most important factors in a coach's success, the hunger for credit is one of the most problematic. Managing ego is a huge part of learning to succeed at poker, Maria Konnikova writes in *The Biggest Bluff*. When players fail, they think it's bad luck, but success they always attribute to skill. And since the environment is wicked—there's a mismatch between action and outcome because of all the external noise (i.e. so many other variables are changing simultaneously)—this is what limits their long-term growth. When it comes to knowledge and wisdom, "Triumph is the real foe," she writes. She describes the studies of the psychologist Ellen Langer, whose experiments studied people's responses to coin tosses, which she rigged so that some people were more likely to guess right at certain times. The question she asked them at the end of the experiment was whether they were good at picking coin tosses—something that's essentially impossible. There were three groups: one with a random distribution of correct guesses, one where correct guesses clustered at the beginning, and one where they clustered at the end. The timing of when people got lucky was critical. While the groups that guessed right at the end and in the middle understood that their guessing was pure chance, the group that appeared to succeed at the outset tended to conclude that they were highly skilled. They lost the plot and latched onto the improbable argument that they could predict the impossible. Success went to their head and caused them to distort reality.

There's a high school coach near where I live who wins enough games to be regarded as successful. After a recent winning season, he wrote this note to his players:

Finally, I want to mention four of the worst words for the development of the young soccer player: "GET OFF THE BALL." I hear this all the time. If your coach is yelling at you to "get off the ball," smile, because you are doing the right thing. Don't get off the ball; keep working on your individual skills.

It takes hubris to write that. A lot of it. Let's just assume for a moment that he is correct on the highly debatable argument that keeping the ball will make you better. (Sorry, Xavi!) Who imagines their own wisdom to be so profound that it should override the guidance of a coach—of every coach—actually observing a player in a specific context? What adult thinks it's responsible to tell athletes to defy their coaches, to be too proud to listen? Who fails to see what the results will be for young people who take that advice? Who disrespects and undercuts the very coaches who developed his players for him in the first place? Let us all take warning: as in Langer's study, success went to his head and led to a gross distortion of reality.. The physicist Richard Feynman warned that, "The first principle is that you must not fool yourself—and you are the easiest person to fool."

Ego unchecked (or unhinged by success) is a dangerous thing. And it's the checking that's hard. "Everyone will recognize this as a problem in at least one other coach," a friend noted dryly when I described this section of the book. "Fewer will see it as an issue worth exploring in themselves." Ego is a surreptitious companion, adept at rationalizing and offering us alternative explanations for self-serving actions, always sneaking its way into our blind spots. To struggle with it is about the most human thing there is. Then again, since it is something players must struggle with, since they too will be asked to put themselves second to the shared mission, there are surely some benefits to experiencing and reflecting on the struggle to put one's self second.

So what to do about it?

I asked this question of some of the best coaches I know. Many mentioned the importance of self-awareness, but of course you cannot decide to be more self-aware. By definition, we don't see what we're not aware of, nor the moment when our awareness ebbs. One profound and useful suggestion, from Ulster Rugby head coach Dan McFarland, was to change your words. Language reminds you of how you want to frame things, and because your descriptions for things will be required frequently and unpredictably, a change in them offers frequent reminders of who you are and how you want to engage the world. "Many teams refer to the 'management' (coaching team, medical, strength + conditioners, operations)," McFarland said. "We refer to ourselves as 'support staff.' It's a simple shift in language that reminds us that, ultimately, we are not the ones going to win the games. We help." Another solution was simply to make a habit of asking "What do you think?" when a parent or another coach or even a player asks you a question. "There are obviously times for telling, but by making regular inquiries about (and implementation of) others' thoughts, the coach relinquishes the 'it's all about me' atmosphere," McFarland observed.

When I talk about issues at the organizational level in the next section, metrics will be a major topic. They are relevant here too. "Coaches who can battle their own ego and do the 'right' thing for the development of the players often get passed over in job searches," one MLS academy coach said. "They get that reputation: 'He doesn't win.' With less vocal coaches, if he wins, they assume it was the players. Evaluation is pretty broken." Which raises the question, how long will coaches like him do what's right over what's beneficial to their careers?

But in the end, the most powerful way to keep ego in check is to focus on—lose yourself in—being process-driven. "Ego-driven and outcome-driven often go together," Stu Singer, who works with coaches on mindfulness and focus, observed. When wins are your metric, you have a hot streak and start looking to spike the ball. You're more likely to do something radically egotistical like writing an *"I am the one true coach; ignore all other coaches"* letter. When process is your objective, on the other hand, you are more likely to respond like Gregor Townsend: "There is never enough space and time to worry about whether the media or parents think the coach shouldn't get the credit. After a win or loss (and every training session), the coach is analysing, strategizing and planning." Focusing on the next step is the best way to keep the previous ones in perspective.

Sideline demeanor and in-game coaching

This book is almost entirely about what is to me the most important part of a coach's job: how he or she teaches in training sessions and practices. But athletes are learning and coaches are guiding them during competition as well. In this section, I offer some reflections on how coaches might think about interactions during matches and games from a learning point of view. That said, if most of this book comes with the caveat that some of what I have to offer must surely be wrong, this section gets a double dose of that disclaimer. Here, especially, I speak from a lack of experience. That said, I hope to offer a few breadcrumbs.

The first thing to consider is that it is very difficult to teach anything new during competition, and efforts to do so run a high risk of actually detracting from performance. Why do I say that? Because consciously learning something new requires the engagement of working memory, and the capacity of working memory is severely limited. If I am explaining to players something I want them to do for the first time during the game, I am diverting working memory from other tasks that demand it during the match.

If I ask players to do something we have discussed and rehearsed in training, however, they may be able to manage the load on their working memory. Especially if I cue them with words I carefully encoded as part of practice. Saying "Higher, Jordan. Press high," is viable if we spent time in training studying how to press and what I mean when I say "press high" is absolutely clear and she can process it nearly automatically. Then I am mostly reminding Jordan of what she already knows.

It's hard to overemphasize the importance of language. The more familiar a cue, the more consistently associated with an action, the more likely players are to be able to use it. If you want to say it in the game, make sure your players have heard it over and over and over in training and that they've heard it used precisely and well.

So if she's heard your words frequently and associates them with a consistent response, Jordan may be able to use your feedback during the game; but if you have not taught pressing in training and familiarized Jordan with the terminology you use, one of two things will happen:

1. Jordan will begin using her working memory to think about pressing and how to do it. This will degrade her perception and give her less working memory to execute the things she already knows. She likely won't press well and there's a good chance other aspects of her performance will be reduced as well. If you see

this and give her further directions—"Higher, Jordan. Anticipate the ball. See if you can jump the pass. Read the pass, Jordan"—there's a good chance you will make the situation worse.

2. Jordan may also probably realize what is happening. She will recognize that she is struggling at trying to do something she doesn't really know how to do and that it is distracting her from something important to her: the game. In that case, there's a good chance she will choose to ignore you instead. This will establish a precedent for her of ignoring what you say during competition (or more frequently, perhaps). It will probably affect her level of frustration and her relationship with you as well.

So a good rule of thumb is that during games, you can remind players of what you are **sure they already know** using **language they are familiar with**.

That said, if a player is trying to distribute the ball and you shout "Wide, Carlos, wide" in the half-second before he strikes the ball, the chances of a poor play are higher, even if Carlos knows what you mean by "wide." Talking to players about what they are doing in the moment they are trying to do it is asking them to multitask uncomfortably, and in fact many cognitive psychologists would say there is no such thing as multitasking, only distraction and reduced concentration. This is likely to harm performance. It also increases the likelihood that they will learn to ignore you so that you don't disrupt their performance. So coach sparingly during live play and strive to give guidance at **breaks in play**.

In chapter 4, I talked about the importance of taking notes during training exercises. It's also important during games to keep track of key events and their frequency. What you see during the game, you will soon forget unless you record it. If you take notes, you'll have data to keep you focused on the most important things when you talk to players at half time or time-outs. But there's another reason to take notes during the match. It can help keep you from over-talking. If you have no other way to keep track of the fact that Jordan is slow to press, you will be more likely to shout it at Jordan in the moment. After all, that's the only channel for your game observations to get back to players. But taking notes—*Jordan slow to press. Doesn't recognize slow pass is a cue. 2×. In front of their goal second half*—gives permanence to the observations you'd otherwise lose. You now have more ways to talk to Jordan about it and you'll feel more in control. You won't have to shout.

The tendency of competition to make us more likely to shout or lose control of our tone of voice is another reason to try to coach only (or at least mostly) at breaks. You'll be a little calmer. The emotion and perhaps judgment communicated by the sorts of strident directions required to communicate during live play—*Jordan! Press! JORDAN! Press!*—increases the risk of distraction. It encourages athletes to wonder: *Why is she blaming me?* All of this reduces players' focus on and presence in the moment. Calmer delivery of technical guidance is usually better, and that tends to happen when players have at least half a second to listen.

What about teaching and learning other times during competition? One of my favorite teaching moves of the many fine coaches my children had growing up was one used by a youth soccer coach named Khris Clemens. When a player made a mistake, instead of trying to tell him while he was playing (distraction) and shouting at him (distraction), Khris would take him out of the game very briefly, stand next to him on the sideline, usually with his hand on his shoulder in a fatherly way, and quietly explain the desired solution. Then he would immediately put the player back in. Obviously, you can't do that at every level—it requires unlimited substitutions—but it was a thing of beauty. The message was very clear: *I will teach you. I still believe in you. I want you to listen and learn but I'm not going to bench you for mistakes*. Not coincidentally, there were immense relationship benefits to this approach. There were few coaches my son loved more.

Half time and after the game are the two other times often put in the service of teaching on match day. What about them?

After a game, emotions are likely to be raw—yours and theirs—which means more opportunity to respond unwisely, half-baked, without getting your ego in check because you lost to a team you wanted to beat and therefore hastily blame the players for "not wanting it bad enough." A lot of post-game talks start with good intentions but—since they are rarely planned—can veer quickly into "Let's establish who is to blame." Establishing blame is rarely the basis of a productive public conversation. So maybe just skip it. Veering off topic— to whatever triggers you emotionally or because talking a lot seems to express the idea that this game was important—is a result of lack of clarity about what you want to say before you start, so why not take 20 seconds to plan? In your phone or on a note card, jot down the two or three most important things to say. Glance down at your notes to keep on task.

One NBA franchise has a simple system for this at both its pro and developmental league teams. The players go into the locker room after the game and the coaches into an adjacent room where they debrief in a way that first lets them vocalize what they're dying to say but perhaps shouldn't—e.g. "Can you believe Smith? Does he even understand the defense?" Then the head coach says some version of, "OK, what's our message in there?" All of the coaches share ideas but they choose one or perhaps two that everyone thinks are most worthwhile. Then they walk in the next room, deliver their shared message collectively in about a minute and that's that. No around the horn: "Coach Wilson, anything else?"

Given the chance to think it through together, the coaches almost always highlight process and mindset. "We lost focus after half time, but our fight was much better in the fourth quarter. You wanted it more than them, that's why we pulled it out." Or "We did the little things today, diving for loose balls, boxing out the shooter after free throws, winning habits." The process lets coaches put a check on one another, keeps the message less personal—it's from the staff—and gives assistant coaches a voice. And of course it ensures that everyone focuses on the main idea.

Another theme of this book: we often assume, falsely, that volume of words and importance of topic are correlated. If we think something is important, we often try to signal that by talking about it a lot. Again, this correlation is false. We want people to listen well. We want our words to be memorable and actionable, to express importance. Not only are those purposes not necessarily brought about through quantity of verbiage, but they often operate in conflict with it. I talk more and you remember each sentence a little less. I talk more and you start to think, *You already told us that; I heard you.* I talk more and your attention wanders to the play you can't stop thinking about or the drive home and where you can get something to eat.

This is important because a lot of the talking that coaches do after a match is *talking done to express the idea that this game and its lessons were important*. Frustrating tie = long talk.

Big loss = longer talk. Often in those cases, the more we talk, the more their eyes glaze over—and therefore, just maybe, the more we talk again because their eyes are glazing over, which suggests that they do not understand how important this game and its lessons were. Cue more talking to reinforce that idea that this game was important. Five minutes later, athletes have begun practicing ignoring us. It's a downward spiral.

If there's a lot to say, it's worth thinking about alternatives to post-game talks. There could be a post-game question: *What did you take from today's game?* But rather than asking rhetorically in the moment and having the words fall on the group like a smothering blanket, why not say *Please text me your thoughts by tomorrow morning.* Or *Please text me one thing you can do more of to make your teammates better.* Or *I have texted you all two key lines from our principles of play document. Can you each take a minute to tell me one moment in which you think we did each of these well and each of these poorly.* Or perhaps practice on Tuesday starts with "I asked you all to think about X. Let me hear some of your thoughts now...."

Or perhaps you want to be more systematic about it. Maybe you want your players to keep journals in which they reflect briefly after every game and which you can occasionally collect and discuss. Or maybe the journals are just for them. Yaya Toure famously kept such a notebook throughout his career; it became a part of him and his life in the game.

Video review might also work. Especially if you want to review critical moments such as the goal #12 scored in which no one marked her. Much more effective to present video of the few seconds before her goal in moments of calm at the next practice, say, than to ask the team to try to remember how she got so open in the moments after the game.

It's worth reviewing here some of the key elements that make feedback effective: it works best when it's close to the antecedent, when it's focused on one or two things only, when recipients can see what we're talking about, and when people get the chance to use it right away. For the most part, none of those things are easily accomplished after a game. The failure of the midfield to mark #12 is now long in the past. No one really remembers it—certainly not objectively. There's no chance to try the guidance of scanning to make sure you see her movements. Players are in their own emotional space. They may not even want to think about #12 and the goal she scored until they've processed something else. In light of that, a good rule of thumb is that the longer post-game talks go on, the worse they get. At the youth level at least, my suggestion would be to steady players' emotions. Offer one or two insights for reflection. Give them a question to respond to or a topic to reflect on before practice. Stop talking. Three minutes max.

Half time talks are a more complex topic, though they raise some of the same issues as post-game talks. The potential benefits are greater: the second half awaits, giving players the opportunity to apply guidance and thus learn more from it. And of course, half time talks give coaches the opportunity to achieve greater success if done well. But while I've seen fewer half time talks than I have end-of-game talks, the ones I've observed or been a part of suggest there are probably significant opportunities for coaches to adjust what they do in order to maximize understanding and foster behavior change in their athletes.

I once joined a group of coaches at a high-level license workshop in which they were asked to practice half time talks based on game analysis. The designers of the course deserve points for including practice. Seeing coaches practice was not only incredibly revealing but also incredibly productive. Coaches got better rapidly by having to hear themselves in a setting of relative calm and reflection. And by imagining themselves as athletes when others practiced and experienced the feeling of, for example, a coach's 8 or 10 or 12 points washing quickly over them with barely a breath, they learned even more. It's one thing to know it would be impossible to remember 8 or 10 or 12 things that "we need to do" delivered in a rapid-fire litany without a moment to process. It's another to feel it.

And thank goodness for the benefits of practice because the half time talks, despite being full of wisdom and insight, were a frontal assault on working memory and therefore mostly ineffective. Coaches fired rapidly through an array of needed adjustments and corrections—sometimes 8, 10, 12 of them at a gallop with occasional diagramming: a lot of information, undifferentiated, presented too rapidly to process or reflect on in a meaningful way. . Working memory was surely overloaded. There was little chance for prioritization or reflection, never mind discussion of how to apply.

My suggestion based on those talks is to dramatically reduce the number of topics you attempt to discuss and to go slowly, with thinking time in between, through the list. If possible, give athletes some way to interact with each concept to encode it a bit and free working memory for the next idea. A minute for reflection for each player based on his or her "priority" that you've identified? Video review if you can. A minute to close their eyes and imagine doing X? Asking players to discuss "what we'll need to do to make that happen"? You know your half time setting better than me. But you at the white board or with a clipboard, running down the things each position group needs to do while everyone else hears it is not the answer.

Then there is the issue of motivating athletes, which is often a primary goal of half time talks. There are better guides than me on the topic of what to say to players in that setting to help them dig deep and find the best within them, but I do think it's helpful to observe that this is a different goal from the "teaching goal": helping players understand what's happening, learn from it and adjust their actions to get a better result. I know—kind of obvious. But it's easy to let them blend into one conversation, and different purposes require different tools. Your voice, your body language, the pacing of your words are all different when you are explaining or discussing how best to react to overlapping runs than when you are telling players to dig deep emotionally and support each other. So the first thing to think about is to separate those functions intentionally. Perhaps that means teaching first. Here you want memory, focus, steady attention, understanding, reflection. You want players to speak up with questions. You want them to listen carefully to one another. Is there a way they could be writing this down? Reflecting on it deeply? In this moment, you're probably more quiet. You speak slowly. You prioritize. You give players time to process. You ask them to consider what challenges they'll face in taking the course of action you're discussing.

Then there's a discernible shift. You're now motivating. "OK, bring it in. Let's do this." A much wider range of body language/voice level/tone are viable. Maybe you're firing your players up. Maybe you're calming them down. Whichever you choose, consider having the psychological preparation to play begin at a clear distinct point, after the learning is done. Let it be part of a transparent routine of "going back out" so players are aware of it and can focus on getting mentally ready. Maybe the transition would sound something like this:

"OK. Last few moments to get our roles and responsibilities straight. Take a few seconds to close your eyes and imagine us defending their overlap and then transitioning to attack. OK. Now let's get our minds right and start getting ready to play! Carlos, bring us in and get us fired up!"

Practice is for coaches

Stu Singer often works with coaches in changing their behaviors. His work with them often starts with video self-study. "Sometimes they'll see themselves on tape, red faced and with the veins popping in their neck and they'll say, 'That's not who I want to be. That's not who I am.'" Coaching is a performance profession. It's done live, like the sports we coach, and our responses and actions during live performance, including but not limited to highly emotional responses like shouting at players, are usually the product of habit. This means there's very little chance you'll find the presence of mind to step back and reflect on how you're doing what you're doing or the impact of it on players in the midst of a game—or even practice—when emotions are intense and raw, Singer observed. You see it clearly afterwards on the video in a way you can't in the moment.

It's hard to change if you're trying to force yourself to remember to change it in the midst of performance. What you want to change you must practice in moments of calm. If you want to react differently, you must build a new habit that you can call on when the performance environment is complex or the context is emotionally intense, and practice is the tool to do that. It's intuitive to us that this is the case for the athletes we coach, but it applies to us too. We can apply it to our own professional development and for more than fixing negative responses. If you want to develop a new skill and be able to implement it in a complex environment, you must practice. True for athletes; true for coaches. Want to improve those half time speeches? Practice a few. Want to give better directions? Practice with a colleague or by filming yourself, or even by scripting and reading them aloud in the mirror or to your partner. Want to give players better feedback in performance review? Also practice. Fortunately that's something you probably know a bit about.

CLUB AND ORGANIZATION

The subject of practice for coaches is a good segue to the final section of this chapter for one particular reason: it's harder to do alone and much better if you have a group of colleagues to do it with you. Best of all is if you are part of a club with a culture in which practice is a tool everyone uses to constantly improve.

So far in this chapter, I've tried to describe some issues I believe coaches should consider in their and their athletes' long-term development. But coaches don't work in a vacuum. They work within clubs and organizations; they work beside parents. For better teaching by coaches to have its optimal effect, decisions by and interactions with those two groups are critical as well. A coach can believe the curriculum matters, for example, but it's impossible to have a curriculum by yourself. The whole idea is that it coordinates teaching across age groups and teams. A club decision to develop and implement it, and to implement it well, is required. To the degree that a club or a team is a business, its clients are parents; their role in choosing a club is often at least as significant as the athlete involved. Making decisions for the long-term benefit of athletes is going to be more challenging if parents don't see and understand them.

With that in mind, I'm going to close this chapter with shorter discussions of a few of the issues these relationships create for coaches. There are far too many to address them all or to address them completely. My hope is that it will still be useful to identify some of the important ones and how they overlap with other topics of this book.

Aligning parents

This book is about maximizing the long-term growth and development of athletes. Ironically, the group that has the greatest incentive for coaches to do that, the athletes' parents, are often poorly aligned in terms of valuing the daily actions long-term development requires. Winning is beneficial, but a good coach knows other things are more important. What do you do when parents are the people shouting loudest to win, or to play cynically to win, or who use winning as their primary criteria in selecting clubs and sometimes threaten to move their children to a "better" club—i.e. one that wins more—if you do things that prioritize long-term development? All of this puts immense and perverse pressure on coaches to make decisions that hurt athletes. As one coach put it, "The club needs to win to market to parents who pay the fees. The system is designed to place winning to be the highest priority metric at the expense of other metrics. Nobody says this out loud, but everyone knows it." I have heard a similar story from enough coaches to know it is more than one person's opinion. But what to do about it?

Two things are necessary: alternative metrics and alignment of incentives. One reason people focus on winning is that it's easy to see. If we want people to look at something beyond or in addition to winning, we have to show them what that looks like. Telling people not to look at A is only possible if you help them to see B instead, and that work is best done in advance. Help people see from the outset, to feel like embracing your vision is part of joining the organization.

"I've always spent an inordinate amount of time detailing what parents will see at training and why," said Todd Beane of TOVO Academy. "I explain our Ideal Footballer Model. That every exercise and every match we play is about developing their child into a player of great cognition, competence, and character. I also promise that every activity we do and all the communications we have will be aimed at that goal. That we will win, lose or draw with that as our metric. Of course, you need to do this before the heat of the first match so that they sign off on that agreement." When people know that your approach is not an excuse for not winning but was part of the plan from the outset and is grounded in deep knowledge of the game, they're likely to buy in.

Ryan Rich, who was until recently Technical Director at Alexandria (VA) Soccer Association, went a step further. He asked teams in the club to gather data on key alternative metrics and share it with parents. It's not just that they said time of possession, number of passes, and the length of passing strings mattered. They proved it by using those metrics, sharing the results and talking about them with parents. Parents got better at seeing what mattered. They often even took pleasure in knowing what to look for—it showed they knew the game—and would often reinforce it with their children when they talked about the game afterwards. Here's an excerpt from a blog post Ryan wrote for parents that included a glossary explaining the why behind the metrics. The post began with a table with data from a recent match comparing an Alexandria team to their opponents

- ***First touches:*** *In this game, our players had nearly twice as many first touches on the ball as the other team. Also, our touches are distributed more evenly based on our style of play vs. other teams whose touches end up being skewed towards their central defender and forwards due to their "kicking it long" approach. These touches benefit our players massively as they practice applying technique and decision-making on the ball at least twice as often as their counterparts in games!*

- ***Number of 5+ pass strings:*** *Counting the number of times each team is able to connect 5 or more consecutive passes helps to determine if players are learning the tactical side of the game. ... If a team does not have any 5+ pass sequences or only a few on a consistent basis, they never really establish possession, [and] the game is simply random with players operating on their own "islands" without any cohesive team framework.*

We live in an era when data and statistics have revolutionized the game at every level. Why not use them to support development? Could such developmental data and statistics work for basketball and hockey and lacrosse too? I don't see why not.

On referees

Speaking of shouting, let's talk about referees. Shouting at referees is an epidemic of self-delusion that's become part of the culture of sports. It's a big problem. Parents and coaches alike often do it. If you're frustrated by the quality of referees in your area, ask yourself why anyone would be a referee in the first place when they are subject to constant abuse. Where are all the good referees, you ask? Probably at home because people who know half as much about the game as they do are constantly shouting at them. In some games, both sides are so busy shouting at the referee for clearly favoring the other, I'm amazed anyone sees the goals. At least it balances out.

The hardest part is that as a coach you could be incredibly adept at dealing with referees and still have a problem. It's not just your own behavior you have to attend to. Again there's risk in poor parent alignment. Parents shouting at referees models poor sportsmanship directly in front of players, gives your team a bad reputation with referees, and makes it harder for you to have normal discussions with referees during the match because they've been put on the defensive. But that's not the worst of it.

The worst part of it is how it affects your athletes' development. After the game (sometimes during it), players should be thinking, *What did I do well that I can do more of? What situations can I learn from and improve upon?* Reflecting on and talking about the referee's performance is a big, juicy distraction from that work. It takes the core self-study work of an athlete and replaces it with a discussion about the performance of someone they have no control over and who potentially provides them with a reason not to be honest with themselves about outcomes.

At a recent game, I decided to count the percentage of all parent comments that were made to or about the referee. I conducted a series of ten-minute samples. Generally, the result was around 50% of comments made to or about the ref, depending on events and who I was standing near. No wonder players want to get in the car and talk about the referee. They think that's what matters most to the adults, and in the end adults talking to refs or even about refs—during the game, after the game—distracts players from reflecting on their own play and thus interferes with their learning. If there were one thing I'd tell parents in a meeting to align incentives when they joined it would be "We never talk to refs and we rarely talk about them. We do that because it keeps our players from learning and growing as well as they could. And in the end, you know you're probably wrong. He sees five games a weekend and is a trained ref. You've got a kid in the game. If anyone is biased, it's you. You're far more likely to be wrong than he is."

Guess what? You run a school

If a coach is more or less a teacher, a club is more or less a school, and a club director is more or less a principal. Since I've run my share of schools, I wanted to share a couple of thoughts.

A few key things differentiate great schools from lesser ones. The first is a clear shared sense of how we do things—a methodology. Weaker schools tend to be like a shopping mall. Each teacher (or coach) runs his or her own classroom (or team) like a little shop. They're all in the same place and branded the same but they do their own thing. Great schools take a more coordinated approach. "Did you see how she did that?" the principal of one of the best schools in Boston asked me as we left a classroom after observing. "The way she responded to that student's question- that's how we do it here." At that school there was a way and teachers were expected to use it. This means students learn more consistently because they use the same words and methods over time and know what to expect. And they feel part of something. In the case of a soccer club (or some other sport), it allows them to have an intact philosophy about how the game is played and how people learn.

If that's true, it's important to know what to hire for. The first criterion is beliefs—coaches who buy into your model and methodology. The second is humility—will they be part of your club or will they see the club as a means to get players for their team? Will they be hungry to learn and share and in so doing make themselves and others better? It does not work to hire a coach who is only loyal to himself, even if he has a following of players who will follow him like ducklings to the club. They will also follow him when he leaves.

How do you find the right mindset in hiring? I recommend this process.

1. Give candidates a description of club methods and philosophy or invite them to come watch a team in the club train. Ask them to respond. What do they observe and value? Are they trying to understand what you do or explain what they do?

2. Ask promising candidates who do well on the previous exercise to coach a session at your club.

3. Give the candidate feedback after the session. Say, "If you were part of this club, our goal would be to invest in you and help you be the best, so we'd give you feedback. Can I give you some now? Good! Here are two things I loved and that I'd want you to do more of. Here are two things I'd ask you to reflect on or try differently." Watch carefully as you say this. Is the candidate taking notes? Does the candidate ask questions? How does the candidate feel about you trying to make him or her better? Defensive? Inspired?

4. Invite the candidate to come back and coach again, implementing the feedback you provided. "Would you like to come run the session again?" If the candidate is willing to, it shows humility. If the candidate improves, if he can hear feedback, observe sessions and quickly get better, you potentially have someone special worth hiring, because they will love getting better and make others around them better. Your club will develop a culture of growth that will feed off itself. If the candidate does not like getting better, do not hire him or her, no matter how good the session. No one is bigger than the team.

If the goal is to have a growth mindset among the adults in the club, there need to be lots of opportunities for growth. The club has to be out to make players better by making coaches better. Meet regularly to study the work of coaching—watch video, observe sessions, discuss reading materials. Invest in people and don't apologize for it. After all you are trying to make them better and that is the ultimate expression of belief in people.

ACKNOWLEDGEMENTS

This book is the result of a figurative journey I have taken to understand more about the craft of coaching, but it is also the result of perhaps a hundred literal journeys: to Kansas City and Atlanta, Wellington and Edinburgh. Each of these journeys meant, for my wife Lisa, doing bedtimes solo, getting three kids to three schools at three different times, and inevitably dealing with some other untoward event: a broken water heater or a foot and a half of snow in the driveway. It meant that scheduling every parent-teacher conference began with what worked for my schedule, never hers. Many frequent travelers will tell you about the weight they feel, sitting in the departure lounge, leaving their family behind. Surely my wife felt at least as great a weight as the door shut behind me. First among the long line of people I have to thank for this book is Lisa.

It is also undeniably true that much of what I learned was accrued on the sidelines while observing my own children's sporting endeavors. Few things have made me happier than watching the three of them grow and compete under the combined influence of a challenging environment and good teaching. Few things have made me prouder than to see the character with which they have played. Their insights were many—there were a lot of driving miles in which to talk—and reminded me of the immense value sports provide in the lives of young people, no matter the outcome.

They have all had many excellent coaches—excellent because they taught young people how to be their best with affection, knowledge and respect for the game. I hesitate to name any because of the strong chance I will recognize when I see this in print that I have left out some of the most deserving of gratitude, but not thanking Steve Covino, Steve Freeman, Garrett Cobb, Phil Ridgway, Khris Clemens and James Beeston for taking an interest in the development and growth of my children as athletes and people would be remiss.

My journey into coaching began with a phone call from Asher Mendelsohn at US Soccer. I could not believe my luck. Since then, Scott Flood, Dave Chesler, Jay Hoffman, Barry Pauwels, Nico Romeijn, Wim van Zwam and Aloys Wijnker (among others) have given me so many opportunities to work with coaches. Some I got right. Some I got wrong. If my performances were off, they did as good coaches do and showed faith in me, giving me the confidence to persist.

To the hard part: there are fifty or a hundred other coaches whose work and ideas are also reflected here in small ways and large. Some shared thoughts after reading the manuscript, some in a comment at a workshop, some shared ideas in the most direct way: I saw them coaching. There are too many to name but a few whose contributions I cannot overlook. First, my colleagues who wrote side bars: Jeff Albert, James Beeston, Sefu Bernard, Lesle Gallimore, Kelvin Jones, Dave Love, Marc Mannella, Joe Mazzulla, Dan McFarland. The influence of conversations with Jesse Marsch, Todd Beane, Christian Lavers, Chris Apple and Gregor Townsend will be clear. Then there were the coaches that ran sessions specifically for me to study and discuss afterwards: Matt Lawrey, Kelvin Jones, Russell Payne, Kika Toulouse, Steve Covino and James Beeston yet again.

On the writing side, Alex Sharratt gave me the opportunity on a project not everyone would have thought half so compelling. Then Oliver Caviglioli, whose work I have admired for years and whose own writing on teaching and learning is of the first order, agreed to illustrate it. (I felt like a Premier League manager signing his most coveted transfer.) Discussing and refining the images as he worked on them was immensely fun. Mark Combes has been a gracious, insightful and flexible editor throughout. He put up with a lot of soccer vignettes to get to the baseball stories that I suspect really spoke to him. And Jonathan Woolgar in editing was somehow always able to make what I'd written sound much more like what I'd been shooting for. Finally, "agent" does not really capture the guidance that Rafe Sagalyn provides on all my projects. This time around, he gave me the support and wisdom to make the project a reality from the word go till the last comma was in place.

nformation can be obtained
Gtesting.com
he USA
44031220
014B/8